THE
ROYAL HOUSE
OF
MONACO

Also by John Glatt

Rage & Roll: Bill Graham and the Selling of Rock
River Phoenix: The Biography
The Chieftains: The Authorised Biography
Holy Killers

THE
ROYAL HOUSE
OF
MONACO

DYNASTY OF GLAMOUR,
TRAGEDY AND SCANDAL

JOHN GLATT

St. Martin's Press ⋈ New York

ISBN 0-312-19326-2

First published in Great Britain by Judy Piatkus (Publishers) Ltd.

First U.S. Edition: October 1998

10 9 8 7 6 5 4 3 2 1

To my parents
Nomah and Louis

CONTENTS

———— ❧ ————

CONTENTS

AUTHOR'S NOTE

Previous biographies of Princess Grace and the Grimaldis have concentrated heavily on the American-born Princess and devoted less attention to events after her tragic death. I felt there was a void in what happened afterwards and how it affected Prince Rainier and his children. I hope this book will go some way toward explaining Grace Kelly's lasting legacy to Monaco and the double-edged sword of celebrity which has plagued her children ever since.

In almost one hundred interviews with members of the Ruling Family, friends and Monégasques, I have attempted to explore what has occurred in Monaco in the sixteen years since Princess Grace died, and where it is going at the crossroads of the 700th anniversary of the Grimaldis' rule.

I would like to thank Prince Albert for spending almost an hour talking to me. Also Grace's warm and vivacious younger sister, Lizanne Kelly LeVine, the last surviving sibling of Grace's generation, who gave me her unique perspective on her family and Monaco. I also received invaluable help from Grace and Rainier's bridesmaids and life-long friends, Judy Balaban Quine and Rita Gam, who helped me put everything in perspective.

I owe a great debt of thanks to Grace's first biographer Gwen Robyns, who became the Princess's close friend and collaborator during her final years. Gwen took me under her wing by offering her unique perspective on Princess Grace and providing a constant source of encouragement. I would also like to thank Stevie Parker who accompanied me to Monaco during the 1997 Grand Prix and showed me a special part of the principality that few tourists ever see. Her enduring friendship with Prince Albert and his closest friends helped win their cooperation for this book.

I would also like to thank Oleg Cassini for a memorable afternoon in his Manhattan office where he spoke candidly and lovingly about his one-time fiancée Grace Kelly.

Some of the people who helped me prefer to remain anonymous for obvious reasons, but I would like to thank the following for their invaluable help: Neil Marr, The Countess of Lombardy (Skovia Grassi), Alec Marr, Michael Powers, Andre Peyregne, Francis Wright, Cannon Brian Matthews, Michel Vivien, Kate Powers, Annette Anderson, Patrick Middleton, Linda Joyce, John Haley, Jane France, Roy Day, Jean Kelly van Remoortel, Noel Museux, Melissa Corken, Robert Lacey, Archbishop Joseph Sardou, Stephanie Theobald, Lucy Yeomans, Andrew Jack, Robert Eringer, Ron Rice, Jack Valenti, Martin Haynes, Lionel Noghes, Patrice Innicenti, George Clare, Martin Ricketts, Tom Hallgarth, Prescilla Coates, R. Couri Hay, Bruce McCormack, Tamara Rotolo and Stuart White.

I also owe a great debt of gratitude to my American Agent Peter Miller of PMA and his team of Yuri Skujins and Davis Posner and my British agent Sarah Hannagan. I also want to thank Rachel Winning, Gill Cormode, Philip Cotterell and Kate Callaghan of Piatkus Books for their unceasing help. My thanks also go to Charles Spicer of St Martin's Press for his continued support and encouragement and his assistant Dorsey Mills.

My heartfelt thanks also go to Patricia O'Connell for her constant advice and support and her superb editing skills. Thanks must also go to Nathania Verlaque for her masterful job of translating Roger-Louis Bianchini's landmark work *Monaco: Une Affaire Qui Tourne*.

I am also grateful to: Shirley Galligan of the Born Free Foundation, Fred and Linda Wehner, Chris Bowen, Annette Witheridge, Laurette Ziemer, Rogr Hitts, Daphna Inbar, Andy Webb, Monica Garney, Jean-Pierre Doria, Katie Sheehey, Milton Goldstein, Barry Everyham, David

Schumacher, Annette Whelan, Pat Malone, Audrey and Mavis Hirschberg, Joanna Coles, Dr Sylvia Virbulis, Brian Hepworth, David Hayes, Winnie Deeks, Bob Anthony, Denise Childs, Wensley Clarkson, Vicky Herman, Christina Lynn, Charles Higham, Janice Gregory, Marian Collins, Dick Belsky, Jock Veitch, Lisa Gaye, Allan Hall, David Hill, Susan Comegys, Stuart Krichevsky, Charles Comer and Anna Gizowska.

PROLOGUE

—— ⚜ ——

On JANUARY 8, 1997, Monaco launched a ten-month-long celebration to mark the 700th anniversary of the Grimaldi dynasty. Wedged like a diamond in a narrow cove on the Côte D'Azur between France and Italy, the tiny principality has weathered the bitter storms of European history to remain fiercely independent.

The Grimaldi family wrote itself into history in 1297 when Francesco Grimaldi, disguised as a Franciscan monk, begged refuge at the wooden gates of the fortress on the rock, where today's palace stands. As soon as the gullible guards let him in, Grimaldi, popularly known as 'il Malizia' (Francois the Spiteful), pulled a sword from under his robes and attacked. Before the surprised guards could close the gates, the Grimaldi troops poured in and took the fortress in a bloody massacre. And from that day on the Grimaldis have stayed in control of Monaco, making them the longest-ruling family in Europe. Over the centuries they have ruled Monaco from their medieval palace, perched on a slab of rock jutting defiantly out over the Mediterranean. From this vantage point they have seen many other ruling families come and go while they have quietly prospered.

The second great invasion of Monaco came in 1956, when the Hollywood movie star Grace Kelly sailed into the harbour on the *USS Constitution* to marry Prince Rainier III and become a Princess. Prior to Princess Grace's arrival, Monaco was a run-down relic of its glory days from the last century, when is casino had made it *the* European resort for the wealthy. But after her marriage, which captured the imagination of the world, Grace single-handedly elevated Monaco to unprecedented heights of glamour and sophistication.

Skilfully using the media, Grace and Rainier portrayed their lives as the ultimate love story – a romantic Hollywood movie come to life in the scenic splendour of the French Riviera. And when Princess Grace gave birth to three beautiful children the ruling family of Monaco seemed blessed by heaven. But unlike fairytales, their story would have anything but a happy ending.

By the time their eldest daughter Princess Caroline and her brother Prince Albert had reached their teens, the publicity machine Grace and Rainier had once used so skilfully for the principality's benefit had begun to turn on them. And by the time their youngest daughter, Princess Stephanie, blossomed into a beautiful teenager it had run out of control with the coming of the paparazzi who stalked them constantly.

After Princess Grace's tragic death in September 1982, Monaco's fortunes descended into a spiral of scandal, betrayal and divorce. The Monaco fairytale had become a nightmare whose principal players – Caroline, Stephanie and Albert – played out their trials and tribulations in an increasingly bizarre public soap opera.

Caroline, whose first marriage to French boulevardier Philippe Junot ended in bitter divorce, lost her second husband, Stephano Casiraghi, the father of their three children, in a powerboat racing accident.

Openly blamed by much of the media for her mother's death, Princess Stephanie reacted by throwing royal protocol to the wind and becoming a rebel. She partied throughout the eighties, going through almost as many careers as she did lovers. She shamed her family by having two illegitimate children with her bodyguard, Daniel Ducruet, before Prince Rainier grudgingly allowed their marriage in 1995. A year later, in Monaco's biggest scandal to date, she divorced him after photographs showing him making love to a Belgian stripper were published around the world.

To naysayers, the Ducruet affair seemed yet another – and perhaps final – nail in Monaco's coffin. Many felt that with the passing of Princess Grace the tiny principality had lost its lustre and become an anachronism; that it would only be a matter of time before independent, sovereign-ruled Monaco would cease to exist. And the deposed Grimaldis would have no one to blame but themselves.

As the 700th anniversary of the Grimaldis' reign approached, the current ruler, Rainier III, was only too aware of the clouds that hung over his once-blessed land. Now in the twilight of his life, the seventy-three-year-old silver-haired Prince was battling heart problems and ill health. After reigning for almost half a century, the absolute sovereign has so far refused to relinquish power to his son and heir Prince Albert, who remains unmarried and enjoys an international reputation as a playboy.

Seizing the 700th anniversary as a heaven-sent opportunity to stem the negative tide of publicity about Monaco, Rainier entrusted his son with the responsibility of organising a no-expense spared programme of celebrations designed to capture the world's attention once more. As he approached his fortieth birthday the balding heir to the throne saw this as the perfect opportunity to demonstrate once and for all that he had 'the right stuff' to rule Monaco.

But as the big day approached a frustrated Prince Albert found himself constantly battling red tape and bureaucracy. Initially he had difficulty firing up government officials with enthusiasm for the anniversary and as the anniversary neared he felt too little had been done too late.

'There are things that we could have done better,' admitted the Prince. 'When my father put me in charge three years ago, I tried to talk our government into setting up [a] committee.'

The National Council finally agreed to Albert's Committee of 700 Years with only two years to go, leaving little time to prepare. With a glamorous special event planned for each month from January to November 1997, Prince Albert speculated over how advantageous it would have been if his ancestor had waited a few months to seize Monaco.

'You can't rewrite history,' reasoned the Prince: 'but it's too bad it came so early in the year as it could have been a culminating point.'

In his official proclamation, Prince Rainier rather loftily decreed that he wanted the 700th anniversary ceremonies to be 'the living expression of the national unity of the nation whose rich and authentic history will allow the new generation to find a newborn faith for the future.'

His American-college-educated son, destined to lead the new generation of Monégasques into the twenty-first century, put it this way:

'You have to make people realise where they come from. The meaning of the history behind our family and the reasons why we had to come here and what happened and so forth and so on. And to be able to come out with the statement that we are 700 years old – that's significant.'

The January 8 celebrations began at 11 AM at the Cathedral of Monaco, where Princess Grace is entombed, with a Mass attended by Prince Rainier, his children and specially invited guests. As the Cathedral choir, composed of young Monégasques, and the Philharmonic Orchestra of Monte-Carlo performed Mozart's moving *Benedictus sit Deus*, the future hope of the Grimaldi dynasty, Prince Albert, felt a sense of awe, as he stood at the crossroads of his country's destiny.

'It's somehow very emotional to go back and to realise what has been accomplished and where we come from,' the Prince would say later, as he recalled his thoughts at the time. 'To think that I will be the guardian of this history and of this tradition and to continue the work that my forefathers and my parents have done is a tremendous honour and a challenge. It is a heavy weight, but I will try to hold that.'

That night Prince Albert and his family took their positions in the princely box for a state-of-the-art live pageant, using computers and lasers to trace the history of the Grimaldis. Officially entitled *A Harbour of History*, 700 Monégasque schoolchildren gathered in the old port to witness the pageant, which was projected on two giant screens: the idea was to create a huge classroom with French actor Jean Piat playing the role of Professor. But as the heavens opened up and rained on the Grimaldi parade, it was hard not to see a metaphor of the sad realities of Monaco's fractured fairytale.

Now, looking back on the fifteen years since Princess Grace's untimely death, it seems that tragedy and misfortune have beset the Grimaldis on an epic scale from the day she died. Indeed, even the most cynical of Monégasques might wonder if the infamous Curse of the Grimaldis had finally come home to roost.

Monégasque legend has it that toward the end of the thirteenth century Prince Rainier I kidnapped and raped a beautiful Flemish maiden as part of his spoils of victory. The poor woman later became a witch and cursed the Prince's family for all eternity, saying: 'Never will a Grimaldi find true happiness in marriage.'

The witch's curse appears to have struck many times down the centuries.

CHAPTER ONE

THE CRASH

O N THE NIGHT before she died Princess Grace of Monaco had an eerie sense of foreboding. As she sat in her bedroom selecting her wardrobe for an extended visit to America, the Princess felt overwhelmed and far older than her fifty-two years.

Over the previous few months she had sunk into a deep depression caused by the onset of the menopause. The once-slender movie star was upset by a recent weight gain that had given her a matronly look; the heavy doses of hormones prescribed by her doctors to counteract the effects of the menopause had only served to make her more bloated, which in turn made her even more self-conscious. She was also suffering from high blood pressure and had been put on a course of medication that sapped her energy and made her lethargic.

It had been a long hard summer for Princess Grace, who, despite her family's pleas, had refused to cut down on her exhaustive schedule of official engagements.

She was totally exhausted and ill all the time. Even Princess Caroline began to fear for her mother's health but felt powerless to do anything.

In an attempt to cheer her up, Prince Rainier had taken Grace and their elder children Caroline and Albert on a late August cruise to Norway on their yacht, the *Mermoz*. With some misgivings Grace had given in and allowed her youngest daughter Stephanie, just turned seventeen, to miss the family holiday and go to Antigua with her handsome new boyfriend Paul Belmondo, the son of French movie star Jean-Paul Belmondo.

But on her return to Monaco Grace felt at an even lower ebb than before. She was tired all the time and suffering severe migraine attacks that sometimes left her barely able to function. Now, late on September 12, 1982, as she sat alone at Roc Agel, the family's retreat outside Monaco, the one-time Hollywood star felt worn out, old before her time.

For moral support she telephoned her close friend Gwen Robyns at 7 PM to discuss her impending trip to London. Robyns, one of Grace's closest friends and a trusted confidante, was organising a poetry reading the Princess was due to give in front of the Queen Mother at Windsor Castle the following Wednesday.

The English author had won Grace's friendship nearly a decade earlier when she had agreed to remove several revealing sections from a biography she had written on the Princess. Grace had been so grateful that Robyns had omitted details of her early Hollywood love affairs that she had declared the writer to be 'one of us' and the two had become very close.

Since then Robyns, who was thirteen years older than Grace, had been a frequent visit to Monaco, often staying at Roc Agel. Over the years Robyns had also become great friends with Prince Rainier and watched the royal children during their formative years. But Grace and Gwen's friendship had reached a new level of intimacy two years earlier when they had collaborated on the bestselling *My Book of Flowers*.

Although they spoke two or three times a week, Robyns had never heard Princess Grace sound so down as she did that Sunday evening.

'I said, "How are you?"' recalled Robyns. 'And she said, "Oh, I'm *so* tired and I've got *such* headaches."'

Concerned for her friend's health, Gwen offered to make an appointment for Grace with a Harley Street specialist during her forth-coming London visit. She suggested that the Princess could seek a second opinion on the treatment she was receiving for her menopause at the same time.

During the past few months Princess Grace had confided in Robyns her deep fears about getting old and the difficulties she was having coming to terms with middle age.

'She was dreadfully depressed about putting on weight,' said Robyns. 'I said to her that it didn't matter but she said, "It *does* matter. I'm sup-posed to look nice and I hate to be fat."'

The former Queen of Hollywood – who had abandoned her acting career when she married Prince Rainier twenty-six years earlier – was also sensitive to gossip linking her weight gain to alcohol. Although she still indulged a life-long passion for champagne, Grace was a moderate drinker. If pushed, she might have the occasional brandy at dinner. She would get extremely giggly on the rare occasions she did drink and she always suffered a bad hangover the next morning, so usually she stuck to champagne, which she liked to sip with caviar.

Apart from her health problems Princess Grace was very concerned about her daughter Princess Stephanie, who she had begun describing to friends as 'My wild child'.

All that summer Grace had agonised about Stephanie's increasing rebelliousness and her refusal to submit to parental authority. She was especially concerned about her daughter's burgeoning relationship with Belmondo, which she called the 'S and P situation'.

Since the trip to Antigua, the iron-willed teenager had constantly crossed swords with her mother. She refused to be reined in. As the dis-ciplinarian of the family, Grace felt increasingly powerless to control the young Princess's behaviour. And she was not helped in the slightest by Rainier, who left all parenting matters to her.

That weekend tempers boiled over when Stephanie announced that she was enrolling at racing-car driving school with Belmondo. Grace was horrified; Stephanie had barely succeeded in graduating from high school and it was only thanks to Grace's connections that her youngest daughter had won a place at the prestigious Institute of Fashion Design in Paris. Now she was throwing away the chance of a real career to drive racing cars with her new boyfriend. It was too much.

Grace's friend, the young film director Robert Dornhelm, who was staying at Roc Agel during Grace's final weekend, witnessed the raging rows between Grace and Stephanie in acute embarrassment. At one point Stephanie even insisted on reading her mother a love letter from Belmondo inviting her to move in with him.

There was no way that the staunchly Catholic Princess Grace would ever let that happen – especially as it would cause certain scandal in Monaco. Eventually, at the end of her tether, Princess Grace had decided she would personally escort Stephanie to the Fashion Institute before leaving for England.

That Sunday night Grace was having difficulty co-ordinating her wardrobe for the trip; she couldn't concentrate, due to her severe headaches. She told Gwen Robyns the problems she was having deciding how to convey her clothes to the Palace the next morning. Although she was a terrible driver and usually avoided getting behind the wheel at all costs, she surprised Robyns by saying that she had decided to drive to make things easier.

'I said, "Why can't somebody else take the clothes? Why are you driving?" recalls Robyns. 'And Grace said, "Oh well, there are problems with things." She sounded so tired.'

After a fitful night's sleep, Princess Grace rose early the next morning. She dressed and went into Princess Stephanie's bedroom at 9 AM to wake her up for the drive to Monaco and then went next door to see her son Albert. The twenty-four-year-old Prince, who had returned late on Sunday night from a soccer weekend in Italy with friends, chatted to his Mother and made arrangements to see her at the Palace later.

By the time Grace had come downstairs, carrying a pile of dresses on hangers, closely followed by her maid holding several large hat boxes, her chauffeur, Christian Silvestri, was waiting in front of the house in her eleven-year-old green Rover 3500. Princess Grace and the maid carefully spread out the dresses across the leather back seat and placed the hat boxes on the floor. She then told the chauffeur to drive down separately in another car as she did not want to crease the dresses.

As Princess Stephanie had still not risen, Grace, impatient to leave, shouted for her to come down. Anxious about driving, Grace wanted to get going on the dreaded drive back to Monaco.

When Silvestri, who knew Grace's fear of driving, tried to persuade her to let him drive, offering to return and fetch the clothes later, Grace was adamant. Declaring it would be easier if she drove, Grace got into the driver's seat, followed by a sleepy-looking Stephanie, who sat on the passenger's side. Even as Grace started the engine Silvestri made one final attempt to dissuade her from driving; but Grace was insistent, saying she wanted to talk to Stephanie.

When they set off from Roc Agel at 10 AM it was a picture-perfect day with the sun climbing high in a cloudless azure sky. Grace drove carefully down the winding hill road into La Turbie. In the town centre she passed the large Roman monument and turned left on to the treacherously steep CD37 two-lane highway that dipped down into Monaco.

Gwen Robyns, who had often travelled the same road with Grace, knew how much she detested it.

Said Robyns: 'One time in particular we were coming up to that particular bend when Grace said to me, "You know, some day, darling, somebody's going to have a dreadful accident here. They are going to die."'

The sun was beating straight down into her eyes as Princess Grace drove down the Corniche. She had a terrible headache and complained about it to Stephanie. Just a mile from the borders of Monaco, as Grace desperately tried to negotiate the first in a series of hairpin bends, a sharp pain seared through her head, causing her to lose consciousness momentarily.

She lost control of the Rover and it began snaking across the perilously steep two-lane road. A truck driver behind the Princess's car, alarmed at the Rover's erratic behaviour, sounded his horn loudly.

When Grace regained consciousness she saw to her horror that the car was hurtling toward the next hairpin bend. Panicked and disoriented, Grace tried to brake but instead, her foot hit the accelerator. As the Rover surged forward toward the bend, Grace screamed out: 'I can't stop! The brakes don't work!'

As the car speeded up Princess Stephanie desperately tried to reach the hand-brake to stop it going over the edge of the Corniche. But it was too late. The Rover plunged through a small restraining wall and over the side into space. It catapulted 120 feet and sliced off the top of a tree before rolling over on impact, ending up on its roof with steam hissing out of the radiator.

Stephanie, who had blacked out before impact, came to and realized she was lying in a small space under the glove compartment, the one part of the car that had survived intact. Certain the car was going to explode, she would later recall, 'I knew I had to get out of there and get my mom out.'

Grace, not wearing a seatbelt, had been launched over the driver's seat into the back of the car. Barely conscious, she lay on her back with her head against the back window. There was a terrible cut in her head — which had hit the steering column — but surprisingly little blood.

In desperation Stephanie managed to kick out the driver's door and staggered from the wreckage of the car, bleeding heavily from a scalp wound.

'My mother's in the car,' she screamed hysterically to a startled local woman who had rushed to the scene to help. 'Please get help, call the Palace, I'm Princess Stephanie.'

It took some time before the woman realised that the injured young girl was not in fact delusional; she was telling the truth.

'I kept pleading with the woman, "Call my father at the Palace. Please get help. My mother is in there." Everything else is blurred until the police came,' Stephanie would later say.

It was mid-morning and student nurse Skovia Grassi was attending a patient at the Princess Grace Hospital when the hospital went on full alert. The young Monégasque — who holds the official title Countess of Lombardy — was stunned to see a procession of guards and police rushing into the ward followed by a stretcher bearing the Princess's injured body.

'I asked my supervisor what was happening and he said that Princess Grace had been in a car crash and was very badly injured,' said the Countess. 'I had known Princess Grace since I was a young girl and I was in tears. My uncle was one of the bishops who had married Grace and she was like one of our family.'

The Countess watched in horror as the comatose Princess was taken to a private room where the hospital's chief of surgery, Dr Jean Chatelin, began to try to restore her vital functions. Princess Stephanie, still in deep shock and suffering from a serious back injury, was brought in on a stretcher and placed in a room next to her mother.

Then an ashen-faced Prince Rainier, who had been told the tragic news at Roc Agel, arrived. He was initially told that Grace had merely suffered fractures and was not in danger.

It was a long time until Prince Rainier knew the full extent of her injuries.

Prince Albert was next to arrive at the hospital, where he conferred with his father and his uncle Louis de Polignac. Princess Caroline was in London when she heard the news; she was told her mother's injuries were not serious and that they did not warrant her returning home immediately.

Princess Grace's younger sister, Lizanne Kelly LeVine, received a telephone call from the Palace at her Ocean City, New Jersey home.

'At first we were told that she was going to be all right,' said Lizanne. 'But that turned out to be a cruel, false hope.'

Acknowledged as Monaco's best medical facility, the Princess Grace Hospital had recently been refurbished with the latest equipment. However it did not have a CAT scan machine – the one machine that could have made an early diagnosis of the Princess's severe brain injuries and perhaps saved her life.

When leading French neurologist Dr Jean Dupay helicoptered into Monaco from Nice to treat the stricken Princess he was shocked to discover there was no CAT scanner. To complicate matters Grace had been given the strong pain-relieving drug Gamma OH when she was placed on a mechanical respirator and doctors had inserted a tube into her windpipe to help her breathe. The drug allowed doctors to repair her broken bones and other internal injuries, but it also meant that they couldn't measure her brain activity until the effects wore off.

In preparation for a brain operation Princess Grace's head was shaved. At midnight, almost fourteen hours after the crash, doctors decided they needed to drive the gravely-ill Princess across Monaco to Dr Michel Mourou, who owned the principality's only CAT scan machine. Mourou's clinic, which specialised in pregnancy and blood tests but also enjoyed a brisk business in VD testing, was situated on the top floor of a tall building. When the doctors arrived at his office, with the comatose Grace hooked up to a portable IV and breathing with the aid of a hand-operated oxygen tank, they had to carry her up several flights of narrow stairs as the elevator was too small to take a stretcher.

The brain scan revealed the true extent of Grace's brain injuries. She was beyond help; her brain damage was irreversible. Doctors surmised that the Princess had initially suffered a mild stroke that caused her to black out momentarily and lose control of the car. If she had been anywhere other than at the wheel of a car it would not have been a problem. The far more serious 'traumatic' damage to the frontal area of the brain had been caused by the terrible impact of the crash. Grace was clinically dead – she was only being kept alive by the machines.

After Grace was returned to her eponymous hospital, Professor Chatelin, the chief surgeon, showed the CAT scans to Prince Rainier, Albert and Caroline, who had recently flown in from London. He explained that Grace was brain-dead, and that there was no hope for a recovery. His advice was to turn off her life-support system.

After a brief discussion with his children late on Tuesday night, Prince Rainier agreed to let Grace die with dignity. And her family went into her room to say their final goodbyes.

Then Rainier went into the adjoining room to tell the injured Princess Stephanie that her mother had died and that she must be courageous. On hearing the news the young Princess let out a terrible scream. She started crying uncontrollably and as her father held her hand tightly, he too broke down in tears.

As the world heard the news of Princess Grace's death in stunned disbelief, the heartbreaking job of arranging her funeral was already under way. Prince Rainier was in such deep shock that he was hardly able to function and it was left to Prince Albert to call the Kelly family and friends in America with the news. Grace's brother Jack and other members of the Philadelphia clan were furious that they had not been consulted on the decision to extinguish Grace's life. Arrangements were made through Grace's first cousin, John Lehman, to fly close friends and family to Monaco for the funeral.

In the house after Grace's death a macabre parade of make-up artists, hairdressers and morticians tried to restore her damaged body; it had been decided that she would lie in state in an open coffin prior to the funeral.

'Stephanie was in terrible shock,' remembers the Countess of Lombardy, who spent much of the week working on the floor on which Stephanie was recuperating.

'She cried all the time and wanted to see her mother after she had died. Rainier wouldn't let her. He thought it would be too upsetting.'

When the people of Monaco heard they had lost their beloved 'mother' they plunged into mourning. It had taken years for the Monégasques to trust the former Hollywood star. Now they were devastated by the news of her death; they felt they had lost a member of their own family.

All the lights seemed to go out in Monaco as the principality went into official mourning. For days nobody spoke on the streets and most of the shops stayed shuttered as people stayed at home in silent respect. It would be more than a year before things returned to normal.

'For Monégasques the death of Princess Grace was like losing an arm or a leg,' said the Countess. 'it was an amputation.'

Princess Grace's body lady on display in an open casket in a tiny private chapel in the Palace, surrounded by a guard of honour. But she was hardly recognisable as the beguiling Princess who had captured the world's heart with her fragile beauty. In their clumsy attempts to cosmetically repair her broken head, the morticians had placed a bizarre blonde wig over her shaven head and plastered her face in heavy make-up. Grace's elder sister Peggy was so horrified by her sister's appearance that she tearfully told a friend it was 'dreadful'.

On Saturday, September 18, an estimated worldwide television audience of 100 million watched an openly tearful Prince Rainier, supported by Albert and Caroline, lead the funeral procession that took Grace on her last journey, from the Palace to St Nicholas' Cathedral. Thousands of mourners lined the route through the ancient town on the rock as the ebony coffin passed through to the single beat of a military drum.

Waiting in the Cathedral – where Grace and Rainier had married twenty-six years earlier – were the cream of European royalty, heads of state and many of Grace's old friends from Hollywood who had gathered to pay their last respects. Her Royal Highness the Princess Diana of Wales, who had become friends with Grace when they met the year before in London, was the sole representative of the British Royal Family; the Queen did not consider the Serene Grimaldis her royal equals.

Forbidden to attend by her doctors, Princess Stephanie, who was recuperating in traction, saw the funeral on television. As the Archbishop of Monaco began the service Stephanie first dissolved into tears, then lost consciousness. Paul Belmondo, who was with her, spent the next few hours trying in vain to comfort her.

After the public funeral there was a private reception for close friends and family in the West Garden at the Palace. Rainier, Caroline and Albert formed a receiving line to accept condolences.

'I was going through that receiving line,' says Judy Balaban Quine, a longtime friend of Princess Grace and one of the bridesmaids at her wedding.

'They were embracing one person after another and Albert was standing at one end. I was about five people away and I was looking at Albie. Suddenly he looked up and caught my eye. I'll never forget that look in his eyes as long as I live.

'It was the whole thing of wanting to have faith in some sort of sensible, universal order. And then just getting shattered.'

CHAPTER TWO

ONCE UPON A TIME

ONE WEEK AFTER her mother's funeral Princess Stephanie returned to the Palace to convalesce. As she left the hospital in a neck brace, the injured Princess refused any assistance from nurses and defiantly walked the ten paces to a car where Rainier, Caroline and Albert were waiting.

They drove home and behind closed doors Prince Rainier and his three children began their grieving process. Now, finally left alone with their memories, each of them knew that life without Grace would never be the same again.

Surprisingly, it was Prince Rainier, the strong, absolute ruler of Monaco, who completely fell apart in the wake of Grace's death. Just three weeks earlier, Rainier had suffered another major blow by losing his oldest and closest friend Jean-Louis Marson, who had died after a long illness. In the space of three weeks the Prince had lost the only two people whom he trusted implicitly to tell him the truth. It would be many months before the anguished Prince could find his direction again.

'I think he's having a very hard time,' Grace's younger sister Lizanne Kelly LeVine said during that period. 'He let Grace do a lot of things that he'll have to take over himself. I don't know how he's going to handle it.'

For years there had been persistent rumours that the Grimaldis' marriage was on the rocks. The couple, through necessity, spent a lot of time apart and by the time they reached middle age, the only thing they seemed to have in common were the children. Indeed, there were those who said that was all they had ever shared.

While Princess Grace passionately loved the arts, Rainier found them tedious, preferring to screen cowboy films or watch a soccer game. Naturally shy, Rainier felt intimidated and insecure about Grace's flamboyant Hollywood friends and avoided them.

Throughout their marriage – which had begun as an arranged one – Grace and Rainier eventually found a bond of love through their children.

'Grace said that she would learn how to love him,' recalls fashion designer Oleg Cassini, who was once himself engaged to her. 'After all, Rainier was an attractive man. He had a lot to offer her.'

But the truth was that Grace Kelly, who married Rainier at the pinnacle of her movie career, had far more to offer the Prince and Monaco than the other way around. As ruler of a then largely unknown and hard-up principality, half the size of New York's Central Park, Rainier fully realised the power of Grace's Hollywood allure and how it would help Monaco.

The eyes of the world were on Grace Kelly when she sailed into Monaco aboard the *USS Constitution* on the morning of April 12, 1956, after an eight-day voyage across the Atlantic. As the massive liner cut its engines to glide into the harbour, it was instantly surrounded by a ragged flotilla of boats eager for a first look at the new Princess. In the skies overhead a flock of helicopters and seaplanes appeared and began to circle. Then, on the instructions of Greek billionaire Aristotle Onassis, a canary-yellow seaplane began dropping thousands of red and white carnations onto the decks of the *USS Constitution*.

All morning a dull, grey mist had hung over the harbour. But as soon as Grace emerged on deck the sun came out as if on cue. She looked magnificent. Dressed in a dark silk coat, Grace had deliberately hidden her face under a huge hat to complete the picture of the shy, virginal bride: the part she had played so successfully in public for so long.

Although she had made many entrances during her acting career, this was by far the grandest, and the most nerve-racking. During the eight days at sea Grace had become increasingly nervous as the liner steamed toward Monaco. Stage fright had never been a problem in the past but now the twenty-six-year-old star was filled with fear and trepidation about what she was about to do.

As Rainier's old war-horse of a yacht the *Deo Juvante II* – a present from Onassis – pulled alongside the *USS Constitution*, Grace stepped across the gangplank to join her new lord and master. She was a bundle of nerves. After all, this was only her third meeting with the man she would marry in a week.

Grace had met her dashing young Prince the year before, in May 1955 while attending the Cannes Film Festival. She had been invited to attend a special screening of *The Country Girl*, for which she had just won an Academy Award for Best Actress.

As a favour to her friend, Pierre Galante – the *Paris Match* movie editor – she had agreed to be photographed in Monaco with Prince Rainier as a publicity stunt. As it turned out, the pairing of the current Queen of Hollywood with the Prince of Monaco was inspired.

But the meeting almost did not take place. Grace's Cannes schedule was so hectic that she had tried to cancel only hours before she was due to leave for Monaco. Everything was a panic. Her clothes had not been pressed and a power cut at her hotel meant she couldn't even style her hair.

Grace had felt it impossible to look her best for the Prince under these trying circumstances. Besides, it would be a terrible rush to get back to Cannes in time for the official American VIP reception she was hosting that evening. In the end Galante had managed to persuade her, saying it would be the height of bad manners to disappoint the Prince of Monaco.

When Grace finally met Rainier she was pleasantly surprised. He was anything but the stuffy, boring aristocrat she had been expecting. Slightly pudgy and boyish-looking, the thirty-two-year-old Prince had a sense of humour and was totally without pretensions. After greeting Grace and her party, and apologising for being a little late, he had taken them on a personal tour of the Palace gardens.

The first stop was Rainier's private zoo on a cliff ledge below the Palace, where he kept two lions, an Asian tiger and some monkeys. Putting on a special show of bravado for Grace and the *Paris Match* photographers, Rainier put his bare hand into the tiger's cage to pet the animal; Grace, who had spent time in Africa making *Mogambo* a few years earlier, was most impressed. Then Rainier escorted her through his exotic flower gardens, showing her some of the fabulous views of the Mediterranean his Palace offered.

As they said their goodbyes Prince Rainier casually announced that he was planning a trip to the United States in the near future. He hoped they might see each other again. Grace smiled, saying she would be delighted.

On the drive back to Cannes, Pierre Galante asked Grace what she had thought of Rainier.

'He's charming,' she replied dreamily, her thoughts a long way away. 'So very charming . . .'

When Prince Rainier became Monaco's ruler at the age of twenty-six, following the death of his grandfather Prince Louis II in 1949, he had inherited a principality on the verge of bankruptcy. Post-war Monaco was in dire straits. No longer was it the magnet for the wealthy set that it had been during the previous century.

The *Société des Bains de Mer* – Society of Sea Bathing (SBM), the corporation that owned and operated Monaco's casinos and hotels, was desperately in need of cash. At one point in the early 1950s the principality's economy was so bad that SBM employees had one month's pay deducted from their annual salaries.

Rainier's solution was to encourage the Greek shipping tycoon Aristotle Onassis to buy a majority share in the SBM and use his connections to re-establish Monaco as a desirable tourist destination for the wealthy. Onassis loved the idea and poured many millions of dollars into the SBM, making it both his latest toy and the tax-free headquarters of his sprawling business empire.

But initially the Prince and the billionaire had little success in depicting Monaco as *the* place to go. Anxious to maximise the return on his SBM investment, Onassis hired Greta Garbo's business manager George Schlee to develop a public relations programme for the principality. They agreed that the best way to attract American tourist dollars was for Rainier to marry a Hollywood film star and inject some glitz and glamour back into the faded principality.

'Marilyn Monroe was the first choice,' says Gwen Robyns. 'They thought Marilyn's sexy image would be terrific for Monaco.'

Schlee enlisted the help of his *Life* journalist friend Gardner Cowles, who knew the troubled star – now single since her recent split from Joe DiMaggio. Conveniently, Monroe just happened to be staying nearby on photographer Milton Green's Connecticut estate, so Schlee and Cowles paid her an impromptu poolside visit.

Gwen Robyns: 'They said, "How would you like to marry Prince Rainier of Monaco?" And Marilyn said, "Where's Monaco?" So they explained where it was. And she said, "Is he good-looking?" And they said, "Yes, he's quite good-looking." "Is he rich?" "Yes, yes, he's rich." And Marilyn just looked at them and said, "Just give me one night with him, he'll want me."

'Then these old bastards decided that maybe Marilyn Monroe wasn't right for him because she was so primitive, so they got to the second name on the list. Grace Kelly.'

Prince Rainier was thrilled by his first meeting with Grace Kelly. The unassuming Prince had little respect for Hollywood and had expected to dislike his movie-star visitor, but Philadelphia-born Grace's radiant beauty, combined with her honest simplicity and sense of humour, had quickly won him over. He was enchanted by her air of purity and innocence – and especially pleased that, like him, she was a devout Roman Catholic.

Even as Grace left the Palace to return to Cannes, Rainier knew that she was the perfect candidate to become his Princess of Monaco. After six years in power Rainier was under a great deal of pressure to marry and provide an heir to ensure the principality remained in Grimaldi hands. So far his achievements had been negligible. He faced constant battles with Monaco's elected National Council. His ambitious plan to build a railway tunnel under Monaco and reclaim land from the sea were openly mocked. It was from a position of weakness that he had first allowed Onassis to take control of the SBM. But he thoroughly approved of the tycoon's strategy of importing the magic of Hollywood into stodgy Monaco. By pure coincidence he happened to be thinking along the same lines and even adorned his study walls with signed photographs of Hollywood actresses who might fit the part.

On her return to the States, Grace's good breeding dictated that she compose a thank-you letter to Rainier. It would be the first letter in an on-going correspondence between the couple over the next few months. With each letter the Prince found himself telling Grace more details of his life, confessing his loneliness as a man and a ruler. Their letters were often flirtatious, with Rainier dropping clear hints that his interest in her might extend beyond mere friendship.

The Prince couldn't have come into Grace's life at a more opportune time. For she was currently playing the role of a Princess forced to choose between love and duty in the film version of Ferenc Molnár's play *The Swan*. And fantasy and reality began to merge for the young star as she began day-dreaming about becoming a real-life Princess across the ocean in Monaco.

During filming, Grace's co-star Alec Guinness, who was playing her Crown Prince, noticed she often seemed strangely distracted.

'Sometimes I saw her just waiting on the set, just looking into space,' recalled Guinness many years later. 'And I asked her, "Grace, are you feeling all right?" Then she came to, but always with a little start of surprise, as if she'd been far away.'

Gwen Robyns believes Grace remained in her *Swan* role long after the camera stopped rolling.

'Grace *became* the character she was playing,' says Robyns. 'She was the Princess in *The Swan* – so it was easy for her to go to the next step and make it a reality.'

That summer Grace and Rainier were pushed closer together by a fortuitous event. Edie and Russell Austin, who often vacationed with the Kelly family in Ocean City, New Jersey, happened to be visiting the South of France for the summer season. Affectionately known as Aunt Edie and Uncle Russ by the Kelly children, the Austins knew about Grace's meeting with Prince Rainier.

During their visit they decided to go to the annual Red Cross Ball at Monaco's Sporting Club but found it was sold out. Russ telephoned the Palace, politely explaining that he was Grace Kelly's uncle and would dearly love two tickets. His request landed on the desk of Father Francis Tucker, Rainier's spiritual adviser and confidante. And Father Tucker was delighted when he saw it.

The Prince had told him about Grace the very night of their meeting and Father Tucker thoroughly approved of the match. Now he found himself with the chance to play Cupid.

The following day the American-born priest personally delivered the tickets to the Austins at their Cannes hotel, using the opportunity to discover everything he could about Grace and her family. When he returned to the Palace he casually mentioned the meeting to Rainier, saying he was most impressed by what he had learned about the prospective Princess.

Later that week Prince Rainier invited the Austins to the Palace for tea, and steered the conversation toward Grace Kelly. As they said good-bye Edie Austin invited the Prince to visit her in Ocean City if he ever found himself in New Jersey.

Several months later, in late 1955, Rainier made his move. He telephoned Grace with the news that he was coming to America in December and would like to meet her family. So he was immediately invited to attend a Kelly family Christmas. Grace's parents, Jack and Margaret Kelly, were intrigued by the prospects of entertaining a real-life Prince at the family home, even if they had never heard of Monaco.

In an interview published in *Collier's* magazine shortly before his arrival, entitled: 'When Will the Prince Find His Princess?' Rainier was asked if there was a romantic reason for his trip.

'I am not shopping for a bride,' snapped Rainier to the *Collier's* reporter.

But he certainly was. Accompanying him on his American trip was Father Francis Tucker and his personal physician, Dr Robert Donat, who was there to ensure Grace was fertile. For Rainier's future bride would have to be capable of bearing Grimaldi children.

Grace Kelly's grandfather John Henry Kelly first came to America in 1867. Leaving behind the tiny village of Drumirla in County Mayo on the western shores of Ireland, the twenty-year-old farm boy arrived as an immigrant with no more than the clothes he stood up in. However, he soon settled down in Rutland, Vermont, fell in love and married seventeen-year-old Mary Costello, also from County Mayo, who had arrived in America nine years earlier.

In 1873 he moved his growing family to Philadelphia after a relative of Mary's found him a job at Dobson's Textile Mill in the Falls of Schuykill. By 1890 Mary, known to her children as 'the dowager', had delivered six boys and four girls. But it was a constant struggle to survive on John's meagre earnings as a labourer.

Mary dreamt of a better future for her children and ruled the family with an iron hand. She dominated her husband, never letting him forget his shortcomings as a provider. It was she who injected ambition and drive into her children; her success can be measured by the fact that five of her children would later achieve fame in business and the arts.

The Kelly clan were Patrick, Walter, Ann, John (who died during birth), Charles, Mary, Elizabeth, George, John Brendan (known as Jack – Princess Grace's father), and Grace, who died of a heart attack at the tragically young age of twenty-two. She had seemed destined for a career on the stage and Princess Grace was named after her.

The strict discipline and wholesome Catholic values Mary instilled in her children are illustrated in an article she wrote for *American Magazine* in 1924 entitled 'Oh, There Ought to be a Million Mothers Like Mary Kelly'. In it she outlined her tips for bringing up children, leaving no doubt that she was the absolute ruler of her large brood.

'I've been a lawyer, for I laid down a code of justice in the family; and I was the policeman that kept order, and the jury that decided the cases, and the judge that handed out the punishment.'

All the young Kelly boys worked at Dobson's Mill and Grace's father Jack began working there after school at the age of nine. Their earnings were handed to 'the dowager' to go toward their keep.

In 1900, at the age of twenty-eight, the eldest Kelly child decided to better himself. Patrick Kelly, a low-paid bricklayer, came up with a brilliant scheme to set himself up in the construction business. A local newspaper was holding a contest asking readers to vote for the most popular employee in town, with the grand prize of a $5,000 house. Jack Kelly followed the paper boy on his early-morning round and prepared a list of newspaper subscribers. That evening another Kelly brother canvassed each reader, urging them to vote for Patrick Kelly.

Patrick easily won the competition and immediately sold the house, using the money to start the P H Kelly Building Co. And before long business was flourishing, providing jobs for most of the Kelly clan.

Jack, a six-foot-two-inch, 185-pound Adonis – who would later be described by President Franklin Roosevelt as 'the most handsome man he had ever seen' – worked for Patrick as a hod-carrier. But every evening after a hard day's work he'd practice sculling on the Schuykill River. The sport, where a single rower uses two oars to propel a light craft through the water, is the supreme test of physical strength.

Jack's passionate love of sculling became a lifelong obsession. When his mother became concerned that his love of the sport was becoming unhealthy, he explained to her that rowing was 'something special' to him. It was a 'real he-man sport' which took 'guts and willpower'.

Jack won every competition he entered and by 1919 he held several national sculling titles. But the defining moment in his life came when he decided to go to England and compete in the Diamond Sculls at the prestigious Henley-on-Thames Regatta. He bought a new boat and prepared with a rigorous training programme. But three days before the event in June 1920, he was told that his application to compete had been rejected. The stated reason was that, as a manual labourer, he had an unfair advantage over the other, wealthier competitors who didn't work with their hands.

Jack was crestfallen at being turned down by the English rowing stewards for not being a 'gentleman'. And his anger at the snub would fester for years, severely affecting the next generation of Kellys. He finally restored his honour by seeing his son Jack Jr, known as Kell, win the Diamond Sculls nearly thirty years later.

After Grace became famous she loved to tell the story of how Jack went on to win an Olympic gold rowing medal at the 1920 Olympics in Belgium.

'Did you ever know an Irishman who would take a thing like that lying down?' Grace would ask proudly. 'So John Kelly, grandson of an Irish pig farmer, two months later won the Olympic singles gold medal. And whom did he beat? The English champ! So he sent his victorious green rowing cap to the King of England with his compliments!'

On his return to Philadelphia he was declared a hero and greeted by 100,000 cheering people who lined the streets to welcome him home.

A year later, in 1921, helped by cash gifts from his brothers, Walter had become successful with his "Virginia Judge" stage routine in which he donned a baggy white suit and panama hat to play the role of a Southern magistrate hearing cases against blacks who became the butt for his bad racist jokes. Virginia Judd: "Want to make a quarter?" Poor Black: "No, suh. I've got a quarter." George was an actor and playwright. Jack left P H Kelly Building Co. to start his own firm, Kelly For Brickwork.

By January 1924 Jack's new business was thriving and he decided to settle down and marry his long-time girlfriend Margaret Majer. A pretty, vivacious girl with blonde hair and blue eyes, Margaret could trace her Germans roots back to sixteenth-century nobility.

As a concession to her new mother-in-law she converted to Catholicism from the Lutheran faith in which she was raised. But Margaret was more than a match for the Kelly matriarch and severe clashes between the two iron ladies would have been inevitable had Mary Kelly not died in 1926. Like Jack Kelly, Margaret was highly athletic and she had a degree in physical education. She posed in the early 1920s for the cover of *Country Gentleman* magazine as a blonde, Nordic beauty. They both worshipped the idea of the perfect body achieved through athletic development; a doctrine they instilled in their four children.

Margaret (Peggy) was born a year after the marriage; John Jr. (Kell) followed in 1927; Grace was born on November 12, 1929, and Elizabeth Anne (Lizanne) in 1933. With Kelly For Brickwork business booming, Jack built his family a rambling seventeen-room house on Henry Avenue in the highly fashionable Philadelphia district of Germantown. Within a few years Jack had become one of the city's wealthiest men; he even ran for Mayor in the mid-1930s (on the Democratic ticket for Roosevelt's New Deal), but was soundly beaten.

'It used to be said in the city of Philadelphia,' said Jack Seabrook, a friend of the family, 'that if four people congregated on a street corner,

Jack Kelly would show up and make a speech. He was a very good speaker, and a very handsome man—but he was also very vain. He was as blind as a bat but he hated to put his glasses on . . . because that detracted from his youthful image.'

A flamboyant playboy, Jack was constantly unfaithful to Margaret, who preferred to turn a blind eye to his indiscretions. Now approaching middle age and known to one and all as 'Ma Kelly', Margaret knew keeping up appearances was vital. She would never do anything to jeopardise her family's good name.

Ma Kelly was a strict disciplinarian. Known by the Kelly children as 'our Prussian General mother', she liked to boast that she wasn't the kind of mother who waited to discipline the children until their father came home. And it was said in the neighbourhood that 'Ma Kelly could really hit'.

'She was a strong martinet on discipline,' said Gwen Robyns. 'It came from her Teutonic stock.'

Growing up in the Kelly household was very hard on Grace. Not a natural athlete like her sisters and brother, Grace was a sickly child who suffered from asthma. To Jack Kelly his puny daughter was a permanent source of disappointment and embarrassment.

'Grace was always sniffling,' said her childhood friend Gloria Otley. 'We were always saying, "Gracie, blow your nose. Stop your sniffling.'"

From the age of five Grace began inventing her own world of fantasy to escape the demands of her parents. She used to borrow her elder sister Peggy's dolls to play with so she wouldn't dirty her own. Grace became manipulative, deliberately assuming a look of abject helplessness which made people want to reach out and help her. It was a valuable tool she would employ throughout her life.

'Grace knew exactly where she was going from the age of five,' says Robyns. 'Once she got her act together she never deviated. She manufactured Grace. Nobody else could have done it.'

Just before her fifth birthday in 1934 Grace was sent to the Academy of the Assumption in Ravenhill, Philadelphia. The strict Sisters of the Assumption drilled the little girl in her catechism, schoolwork and the importance of good manners. One of her teachers, Sister Francis

Joseph, remembers Grace as a well-behaved girl of average intellect and 'pretty matter-of-fact.'

As she grew up Grace developed a love of the theater. Her acting skills were greatly helped by her playwright uncle George, who became her mentor. George Kelly won the Pulitzer Prize for his play *Craig's Wife* in 1926. By the age of twelve Grace was regularly performing with the East Falls Old Academy Players, together with her sister Peggy. Grace had an obvious talent and began getting bigger and bigger parts as she entered her teens.

When Grace was fourteen she moved to Stevens Public High School in Germantown as Jack Kelly had decided its sporting facilities were far superior to Ravenhill. And when she graduated at the age of eighteen from Stevens, the caption on her yearbook photograph prophetically declared: 'She is very likely to become a stage or screen star.'

When Grace announced she wanted to study at the American Academy of Dramatic Arts in New York her parents tried to dissuade her.

'I was not too fond of the idea of my little girl all alone in New York,' Ma Kelly would remember. But finally the determined Grace persuaded her father to let her audition and she was accepted after reciting a part of her Uncle George's award-winning play. *The Torch Bearers.*

The Grace Kelly who arrived in New York in October 1947—a month short of her eighteenth birthday—to begin her studies at the American Academy was very different to the shy, feeble girl who had once embarrassed her parents. The Kelly ugly duckling had grown into a ravishingly beautiful swan. Five-foot-six-and-a-half-inches in her stockinged feet, Grace had hypnotic blue eyes and the flaxen blonde hair of a sleek, Teutonic goddess.

Just before her first semester in New York, Grace lost her virginity to the husband of one of her friends. Relating her first sexual encounter she would tell a later lover: 'It all happened so quickly. I dropped in unexpectedly at a girlfriend's house—I remember it was raining very hard—and her husband told me she would be gone for the rest of the afternoon. I stayed talking to him, and before I knew it we were in bed together.'

No one knows for sure how many men Grace Kelly slept with before she married Prince Rainier. In recent years biographers have shattered Grace's frigid 'ice queen' image with sensational claims that she had a voracious sexual appetite and bedded several of her leading men, including Clark Gable, William Holden and Bing Crosby. She has been labelled an ambitious marriage wrecker who did not think twice about sleeping with married men. But, as was the case with her admitted affair with *Dial M for Murder* co-star Ray Milland, Grace was often the victim of unscrupulous men who misled her.

'She had gotten a sort of bad reputation with Ray Milland,' recalls actress Rita Gam, who shared a Hollywood apartment with her and would later be a bridesmaid at her wedding. 'I mean, the wives were just out with their knives for her.'

The major love affair of her life, before she met Prince Rainier, was with the international fashion designer, Oleg Cassini, to whom she was briefly engaged. Now in his eighties, Cassini believes that Grace would only sleep with a man if she truly believed it would end in marriage.

'There have been attempts to make it appear that every time she made a picture she had an affair with the guy,' said Cassini.

'She was a militant Catholic with very profound and rigid beliefs. She would never consider romance with anybody unless she really, honestly thought she would marry them.'

The self-made millionaire fashion designer, who later dressed Jackie Kennedy and created her sophisticated look, was charm personified. After falling for Grace Kelly when he saw her in *Mogambo*, he hatched a campaign of military proportions to win her heart. A master of courtly love, Cassini's playful romantic poker game enthralled Grace and the relationship seemed to be heading for the altar – until her parents stepped in.

After the couple became engaged in the summer of 1954, following a whirlwind romance in the South of France, Grace brought Cassini, the son of an exiled Russian nobleman, to the Kelly's Ocean City summer home to meet her parents. The weekend was a disaster. Jack and

Ma Kelly thoroughly disapproved of the twice-divorced Cassini's thick European accent and playboy image and didn't hesitate to let him know it.

At their first meeting, over lunch in a New York restaurant, Ma Kelly launched a pre-emptive strike.

'She said to me, "Frankly, we don't think you're good material for marriage,"' recalls Cassini. '"You have too many girlfriends and you go around too much – you're a playboy!"'

Although she was an internationally-famous movie star and one week short of her twenty-fifth birthday, Grace was still a feeble little girl when it came to her parents. Time and again in the past she had let them interfere with her love life, telling her which boyfriend was suitable and which was not. Now Cassini demanded she take a stand for once and for all against her parents.

Grace even suggested a way of 'blackmailing' her parents into letting them marry; she would deliberately get pregnant so the strictly Catholic Kelly parents would have no choice in the matter.

A few days after Ma Kelly came to New York, Grace invited Cassini to Ocean City for the weekend, saying her mother had softened her attitude a little. However, Jack Kelly was still vehemently opposed to Cassini – calling him variously a 'wop', a 'dago', and a 'worm' – though he had finally agreed to let him spend the weekend.

The weekend was a nightmare for Cassini. Jack Kelly totally ignored him, refusing to even acknowledge his presence; Cassini sat uncomfortably through breakfast, lunch and dinner, during which not a word was spoken by the family. Every time he tried to make conversation there was a resounding silence. It was a real relief for Cassini when he finally left Ocean City.

'When my father and mother wanted to put on the cold shoulder they did a very good job,' explained Lizanne.

Back in New York, Grace and Cassini carried on their romance as if the weekend with the Kellys had never happened. Most nights they would dine in Grace's apartment where they would take turns doing the cooking, acting like a proper married couple; at weekends they would go to Long Island to stay with Cassini's friends. When Grace went to Hollywood to film the interior scenes for *To Catch a Thief* she rented a house and Cassini moved in.

In early 1955 Grace became pregnant with Oleg Cassini's child. She declared that she was now ready to marry the forty-one-year-old couturier.

'I feel for the first time ready to approach love and marriage in an adult way,' she wrote to Cassini. 'I love you more every day and hope you feel that way too. I love you and want to be your wife.'

Cassini agreed to convert from the Russian Orthodox religion to the Roman Catholic faith and found a priest in Virginia who would perform the wedding ceremony. The couple planned to have a small secret wedding, with Grace taking time off to have the baby.

But at the last minute she changed her mind. Torn between her devout Catholic upbringing, her movie career and her love of Cassini, Grace decided she could not risk a scandal. So instead of going through with the marriage she had an abortion.

Asked about the secret baby more than forty years later, the ever-chivalrous Cassini remains defensive and evasive.

'It's too delicate a matter,' he says sadly. 'I don't have to answer this and I will make no comment about that. Absolutely no comment. Let people think what they want.'

Explaining the breakdown of his relationship with Grace Kelly, all Cassini will say was that at the last minute 'she didn't feel well'.

'I must say that I got exhausted emotionally with all this effort by the studio, her agent, the priest, the family, to get me away from her. And I thought, "Well, let destiny play its role here. I'm not going to push for any conclusion."'

CHAPTER THREE

THE WEDDING
OF THE
CENTURY

WHEN PRINCE RAINIER arrived at 3901 Henry Avenue on Christmas night to meet the Kellys, he enjoyed a much easier reception than Oleg Cassini had a year earlier. As the Prince walked up to the front door accompanied by Father Tucker and Dr Donat, an anxious Grace Kelly awaited inside.

Grace had almost changed her mind about coming home from Hollywood for Christmas. She was very nervous about meeting Prince Rainier again; after their six-month-long transatlantic friendship Grace was not sure she had the courage or inclination to go to the next step.

'I made up my mind I wouldn't go,' she would later remember. 'And then – I can't remember how it happened – I just went and bought a plane ticket anyway.'

Even though the dinner visit to the Kellys was to be informal there were still matters of protocol to consider. After all, the Prince, still a stranger to Grace's parents, could not just invite himself round for dinner. To circumnavigate this it was decided that Rainier should first have lunch with Aunt Edie and Uncle Russ Austin, with whom he was already acquainted; they in turn would call Jack Kelly to ask if they could drop by later with 'some foreign friends'.

As late as Christmas morning Grace was having serious second thoughts about the imminent reunion. She spent the day in a panic before she finally calmed down enough to prepare herself for Rainier's visit.

Grace's elder sister Peggy Conlan would later recall that momentous night, noting that, compared to Grace, the rest of the Kellys were relatively relaxed about the Prince's visit.

'We knew almost nothing about him,' said Peggy. 'It wasn't like he was well known in the United States; we weren't reading about him in the papers every other day. So it wasn't like Prince Charles coming to your house for dinner.'

Jack Kelly greeted Prince Rainier's party at the door, making a point of calling him 'Your Highness'. The Prince looked bashful as he walked into the hall followed by the inimitable Father Tucker, who had a mischievous twinkle in his eye.

'My father knew an Irish priest if ever he saw one,' said Peggy. '"Father Tucker," he said, "sit down and I'll give you a cigar."'

Although Grace was feeling awkward and self-conscious, she was doing her best to look at ease. But Father Tucker's good-natured *craic* and humour immediately cut through any tension there might have been.

It wasn't long before Prince Rainier had manoeuvred himself next to Grace. Soon, 'sparks were flying', according to her sister Peggy. Ma Kelly watched with pride as the thirty-two-year-old Prince 'monopolised' Grace during dinner, as they caught up on each other's adventures since they had last met. Time flew by and at ten o'clock Father Tucker left to catch a train to Wilmington, Delaware.

The Prince seemed in no hurry to end the evening so Ma Kelly asked if he and Dr Donat would like to stay the night in the guest room. The Kelly matriarch was impressed with the Prince and was now trying to assess his interest in her daughter. When Rainier jumped at her offer to stay, Ma knew the Kellys' imminent entry into the ranks of European nobility was firmly on the cards.

'His intentions were not just those of a smitten young man,' Ma Kelly recalled later. 'There was purpose in his every word and movement.'

At this point Ma suggested that the 'young ones' retire to Peggy's house around the corner where they could amuse themselves away from the 'grown-ups'. On the way over Grace and Rainier plotted to be alone; when they arrived they disappeared into the next room, leaving Peggy, Kell and Dr Donat to play cards.

It was two in the morning when a sheepish-looking Rainier emerged, his jacket covered in black dog's hair. Seizing the opportunity, Peggy offered to get some scotch tape to make the Prince look presentable, at the same time ushering Grace into the bedroom to discover what had happened.

'I think he's very, *very* fascinating,' was all Grace would say as she tried to stem her giggles.

'Well, I think he is too,' agreed Peggy as they returned to Rainier and prepared for the walk back to Jack Kelly's house.

A few days after Christmas Prince Rainier asked Grace to marry him. She immediately accepted. Since Christmas dinner the couple had been inseparable. On Boxing Day Grace took Rainier on a tour of Philadelphia and then on to dinner with her younger sister Lizanne and her husband Don LeVine, who had both missed Rainier's visit as they had been in Pittsburgh.

While the Prince was helping Don with the dishes, Grace and Lizanne went into the front room to talk. When Grace asked her sister what she thought of Rainier, Lizanne said she thought he was very nice. Then, to Lizanne's astonishment, Grace announced they were engaged to be married.

'Well, I just about fell off the couch,' said Lizanne. 'I said, "Oh, my God, Grace – you don't even *know* this guy!"'

The next step was for Rainier to ask Jack Kelly for permission to marry his daughter. Although Rainier was an absolute monarch in Monaco, here in Philadelphia he was another young suitor who had to prove his worth. But Jack had been most impressed with the Prince and looked forward to the new status that would come with entry to the Monaco ruling family.

He gave his permission right away but felt compelled to lecture Rainier on faithfulness, although he himself had broken his marriage vows on numerous occasions.

'I hope you won't run around the way some princes do,' Jack warned. 'Because if you do you'll lose a mighty fine girl. Don't forget, she's got Irish blood in her veins and she knows what she wants.'

Many years later Grace would admit that when she got engaged she had acted on 'instinct' and had not thought through the implications of leaving Hollywood and her dazzling career to marry a European Prince.

She would later analyse the situation:

'We happened to meet each other at a time when each of us was ready for marriage. There comes a time in life when you have to choose.'

Grace's sister Lizanne believes that the couple found a 'great attraction' in each other but it was not a love match.

'She didn't have time to *really* be in love,' she explained. 'She had been more in love with other people than she was with Rainier when she first met him. I don't know why she decided to marry him so quickly.'

Even today Prince Rainier admits he wasn't in love but says there was a 'flint' of something when they met.

'I don't really believe in love at first sight,' said Rainier in December 1996. 'I think true love has to be based on something.'

Before Rainier and Grace could officially announce their engagement there were several barriers that had to be surmounted. The first of these was to ensure that Grace could bear children – heirs to the throne of Monaco.

This was a particularly touchy subject for Rainier. The love of his former life had been the French actress Giselle Pascal who lived with him in the early 1950s in his villa outside Monaco, at Beaulieu. In 1953 Rainier proposed to her and Monaco had prepared for a new Princess. But a medical check-up, insisted on by Monégasque officials, found her infertile and Rainier broke off the relationship. Ironically, some years later Pascal did marry and have children.

Prince Rainier was unwilling to discuss so delicate a subject with Grace, so it was left to Father Tucker to do the dirty work. When he explained the significance of the test to the future of Monaco, Grace readily agreed and was tested at a private sanitarium outside Philadelphia. But her main concern was that the test would reveal she had been sexually active and was not the virgin she had led Rainier to believe.

She passed the fertility test but there was now an even more difficult hurdle ahead – the question of her dowry. The idea of the father of the bride paying the bridegroom for the privilege of marrying his daughter was a time-honoured tradition among Europe's best aristocratic families.

But Jack Kelly flew into a rage when Father Tucker broached the subject, placing the wedding in jeopardy. The Kelly patriarch had started from nothing to build one of Philadelphia's biggest fortunes; his Irish pride dictated that he was not going to subsidise a pauper Prince from a tin-pot principality.

Feeling herself losing control of her destiny, which was now being hammered out by lawyers, Grace made a series of phone calls to Don Richardson, her former drama teacher with whom she had had her first love affair in New York.

'She'd say, "Daddy's being impossible!"' Richardson remembered. 'Her father kept storming out of meetings with the Prince's lawyers in a rage.'

Finally, after Father Tucker produced proof of Rainier's assets, a dowry was agreed on. It was reported to be $2 million – a figure later disputed by the Palace. Perhaps more ominous for Grace was that part of the agreement stipulated that, in the event of a divorce, any children of the marriage would stay in Monaco with their father. But when concerned friends raised the matter with her, Grace, the devout Catholic, said there would never be question of a divorce.

On January 5, 1956 – a Thursday – the news that Prince Rainier was to marry Grace Kelly was announced simultaneously in Monaco and the United States. The fact that America's number one box-office star was marrying Europe's most eligible bachelor captured the public imagination to the point of intoxication.

'It absolutely was a fairytale romance,' declared Prince Louis de Polignac, Rainier's cousin and chairman of the SBM, the casino organisation which stood to benefit most from the match. And Aristotle Onassis must have been delighted when he heard the news which would transform the fortunes of Monaco and dramatically increase his own financial stake in the principality.

They called it the wedding of the century. An army of more than 1,600 reporters and photographers flooded into the tiny principality to cover the unprecedented event; not even World War Two had warranted such heavy press representation.

Metro Goldwyn Meyer had a heavy stake in the action. In return for putting Grace Kelly's movie contract on indefinite hold, the studio won exclusive film rights to her wedding. The documentary, named *The Wedding of the Century*, was later successfully shown in cinemas around the world.

The agreement called for an MGM-financed, Monégasque crew to film the Cathedral nuptials and wedding reception. The studio would then split the profits – minus a thirty per cent distribution cut – with Grace and Rainier, who had agreed to donate the proceeds to the Monaco Red Cross.

Although Rainier was pleased to have put Monaco so firmly in the spotlight, he was less than happy about having to co-operate with the press for staged photographs. At one point, during a press conference to announce the wedding, the Prince became visibly irate after he had been asked rather irreverently to kiss his new bride. 'After all, *I* don't belong to MGM,' he had hissed to Father Tucker.

As thousands of tourists poured into Monaco to witness the history-making event, crass commercialisation threatened to overshadow the regal dignity of the wedding. America's three television networks were covering it and had already sold airtime during the ceremony to a host of unsuitable sponsors, including lingerie and soap powder manufacturers.

'It was a media circus,' remembers Grace's friend and bridesmaid, Rita Gam. 'It had the quality of an insane happening and the Monégasques were slightly bemused by it all.'

Some of the Monégasques tried to cash in themselves, hawking over-priced souvenirs to tourists; others became scalpers, selling their wedding-event tickets to the highest bidder. Prince Rainier stepped in to ban any use of the official Grimaldi coat of arms, but he was powerless to stop the publicity machine once it had revved into high gear.

Many years later Prince Rainier would describe the eight days of wedding festivities with regret. 'Grace kept saying: maybe we should run off to a small chapel somewhere in the mountains and finish getting married there. I wish we had, because there was no way either she or I could really enjoy what was happening.'

At 9.30 AM on Thursday April 19, 1956, Monaco was bathed in bright sunshine as the 800 wedding guests took their places in St Nicholas' Cathedral to await the arrival of the bride. Grace's Hollywood friends – Ava Gardner, Gloria Swanson and David Niven, amongst others – rubbed shoulders with Aristotle Onassis, Somerset Maugham and Randolph Churchill in the Cathedral, which had been spruced up for the occasion. But there was a conspicuous lack of European royalty at the wedding. The British Royal Family did not consider Prince Rainier their equal, and had declined their invitation.

Every head turned as Grace entered the Cathedral on the arm of her father. Resplendent in her pure white wedding gown, with her golden hair swept back under a Juliet cap, she looked as if she had stepped out of the pages of a storybook. Her shimmering gown had been a gift from MGM and had been lovingly hand-made by studio wardrobe designer Helen Rose, a close friend. As befitted a Princess, the dress included 125-year-old rose-point lace purchased from a museum; 100 yards of silk net; and twenty-five yards of silk taffeta. Thousands of pearls had been sewn into the veil.

'Grace looked like Snow White,' said bridesmaid Rita Gam. 'It was the Hollywood fantasy to end all Hollywood fantasies.'

Although the bride was traditionally elegant, dressed in perfect taste to suit the occasion, the same could not be said for the groom. Prince Rainier had designed his militaristic outfit himself, drawing his inspiration from the costumes worn by Napoleon's marshals. Although Monaco did not even have a standing army, the Prince wore a plethora of French and Italian military medals and orders, some of which he had won as a colonel in the Free French Army. His chocolate uniform was weighed down with a crazy collage of gold leaf, epaulettes and ostrich feathers, and he wore the red and white sash of the Order of St Charles across his chest.

'Watching Grace come down the aisle, I wondered how many hours she had spent rehearsing in her dress,' recalled bridesmaid Judy Balaban Quine. 'As an actress, Grace would have known how important it was to see how the dress worked as she walked, stood, sat, kneeled and rose again. As a Princess bride, she had probably practiced extensively.'

In fact, to all intents and purposes the Cathedral was no more than an elaborate movie set, hardly reflecting the solemnity of the occasion. There were arc lights hanging from the rafters and cameras everywhere; throughout the ceremony television technicians were constantly adjusting the microphones placed around the altar.

But the bride was oblivious to the heat of the lights and all the other distractions. When Father Tucker called 'Action' Grace Kelly concentrated on her part – just as she had done in so many movies – to deliver a flawless performance.

(Although the service was being officially conducted by the Bishop of Monaco, Monsignor Gilles Barthe, it was the bilingual Father Tucker who directed the wedding, making sure that everyone was in the right place at the right time.)

After making a seventeen-minute address, Monsignor Barthe began the solemn exchange of wedding vows that would transform Grace Kelly into Princess Grace of Monaco.

'Rainier Louis Henri Maxence Bertrand,' intoned the Bishop, 'will you take Grace Patricia here present for your lawful wife, according to the rite of our Holy Mother the Church?'

Through the whirl of the cameras and the glare of the floodlights, the Prince quietly replied, 'Yes, Monsignor.'

As the Bishop asked Grace to pledge her love she reached for Rainier's hand. She gripped it tightly as she replied, 'Yes, Monsignor,' in a clear, soft voice, without any hesitation.

The Bishop then said the words the whole world was waiting to hear: 'I declare you united in marriage in the name of the Father, the Son and the Holy Ghost.'

CHAPTER FOUR

LIFE IN MONACO

PRINCESS GRACE GAVE birth to a baby daughter in the Palace library on January 23, 1957, exactly nine months and four days after the wedding. Caroline Louise Marguerite was officially welcomed into the world by a twenty-one-blast salute from a cannon in the harbour; the bells of the principality's fourteen churches and chapels rang out in celebration. Down below in the harbour Aristotle Onassis's yacht *Christina* led an unruly cacophony of horns and sirens from the various craft moored there. But it would be another year before the cannon would fire the 101-blast salute reserved for the arrival of a male heir.

It had been a difficult nine months for the new Princess, who found herself isolated in a foreign culture, having to rely on her meagre schoolgirl French in order to communicate.

'Grace had no idea of what she was getting herself into,' said Gwen Robyns. 'She suddenly found out that her Prince was His Serene Highness and she was just there to be seen – this beautiful thing that all the men wanted as a frontispiece for Monaco.'

For the first year of their marriage Grace felt anything but beautiful. The strain of the wedding and the huge adjustments of marriage brought back the chronic asthma she had suffered as a child. Her honeymoon, spent cruising the Mediterranean aboard Rainier's yacht the *Deo Juvente II*, was spoiled by sea-sickness, which plagued her almost every day. When she returned, pregnant, to begin her new life as Monaco's Princess, she faced distrust and sometimes outright hostility.

The Monaco of the mid-1950s was like a nineteenth-century village, populated by a motley collection of exiled European royalty, old-money millionaires, and impoverished aristocrats. It was incredibly snobbish and Grace was looked down on for being from Hollywood – and worst of all, an Irish bricklayer's daughter.

'There was some suspicion of Grace being a movie star and that she was inappropriate,' said Judy Balaban Quine. 'Even though she looked beautiful and had this sweet smile and handled herself magnificently, there was in some quarters a sense that a Prince doesn't marry a movie star; he marries a Princess.'

Ten years later Princess Grace would tell American television interviewer Barbara Waters that she faced a 'definite anti-American feeling' when she arrived in Monaco.

'Naturally I was a stranger coming into their midst,' she said. 'And to many people I am considered a foreigner and will always be.'

Prince Rainier's family were especially hostile. And when she became a Grimaldi, Grace found herself traversing a dangerous minefield of decades of family strife. Rainier's parents, Prince Pierre and Princess Charlotte, had had a bitter divorce that had traumatised him as a young boy. They hated each other with a vengeance, and Rainier and his sister Antoinette – known in the family as Tiny – had been innocent pawns in their parents' furious battles.

When Grace married Rainier she was frozen out by both Charlotte and Tiny. In contrast, Prince Pierre gave her a warm welcome, embracing her like a daughter. Grace was so distraught by the women's rejection that she fell into a depression and became very homesick.

'Grace had great problems with Rainier's mother,' recalls her sister Lizanne Kelly LeVine. 'Cold wasn't the word for Charlotte's attitude towards Grace ... And Princess Antoinette wasn't any happier about the Prince marrying an American actress than Charlotte had been.'

To complicate matters even further, Rainier's sister was embroiled in an affair with Jean-Charles Rey, a National Council member who hated Rainier. The two had unsuccessfully attempted to depose Rainier several years earlier. Before the marriage, Antoinette had been Monaco's acting First Lady but when Grace arrived she was forced to give up the position. She was not happy, and Grace bore the brunt of her anger.

During her first couple of years in Monaco, Princess Grace remained silent at her public appearances, mostly because her French was so bad. She was afraid of making a mistake and saying the wrong thing but the Monégasques misunderstood, believing that their new Princess was aloof and did not care for them.

The rigid protocol that her position as First Lady of Monaco demanded, both inside and outside of the Palace, was also difficult for Grace to endure. Palace officials drilled her daily about what she could and couldn't do as a Princess. She learned that she must always wear a hat at public events; that she must never appear alone without her husband or a lady-in-waiting. In her letters and other correspondence she must sign her name as 'Grace de Monaco' and only refer to her husband by the capitalised pronoun 'He', or 'Him'. When women met her they must curtsey; she would be known as 'Your Serene Highness' or the more formal 'Her Serene Highness'.

Years later Grace would say that she could never get used to hearing her title of 'Serene Highness' in American although it seemed normal in French.

Settling down to married life with Rainier was also a strain. After their six-month transatlantic courtship Grace was ill-prepared for her new husband's bouts of moodiness and melancholy. His fiery Latin temperament made him unpredictable and his hair-trigger temper could go off without any warning. On one occasion Grace's unfortunate choice of flowers for the guest quarters of a visiting dignitary sent the Prince into a tirade in front of her embarrassed secretary, Madge Tivey-Faucon.

'For God's sake,' he screamed at Grace, 'white chrysanthemums are the flowers of the tomb!'

In those early days Grace often telephoned her friends back home in tears to complain about Rainier's tantrums.

'She said Rainier was terrible, difficult to get along with,' Grace's friend Bill Hegner told author James Spada. 'She was homesick, and he's a strong-willed person.'

She soon discovered that European husbands were very different from American ones and being married to an absolute ruler brought its own unique set of problems.

'A European husband is definitely head of the household; there are no two ways about it,' said Princess Grace in 1966. 'American women are outspoken, forthright and honest and say what they think. And this shocks European men.'

In the fall of 1956 – just five months after their wedding – Grace and Rainier had embarked on a two-month shopping expedition to America to buy baby clothes and new modern furnishings for the Palace. While she was in New York, Grace had closed up her old apartment and shipped her furniture and belongings back to the Palace so she could feel more at home – but even that would cause great friction within Palace walls.

Day-to-day life in the dilapidated old Palace had remained largely unchanged for centuries. And the vivacious young Princess's efforts to drag it into the twentieth century were strongly resisted by the staff, who were set in their ways. Her poor command of French made it hard for her to understand the servants and she became convinced that they were laughing at her behind her back. One butler, who was responsible for the wine and preparing the table-settings, became a particular thorn in her side. He would steadfastly resist even the smallest change in

Palace routine that Grace tried to introduce.

'We don't do things that way here,' the butler would say condescendingly to the American upstart.

An elderly gardener who had arranged the blooms in the palatial Palace gardens for decades was also furious when Grace dared to make a suggestion.

'He was "Mr. Flowers" at the palace,' said Judy Balaban Quine. 'And who was this American movie star coming in here and showing him how to do flowers?'

The Palace staff were appalled to see crates arriving from the United States containing bulk quantities of Grace's favourite brands of canned foods, cookies and diet supplements. There were also hundreds of rolls of soft toilet paper, which Grace said made her feel more at home.

In addition, the Palace chef and servants were upset at having to use her new American cooking equipment, as well as at her appointment of an English housekeeper, to whom they had to report. All this resentment – combined with a difficult pregnancy that stretched into a scorching hot Monaco summer – finally took their toll on Grace's health.

'Grace told me that she had an awful time with the heat and that she was constantly sick,' said Robyns. 'I remember saying to her once, "Well, what did you do?" And she said, "I just sat there knitting. The one thing that they wanted was an heir and I gave them that nine months to the day."'

Prince Rainier was delighted to be a father. Unlike Jack Kelly, who when told about his new granddaughter had tactlessly reacted by saying, 'Oh, shucks, I'd been hoping for a boy', – or Grace, who cried when she first heard – the Prince did not care in the least about his firstborn's gender.

As Grace held her new daughter and sipped champagne, Rainier gave thanks in the Palace chapel before addressing his subjects.

'My beloved wife, the Princess, has given birth to a baby Princess who has been given the name of Caroline Louise Marguerite. Thank God and rejoice,' he jubilantly declared.

Tradition dictated that officials from Monaco's National Council be brought in to view the infant so she could be officially declared the heir apparent. So, as tiny Caroline lay sleeping in her mother's arms, press photographers and television cameras were allowed into the library for a photo-call.

To celebrate the great event a national holiday was declared. Monte-Carlo's casinos were closed; free champagne was served in the streets; children were let out of school early; and the three prisoners in Monaco's gaol were released.

Now she had given the principality an heir – albeit a female one – Grace felt she had the leverage to start exerting her influence on the Palace and on Monaco. She had done what was expected of her, and she now wanted a reward. Her first order of business was to redecorate the gloomy 800-year-old palace; she began by repainting the outside, transforming it from a crusty ochre to its present lively pink.

She then set about the complete renovation of the inside of the labyrinthian 220-room building, many parts of which had not been used for more than a century. Once-majestic tapestries were almost hidden under dust and cobwebs and many of the old medieval tapestries were peeling away from the walls.

Masons were brought in from Italy to restore the crumbling stonework and French craftsmen were imported to mend the Palace's woodwork.

'My predecessors let it get into such a state of neglect,' admitted Rainier. 'It was almost falling to pieces.'

During Rainier's first seven years of rule he had not been able to afford to renovate his crumbling palace but since Grace's arrival the financial fortunes of Monaco – and the Prince himself – had changed dramatically. In the months following the 'wedding of the century' tourists flocked to the tiny principality and it became one of the world's most popular tourist destinations.

By the end of the 1950s Monaco's annual tourism, on which is economy was wholly dependent, had almost doubled from what it was the year before Grace first set foot in the principality. Monaco had regained its position as Europe's most glamorous resort and now carefully ensured its exclusivity by charging higher prices than its competitors along the Côte D'Azur. It cost at least $200 a day for a couple to stay in Monaco – and that was before they'd placed a bet at the gambling tables. This was a deliberate policy by Aristotle Onassis's SBM to keep out the day-trippers and low-spending tourists. Just as it had been in the previous century, Monaco was once more an exclusive playground for the super-rich. Its annual profits accelerated into the tens of millions.

Monaco's biggest attraction was Princess Grace; the living embodiment of a fairytale of which the world itself felt a part. Millions of people the world over had watched the Monaco wedding; now they were hungry for more and more pictures and news of the magic couple.

'She attracted people and it was the cult of Grace Kelly,' says Oleg Cassini. 'They were coming to Monaco like the Arabs go to Mecca. It was the pilgrimage of the affluent toward Monaco.'

Publicity was the engine that drove the new cash cow. At the beginning Princess Grace believed she could control it and exploit it, exactly as she had done in Hollywood. She hired her Hollywood publicity agent and friend Rupert Allan to handle the press, who were clamouring for exclusive pictures of the ruling parents and their new baby Caroline. His brief was to make sure the press did only 'good taste publicity'. But this was easier said than done. Everything was fodder for the press: the colour of the nursery, the natural birth without anesthetic and especially Grace's controversial decision to breast-feed.

The American public were horrified to read that the Princess was breast-feeding Caroline: it seemed a throwback to the dark ages. Modern American mothers used formula milk, bottles and rubber nipples instead of the real thing. But Grace dismissed her detractors saying breast-feeding was 'wholly normal and right – I never considered anything else.' Over the years Princess Grace became an outspoken advocate for breast-feeding and worked tirelessly on behalf of the La Léche Legion, which turned breast-feeding into a political issue.

When Caroline was three months old an English tabloid newspaper, The *Daily Sketch*, published a report of a kidnap threat made against the baby during a family vacation at Rainier's Swiss villa in Gstaad. The Palace had apparently received anonymous letters detailing the plot and Swiss plainclothes police had been sent to guard Caroline. As newspapers all over the world picked up on the story, magnifying it into another Lindberg baby drama, a horrified Grace and Rainier realised for the first time the very real dangers of excessive publicity.

'The kidnapping was a pure invention,' Rainier claimed at the time. 'It is criminal, as it could give someone the idea.'

In 1958 Rainier sent Rupert Allan a public relations memorandum outlining his ideas for controlling the press. Verbosely titled *Idea for the Organisation of Press Relations Service to TSH [Their Serene Highnesses] the Prince and Princess of Monaco*, it would prove to be a Pandora's box that plagues the ruling family to this day.

'I do not want that my daughter has her childhood encumbered and poisoned by an excess of journalistic publicity,' instructed the Prince. 'It MUST be dosed and carefully timed so as not to become saturated . . . I think we must choose a number-one magazine and give it to them and not have more than two stories a year on her.'

In an amazing display of naiveté Rainier then laid down his plans to carefully disseminate 'the good-taste publicity that does not seem promoted or sponsored. The dignified and true stories on TSH and the principality. Protection against the bad, ill-meaning press articles, and screening of press demands, with elimination of a quantity of them, and a proper scheduling and programme of those accepted.'

To these ends Grace and Rainier would subject all their children to a barrage of staged photo opportunities purporting to show them being 'natural'. Almost from the cradle they were put through their paces for American photographers; they were shown eating their breakfast, playing in the palace nursery, doing their homework. This early exposure to the media instilled a strong dislike of the press in all of the Grimaldi children.

'It's a family that was made by publicity and is being destroyed by publicity,' says American social commentator and one-time editor of *Interview* magazine, Bob Colacello.

'The story of this tiny principality is a very contemporary little fable. Monaco is a business. It's Monaco Inc. really. And to keep that going you've got to keep the glamorous image going. The great power of the Grimaldis is in the realm of publicity.'

And the Monaco ruling family would stoke the fire of the modern cult of celebrity which would reach is terrible zenith with the death of Princess Diana almost forty years later.

When Caroline was eight months old Princess Grace took her in front of the cameras to deliver her first press conference since the birth. Playing the role of the proud, doting mother, the Princess joyfully announced that little Caroline's first tooth had just broken through.

'Now she's chewing everything she can get her hands on,' laughed Grace. 'She has chewed her bedclothes, all my beads, my husband's ties, and even the ears on our poodles.'

Although she denied it to the press at the time, Grace was already two months pregnant and on March 14, 1958, the cannon gave a 101-blast salute as she delivered an eight-pound, eleven-ounce male heir apparent, Albert Alexandre Louis Pierre.

In 1957 Prince Rainier brought a small farm high up in the mountains over the French border as a retreat for his growing family. Although it was only a few miles from the palace, Roc Agel allowed the Grimaldis to live a far more normal life than they ever could on 'the Rock'.

The Provençal stone farmhouse, with its massive wooden beams, was enlarged into an American ranch-style family home. Prince Rainier himself planted the garden in the sixty-acre estate with 400 fruit trees. And it was at Roc Agel that the Grimaldi children would grow up in a real loving family atmosphere.

'Grace had notions of what was appropriate and proper and tried to raise her children with that,' says Judy Balaban Quine, who was a frequent visitor to Roc Agel.

'But they were frustrated by all the things that set the children apart from the experience of other children.'

Roc Agel was where the Grimaldis could relax and let their hair down without having to worry about the increasingly intrusive paparazzi. Everyone wore T-shirts and jeans; pigs, chicken and goats wandering around all over the grounds.

'It's a sort of playground for everyone,' said Prince Rainier.

Roc Agel was self-sufficient and the Prince took great pride in his model dairy, where he produced milk and butter, and his organic vegetable garden which supplied the Palace with produce. The Prince also moved a drum kit into a shed and delighted in playing along with his favourite jazz records.

'You would arrive and find Rainier barbecuing hamburgers on a little outdoor grill,' remembers Quine. 'Grace would be making little chicken sandwiches and slicing the tomatoes and cutting up fresh basil. And the kids would be racing around in their bare feet.'

Grace and Rainier were determined to provide a nurturing environment for their children as far removed as possible from their own unhappy childhoods. The Prince was still haunted by his tortuous days at Stowe public school in England where he was bullied and mocked as 'Fat Little Monaco'. And Grace's ultra-strict upbringing by Ma Kelly was to have a profound influence on the next generation of Grimaldis.

'I think you have to give a child love and understanding – and, above all, treat him as an individual,' Grace had replied cautiously when asked how her own childhood would affect her parenting.

Although the Princess was determined to be a hands-on mother, she did hire a Swiss nurse called Margaret Stahl for Caroline. And when Albert – or Albie, as he was affectionately known by the family – arrived, she engaged an English nanny, Maureen King. But Grace, who Rainier had humorously appointed as his 'Co-ordinator of Domestic Affairs', made sure that she and not the nannies did most of the child-rearing.

In the early 1960s Dr Benjamin Spock and his revolutionary child-rearing ideas were in vogue among the middle and upper classes. And like thousands of other American mothers Princess Grace became a disciple, spending hours poring over his bestselling book and applying his liberal ideas to Caroline and Albert.

'I've always tried to treat children as individuals and never as inferiors,' Grace explained in 1974 when she was asked to describe their early training.

'They're people and I respect them as such ... their privacy, their needs. But in the household, they have to learn to conform to the rules.'

Grace employed a mixture of discipline and love, but although she was strict she was nowhere near as tough as Ma Kelly had been with her.

'I know people who say, "We have to clear off the tables because the children will break things." Well, I never took anything off mine. My children's fingers were slapped many times ... but they learned,' she said.

Fearing the destructive influence that their privileged status could have on the children, Grace and Rainier tried not to give them special treatment. The young Grimaldis were reprimanded at the least hint that they were getting swollen heads.

'I don't think they realised that they were anything special for a long time,' said Maureen King, who along with the rest of the palace staff addressed the infant Princess as 'Madame Caroline'.

But, as members of the ruling Grimaldi family, protocol dictated they be treated very differently by their playmates. On Caroline's third birthday Princess Grace organised a party where the little Princess played hostess to twenty-five friends: the children all bowed and curtsied to Caroline as she received them.

Recognising the dilemma, Princess Grace started up classes in the Palace so Albert and Caroline could mix informally with other children their own age.

American-born Kate Powers, whose mother, Jeanne Kelly van Remoortel, met Princess Grace when they were both at acting school in New York and later moved to Monaco, joined the Palace class. She became friends with Caroline.

'When you're that young you don't really think of princes or princesses as being any different,' said Kate, who is still close to Princess Caroline.

'I don't think I really thought about it at the time, except when we'd be trying to dodge the bodyguards when we'd be out with Caroline. We'd always be trying to run away and hide.'

Caroline and Albert were now the centre of their parents' lives and the ruling couple loved spending quality time with them. At bedtime Princess Grace would come into the nursery to tuck them in and read them fairytales. Now she was retired from acting these stories were the only outlet for Grace's love of theatrics, and she'd perform them with such drama and emotion that Nanny King loved to stay behind to listen.

If they had an official evening engagement and could not put the children to bed, Grace would ensure that she dressed and put on her make-up early so she could sit with them at dinner. One of Caroline's earliest memories is of seeing her glamorous mother leaving for a night out on the town.

'There were sort of visions as a small child of seeing someone incredibly beautiful and well dressed going [out] with a train of perfume behind,' the Princess would fondly recall many years later. 'And sort of "careful, don't mess with my hair or make-up." And it is the image that comes back.'

Little Caroline hated seeing her mother leave without her and would break down in floods of tears, knowing that Grace would always come back and comfort her.

'She turns back at the first sob,' Madge Tivey-Faucon told *Cosmopolitan* in March 1964. 'This scene usually takes place in the Cour d'Honneur. All the secretaries, hearing the little girl's scream, rush. The Princess bends over the child and consoles her gently until she stops crying. This may last a quarter of an hour. But the Princess never becomes impatient or angry.'

From her earliest days Caroline had a hard-wired assertiveness and sense of self. She inherited her father's dark looks and Latin temperament and was an extremely strong-willed child. She was also incredibly jealous of any attention paid to Albert.

When the stubborn Caroline began biting her sweet-natured brother, Grace was forced to step in with her own unorthodox brand of discipline. Placid and unassertive Albert would allow Caroline to bite him at will – he never complained. It was only after seeing bite marks on his arm that Grace realised what was happening. When her warnings to Caroline to stop biting Albert were ignored, Princess Grace bit Caroline's arm hard, so she could feel the pain.

'I'm afraid I'm very severe at times,' said Grace in 1962. 'Outsiders might think I'm too hard on the children. But I give them just as much love as I do discipline, and it seems to work out very well.'

But to many of their more old-fashioned friends Rainier and Grace appeared to give their two young children too much freedom, allowing them to run amok during official functions and constantly interrupt their father while he was working.

Recalls Judy Balaban Quine: 'Grace and Rainier included their children far more in their adult lives than I suspect most people in Europe did, let alone royals.'

Both children were spoiled rotten. When visitors arrived at the Palace they were usually laden with expensive presents for Caroline and Albert, who came to expect these tributes. Aristotle Onassis gave Albert a miniature electric car that was a scaled-down version of the real thing, while Caroline amassed a collection of expensive dolls, kept in a specially designed dolls' house. And when Caroline demanded a cocktail dress for her fifth birthday, the French designer Hubert Givenchy personally made one for her.

During a family vacation in America, Caroline was put in the care of Grace's friend Micheline Swift, who took her shopping. At Saks Fifth Avenue Caroline was rude to the staff as she tried on dresses and then threw them on the floor. When she was asked to behave she flew into a tantrum: 'I'm Caroline, Princess Caroline – and don't you dare speak to me like that!'

As Monaco's heir apparent, Prince Albert was groomed from his earliest days to prepare him for eventual rule. Prince Rainier personally supervised the little boy's upbringing and the special training he would need to fulfil his destiny and continue the Grimaldi dynasty.

But Albert's gentle nature and his chronic stammer greatly worried Rainier, who was concerned that his son lacked the natural strength and inner resources to be a leader. Rainier tried hard to prepare his son for the outside world.

'I don't think Rainier really knew how to relate to Albert's sensitive side,' said Judy Balaban Quine. 'It would have frightened him. There was a sense that, "I've got to toughen this kid up for the worst."'

CHAPTER FIVE

GRIMALDI INC.

As PRINCE ALBERT grew into boyhood his father carefully tutored him in the history of his family. The blue-eyed blond boy – who had inherited his mother's looks – knew very early on that he was different from his friends who came to the palace to play Cowboys and Indians with him. One day he would have to rule Monaco and lead the principality's 30,000 residents. Like his father he would have the absolute powers of a dictator and would have to learn how to use them responsibly for the good of Monaco. Although Prince Rainier patiently tried to help his son come to terms with the future, it was nonetheless a huge burden.

'It is a heavy weight,' Prince Albert would later explain. 'There was not much in Monaco in the early days and to see what it has become is just incredible.'

Monaco has absolutely no natural resources. Situated on the Mediterranean next to the French/Italian border, it covers less than one square mile and would easily fit into New York's Central Park. With is 30,000 residents – 5,500 of them Monégasques – it is the most densely packed country on the globe. Its excellent climate, almost non-existent crime rate and zero income tax make it a highly desirable place for the very wealthy to live.

The principality is composed of five distinct districts: Monaco-ville, the fortified capital perched on top of Le Rocher, a fist of stone defiantly striking out over the clear blue waters of the Mediterranean; Monte-Carlo, founded in 1866 in the reign of Prince Charles III, for whom it was named, which houses the world-famous casino, the grand hotels and The Monte-Carlo Sporting Club; La Condamine, the old harbour where the yachts of the fabulously wealthy are moored; Fontvieille, a large area of land reclaimed from the sea, housing a light industrial area, a tourist complex and a port; and Moneghetti, the exotic gardens lying on the French frontier at Cap D'Ail.

To this day the Grimaldis proudly retell how Francesco Grimaldi cunningly seized the fortress on the cold winter's night of January 8, 1297, by masquerading as an innocent monk begging, with his companions, for refuge. When the Genoese guards took pity on the group of shivering holy men and opened the fortress gates to let them in, Francesco the Spiteful pulled out his sword and led his men in a bloody massacre to seize control. Monaco's official coat of arms still celebrates the blood bath today, portraying two brown-robed monks brandishing swords.

Over the centuries the Grimaldi family's wealth and power grew through warmongering, intrigue, piracy and – when necessary – murder. From its strategic position overlooking the Mediterranean, the Grimaldis could dominate their neighbours. They demanded tolls; it was said no one passed through their region of the Riviera coast without paying handsomely for the privilege.

Monaco was the smallest principality in Europe and although the Grimaldis never achieved their ambition of being declared a monarchy, they did manage to secure the lesser rank of 'Serene Highness' for their rulers.

Scandal first became synonymous with Monaco in the late seven-

teenth century, when Princess Charlotte-Catherine Grimaldi shocked
the French court of Louis XIV with her passionate affairs with
members of both sexes. The beautiful, dark-eyed twenty-year-old had
arrived in Monaco in 1660 for an arranged marriage with Prince Louis
I, who was three years younger and a virgin. The urbane and sophisticated Charlotte-Catherine found Louis and Monaco very provincial
and, after only three years of marriage, she abandoned her husband, taking their three daughters to Paris. Once she had established herself in
the court of the Sun King, the *Princesse de Monaco's* rampant bisexuality
and her reported liaison with Louis XIV made her the talk of France.

Until the French Revolution Monaco was many times larger than it
is today. But in 1789 they were stripped of most of their assets and
Menton and Roquebrun declared themselves free cities. Monaco's
Princess François-Therese Grimaldi was even guillotined in Paris at the
age of twenty-six as an enemy of the people.

In the aftermath of the Revolution the Grimaldi Princes were left
with a ransacked palace and the ruins of a pillaged country. Monaco
became something of a joke in Europe; the Grimaldis lost ninety per
cent of the principality and were left with only the rock and the harbour.

But Monaco's fortunes changed again when Prince Rainier's great-
great-grandfather Charles III came to power. In 1861 Charles signed a
treaty with Napoleon III to create the modern principality of Monaco.
Monaco's sovereignty now came under French protection.

Perilously close to becoming a footnote in history, Charles III came
up with an inspired idea to give Monaco an identity that would endure
to the present day. He decided to transform Monaco into a fashionable
resort to attract wealthy Europeans. As gaming was illegal in France and
Italy, Charles decided to build a grand casino to give the principality an
enormous advantage over the competing resorts of Nice and Cannes.

In a bold move aimed at turning Monaco into the gambling centre
of Europe, Charles created a casino corporation and leased it out to the
newly formed *Société des Bains de Mer* – the SBM.

New railway lines, better roads and improvements to the harbour opened up Monte-Carlo to the rest of the fashionable world. Members of European royalty and rich industrialists poured into Monte-Carlo to play the tables. By day, in the name of sport, they'd flock to the pigeon-shoot below the casino to kill the birds that were released by the dozen from baskets; but by night they'd gamble their fortunes away in the casino.

Realising the potential threat that gambling might pose to weaker members of his family, Charles III made it illegal for any Grimaldi or Monégasque to enter the casino to gamble.

By the 1880s Monaco had become so wealthy that residents were told they would no longer have to pay income tax – a privilege they still enjoy to this day. By now the casino was firmly established as the principality's financial motor.

In 1889 Charles was succeeded by his son Prince Albert I, an adventurer who was also a pioneer in maritime exploration.

Albert was a committed pacifist, yet his son and heir Louis couldn't wait to enlist in the French Army to serve in North Africa. And while stationed in Constantine, Algeria, Louis had a love affair with his laundress that would drastically alter the Grimaldi line of succession. In 1898 the washerwoman bore Louis an illegitimate daughter, named Louise-Juliette. Later, at the age of twenty-two, this daughter was to become Princess Charlotte, Rainier's eccentric mother, better known in the family as 'Mamou'.

At the end of World War I, Monaco signed the 1918 treaty with France. This guaranteed the principality French protection as long as the Monégasque government conformed to French economic interests; it also stated that if a Monégasque Prince should die without appointing a male or female heir, the principality would revert back to France.

In the aftermath of the war, the victorious allies realised to their horror that if both Albert and Louis were to die, the succession would pass to the German branch by marriage of the Grimaldi family: the house of von Urach. And so it was that young Louise-Juliette, the washerwoman's child, found her life irrevocably changed.

In order to prevent Germany gaining power and influence in Monaco, Louise-Juliette was officially legitimised. On her 1920 marriage to a young French aristocrat, Count Pierre de Polignac, she was restyled 'Princess Charlotte'. Under the bizarre marriage arrangement Pierre became a Prince in exchange for altering his surname to Grimaldi, thus by sleight of hand ensuring the family's continuing rule of Monaco.

In 1922 Louis became ruler on the death of Prince Albert; a year later Princess Charlotte and Prince Pierre had a son they named Rainier.

When Europe lurched into World War II Prince Louis trod a treacherous path by helping the Nazis while officially remaining neutral. He openly supported the collaborationist Vichy government in Paris, allowing Monaco's bankers and lawyers to launder illegal German war profits to the benefit of the principality. During the war Monaco became a favoured resort for top SS and Gestapo officers; they frequented the casino, and business boomed.

When peace returned to Europe in 1945 Monaco's economy was left in ruins. By the late 1940s the casino was suffering heavy losses; few people could afford the luxury of gambling in the days of European-wide rationing.

Prince Louis was unpopular with the Monégasques, who were concerned about the eccentric Mamou succeeding to the throne. So on May 30, 1943 — the day before Rainier's twenty-first birthday — his mother agreed to resign all claims to the succession. Three days later, on April 2, Prince Rainier was named as Louis' heir.

'It was not an especially joyous moment for me,' Rainier would remember many years later. 'It meant a severe change of style in my life. I suddenly had to assume a lot of responsibilities.'

★ ★ ★

Prince Rainier III was born in the palace of Monaco on May 31, 1923. As a young child he was traumatised by the growing bitterness between his estranged parents, Mamou and Pierre, whose arranged marriage had never been a happy one. After his parents finally divorced in 1929, the young Rainier was sent away to England to a prep school; six years later, at the age of twelve, he was enrolled at Stowe public school in Buckinghamshire. Rainier spent his vacations in Monaco where he became best friends with Jean-Louis Marsan, a boy his age who came from one of the principality's most prominent families. Nicknamed Loulou, Marsan would become a life-long friend and protector of Rainier and would later play a key role when he came to power.

Even though the young Rainier spent most of his childhood abroad, he nevertheless found himself the centre of his parents' ongoing feud. One day his father Prince Pierre arrived at Stowe and took him away, prompting a much-publicised eighteen-month custody battle with Mamou in the British High Court.

The young Prince hated Stowe. As the only foreigner among 560 pupils – and a Catholic to boot – he found himself an outcast; ostracised and bullied by the other boys. He fell victim to the time-honoured English public school traditions of 'caning' and 'fagging', forced to act as servant to the older boys and carry out humiliating menial tasks. In order to survive the cruel taunts of 'fat little Monaco', the naturally-shy Rainier withdrew into his shell and became a loner, avoiding contact with the other Stowe pupils where possible.

When he was fourteen, Mamou realised the depth of her son's despair and transferred him to Le Rosey boarding school in Geneva. Here he was far happier and when he finished his studies, three years later, he went to the University at Montpellier where he completed a Bachelor of Arts degree. Then, in the midst of World War II, Rainier moved to German-occupied Paris, where, for a year, he studied political science.

In 1944, six months after his appointment as Crown Prince, Rainier returned to Monaco to be groomed by his grandfather to take over the helm of state. Fiercely idealistic and anti-Nazi, the young Prince was disgusted by Louis's refusal to dismiss his pro-Hitler French minister of State, Emile Roblot.

Recently-released Vichy government papers reveal that, during the war, Monaco laundered funds for the Nazis, including those stolen from Jews. The documents show that the annual revenues of the SBM rose from just three million francs in 1941 to eighty million in 1943.

But co-operation with the Nazis went even further. With an Allied victory at hand, Roblot banned anti-Nazi demonstrations in Monaco; he plastered propaganda posters throughout the principality which said: 'The German authorities have acted with the greatest courtesy toward the Prince and his government.'

The young Prince Rainier had tried unsuccessfully throughout the war to make his grandfather disown Roblot's policies. Three weeks after France was liberated by the Allies in September 1944, Rainier joined the French Free Forces and informed on Roblot. He issued a statement to clarify his position to the world: 'I have witnessed the misdeeds of the dangerous policy of politicians who obtained the trust of Prince Sovereign, my grandfather [which] made us lose the rank and the role that we should have held and deprived us of our neutrality and independence.'

Young Rainier was assigned to French Intelligence, in which he served for seventeen months. He was awarded the *Croix de Guerre*, the Bronze Star. Later he attained the rank of *chevalier* in the Legion of Honour. These medals would proudly adorn his self-designed militaristic wedding outfit twelve years later.

As the superpowers redrew the map of Europe after the war, the US State Department considered Monaco's questionable war record. Minutes from a meeting at the US Embassy in Paris on February 10, 1945, were particularly damning:

'It is well known that the Prince and his advisors, as well as a large proportion of the people of Monaco, had been highly unco-operative with the Allies, and pro-Axis.' It went on to accuse the principality of using its special taxation and banking laws to connive to defraud the French and other Allied treasuries.

When Prince Louis invited the American general in charge of the Riviera to pay him an official visit, Washington carefully considered the request before allowing him to go. As post-Vichy France had decided not to reprimand Monaco publicly for its poor war record, America was not in a position to do so either.

After the war, Rainier spent time in Berlin working in the Economic Section of the French military mission. There he was promoted to Colonel. In 1947 he returned to Monaco to find the principality in a deplorable state; his ailing grandfather Louis seemed indifferent to the problems around him.

Realising that it was only a matter of time before he would have to take charge, Rainier became a daredevil playboy, sowing his wild oats. He took up auto-racing, competing in the Tour de France; he went wild boar hunting. Once he almost drowned in a foolhardy attempt to retrieve an arrow from the bottom of the sea.

On May 9, 1949, Louis II died. Rainier succeeded to the throne of Monaco three weeks before his twenty-sixth birthday. It proved to be an ordeal by fire for the young Prince as he immediately locked horns with the National Council. Rainier had ambitious development plans for Monaco, but the conservative National Council lacked his foresight and the new ruler faced an uphill battle as he struggled to introduce change.

In the mid-fifties Rainier had to put out the fires of a major banking scandal when the government-subsidised Monaco Banking and Precious Metals Society suddenly faced bankruptcy due to poor management. Ruling Monaco was fraught with difficulties for the Prince in those early years.

Six years after Rainier had acceded to the throne, the US consul in Nice, Albert Clattenberg Jr, reported to Washington that Rainier III had 'not so far shown himself to be possessed of force of character or qualities of leadership.'

Bleakly describing Monaco as 'a hot-bed of gossip, scandal and neighborly bad feeling,' Clattenberg added a footnote: 'An energetic young wife with a talent for running things . . . could right the present situation.'

CHAPTER SIX

GRACE IN MONACO

W HEN GRACE KELLY arrived in Monaco there had been few changes to the principality since the casino and grand hotels were built a hundred years earlier. A fine moss of delicate, pastel buildings dotted the port, and the thirteenth-century Grimaldi palace perched on the rock like an eagle.

The perfectly groomed gardens were planted, as they had always been, with red and white cyclamen. The charming cobbled streets of Le Rocher twisted through shadowy stone archways. The square by the casino was used as an outdoor cinema where Monégasques had first seen their new Princess-to-be acting in Hollywood movies shown on the huge screen years earlier. Down below was the pigeon shoot, which drew wealthy sportsmen into the principality off season.

'Monte Carlo looked like a picture postcard of a resort city that had seen grand days but was now fading,' remembers Judy Balaban Quine. 'It was not without charm, but it seemed to belong to the past.'

After spending two years in Monaco adapting to her new existence, Grace was ready to begin playing what she saw as the most important role in her life – that of First Lady. In the next ten years she and Rainier would drag Monaco into the twentieth century and give it a new sheen of affluence and success.

'Well, she did create a character – "The Princess",' says her former roommate and bridesmaid, Rita Gam. 'I mean, she would even dress the part. She'd go to a ball and her hair would be a foot higher than everyone else's. She created the royal bubble wherever she walked.'

Right from the outset Grace began stamping her identity on the principality. When Monaco's first high-rise building went up by the port it was named Schuykill, after the Philadelphia river where Jack Kelly used to scull. She also persuaded Rainier to ban the annual pigeon shoot in January, condemning it as barbaric. This was a controversial move – it upset many Monégasques, who were furious that an American outsider was meddling in their time-honoured traditions.

Grace had a keen sense of duty, inherited from Ma Kelly, who still worked hard for her beloved charity, Women's Medical, in Philadelphia. But when Grace began to involve herself in charity work and fund-raising she did it on a far grander scale, exploiting her friendship with the likes of Frank Sinatra, David Niven and Cary Grant to advance her favourite causes and bring glamour to Monaco.

'Grace brought a great deal of pizzazz to the area because of her connections with the movie business,' says Michael Powers, who would become Prince Albert's best friend.

'She attracted a new element that just didn't exist before and transformed Monaco overnight into a whole new environment with a new spirit.'

Grace's first innovation came in 1956. Though heavily pregnant with Caroline, she invited every Monégasque child between the ages of three and twelve to the palace for what has become the ruling family's traditional Christmas Party. Grace and Rainier played host, handing out sticky buns and pouring soda. Then the children were entertained by a Punch and Judy show before being given a present on their way out.

The party was such a success, and generated so much goodwill for

Grace in Monaco, that she later copied the idea for the elderly, giving them money and something practical, usually clothes, as Christmas gifts.

As Monaco's First Lady, Grace felt a strong sense of duty. She was determined not to distance herself from her people. She broke down barriers by meeting citizens one on one in her palace office, where she would listen to their problems and dispense sound advice and help.

The Princess's accessibility and her genuine concern for others impressed those Monégasques who had initially mistrusted her motives. It was not long before they took her to their hearts. Instead of coldly calling her 'The American Princess', the Monégasques retitled her 'Our Princess'. It was a triumph of goodwill that meant the world to Grace.

'She was always there for Monégasques when things were bad,' recalls the Countess of Lombardy. 'She did so many things for us and we loved her for it.'

Grace found her mission in life in Monaco, pursuing her charity work with an almost evangelical passion. She started paying regular visits to Monaco's old people's home, the orphanage and the hospital, which had been named after her in 1958. During a tour of the hospital, she was shocked at how run-down it was, with its cold, dreary wards. On being told that there were no funds for a new coat of paint she took it on herself to bring in fresh flowers and began raising funds to brighten it up.

Turning her attention to Monaco's home for the elderly, she organised volunteers and local Girl Guides to visit the lonely old people and befriend them. And when Grace went on one of her frequent walkabouts she would often bring Caroline and Albert with her to cheer up the old folk. 'She brought us heart,' said one elderly lady.

In May 1958 Rainier replaced his sister Tiny with Grace in the prestigious post of President of the Monaco Red Cross – he had recently discovered that his sister and Jean-Charles Rey were again plotting to overthrow him and put Tiny's own son, Count Christian (Buddy) de Massy, on the throne.

Grace was determined to take an active part in her Red Cross work; it wasn't in her nature to be only a figurehead. But initially her businesslike approach was not popular with the more casual, Mediterranean style of her fellow board members. When Grace first arrived at meetings with her secretary Phyllis Earl, wearing a smart suit and glasses, she was well prepared for her new role and ready for action. The Monégasques were genuinely confused. They were used to treating meetings as social occasions for gossip and small talk; Red Cross business had always been of low priority.

Grace soon discovered, to her frustration, that the Monégasques' business manner was very different from the brisk, no-nonsense American one. She would have to learn patience.

'The Red Cross will be the end of me,' Grace wrote to a friend in 1960.

The Monaco branch of the Red Cross had been formed by Prince Rainier in the late 1940s to augment the state welfare system. When Grace took over the helm she enlarged it, introducing nurseries for working mothers, first-aid training, classes for expectant mothers and a new orphanage.

At the beginning it was seriously underfunded, but Grace refused to let this problem get in the way. Her favourite saying at Red Cross meetings was: 'Of course it can be done. Why not?'

To finance her ambitious plans, Grace used all her Hollywood pulling power. She single-handedly established the annual Red Cross Gala as *the* premier event of the Riviera's social calendar, attracting high-profile guests from all over the world.

Held on the first Friday of August in the Monte-Carlo Sporting Club, the lavish costume ball drew the *crème de la crème* of Hollywood – Elizabeth Taylor, Frank Sinatra, Sophia Loren, Richard Burton – many of whom performed for free as a favour to Grace.

'It was the highlight of the summer social season,' says New York socialite and writer R. Couri Hay, who attended every ball through the 1960s and 1970s.

'The Croix Rouge was a fabulous, fabulous event and Princess Grace and Prince Rainier were such an attractive couple.'

Princess Grace loved the Red Cross balls; they gave her the opportunity to dress up in costume once more and star in the whole extravaganza. One year she decided to go as Marie Antoinette, donning an enormous headpiece so high that she couldn't fit into the car. After several failed attempts a servant was dispatched to find a van capable of conveying the costumed Princess from the Palace to the Sporting Club. By the time they found one, and made her as comfortable as possible in the back, she was an hour late.

Monaco law dictates that the ball officially starts with the arrival of the Prince and Princess; no drinks can be served beforehand. With no sign of the ruling couple – or any explanation of what was happening – the thirsty guests became increasingly impatient.

'She was heavily criticised for being so late,' recalls Gwen Robyns. 'But she wanted to make her proper entrance as the Princess of Monaco.'

In 1962 Princess Grace was the matron of honour when her old friend from New York, Jeanne Kelly, married the conductor of the Monte-Carlo Philharmonic Orchestra, Edouard van Remoortel. A beautiful red-haired Southern belle from Memphis, Tennessee, Jeanne had renewed her friendship with Grace when she moved to Monaco with her two children from a previous marriage, Mike and Kate Powers.

For the next twenty years Jeanne would become a key member of Princess Grace's inner circle as their children grew up together. Like Grace, Jeanne Kelly (no relation) was of Irish-German descent; as lively, fun-loving young mothers they had much in common and soon became fast friends.

'Monaco was such a glamorous place in those days,' remembers Jeanne, who is still known solely by her maiden name of Kelly. 'There were different galas for different occasions, and of course the opera and the ballet. Nuryev would often come over as he had a home at Roc Agel. Those were the magical days.'

The two friends regularly partied together on yachts with the likes of Aristotle Onassis and opera legend Maria Callas who was his mistress, Greta Garbo, Frank Sinatra and Louis Mountbatten. They would play tennis together at the Palace courts and shared a love of Tex-Mex food, which Jeanne would prepare on Prince Rainier's yacht, *Deo Juvante II*.

One of Jeanne's most treasured possessions is a fading photograph of her and Princess Grace at the Monaco centenary costume ball in 1966. On it Grace has written, 'Two little Kelly girls looking pretty fancy! Love – Grace.'

During the August/September season there would be a grand gala every Friday night and Princess Grace and Prince Rainier would attend them all. The world's beautiful people – the Aga Khan, The Charles Revsons, the Majarhani of Boroda and the von Krups – would all drop anchor in Monte-Carlo and stay for the season. Their Rolls-Royces would be shipped into Monaco for the month just so their owners could sweep out of the Hotel de Paris bedecked in glittering jewels, wave to the admiring crowd, and then make the short drive to the Bathing Club or the old Sporting Club.

'Everyone came to see Grace,' remembers R. Couri Hay. 'She was the main attraction in Monte-Carlo.'

But after the last dance, Princess Grace would return to the Palace and find herself terribly alone. She might be one of the most famous and admired women in the world, but she was an outsider in a foreign country with few close friends.

Besides Jeanne, there were few American women in Monaco with whom she could socialise. At the beginning she had made a special effort to make new friends by inviting the Monégasque wives over to the Palace for informal dinners. But her attempt at friendship had been a failure. The local ladies felt intimidated by their Princess and found it impossible to treat her without deference.

Missing America and the showbiz gossip she had loved so much, Grace started subscribing to the Paris-based *Celebrity Bulletin* – a daily newsletter that listed who was passing through Europe. If Grace found one of her old friends was in the vicinity she would immediately invite them to visit.

When Cary Grant and his wife Betsy Drake came to Monaco in Easter 1961, Grace was so delighted she met them personally at Nice Airport. Grace was thrilled to see her *To Catch a Thief* co-star again and greeted him with a kiss that was dutifully caught by a paparazzo photographer. But when the photograph appeared on the front page of *Nice-Matin* the next day, Prince Rainier was furious.

'He was always jealous, in spite of himself, of his wife's friends from the days before their marriage,' said Madge Tivey-Faucon.

'He was doubtless also afraid that this friendly embrace might remind the gossips of the passionate kisses Cary Grant and Grace Kelly shared in front of the camera. The Prince did not hide his bad humour during the Grants' stay at the Palace. He spoke to no one. He sulked . . . The Princess was cool – her usual attitude to her husband's moods.'

After that, *To Catch A Thief* was never again shown in the Palace, on Rainier's orders.

When Grace's younger sister Lizanne came to stay at the Palace for the first time in the early 1960s, the atmosphere was far lighter.

'The Palace accommodations are so beautiful and they gave me a lovely suite,' said Lizanne.

During Lizanne's stay with husband Don, Grace went to a lot of trouble to make them feel at home. Every morning she would cook breakfast for Lizanne and her children; then they'd all go up to Roc Agel and take long walks through the peaceful grounds. At night Prince Rainier would join them for dinner and then they'd play games of charades that would go on for hours.

But things were not so blissful when Grace's father visited. Jack Kelly loathed the Palace and did not like his authority being overshadowed by that of Prince Rainier. The irascible old man considered Monaco pretentious and especially disliked the stuffy royal protocol. Whenever the Palace servants tried to bring him anything he would scream, 'Go away! I'll call you when I need you!'

In April 1960 the seemingly indestructible Jack Kelly felt unwell and went to hospital for a check-up. The doctors ordered exploratory tests on the seventy-year-old Kelly patriarch – and discovered he had terminal cancer of the stomach. When Grace heard the news she flew straight to Philadelphia, accompanied by her personal secretary Phyllis Earl.

When she arrived at the hospital the Princess was so distraught that hospital nurses failed to recognise her. But before she walked into the private room to see her father she took a deep breath, focused – and put on the performance of a lifetime.

During the fifteen-minute visit Grace was light-hearted and breezy in a brave attempt to cheer up the father who had always seen her as the runt of the litter. She never acknowledged his illness, let alone the fact that he was dying. Grace cheerfully brought him up to date on his grandchildren Caroline and Albert, telling him the latest family gossip. When she left his room she broke down in tears, realising that it would probably be the last time she would ever see him alive.

Jack Kelly died on June 20 and Grace returned to Philadelphia for his funeral. Kelly's death was front-page news in Philadelphia; he was such a celebrity in his own right that within days of his death copies of his twelve-page will were being hawked on the streets for $7.

Back in Monaco, Grace fell into a severe depression. It was very painful for her to accept the death of her father whom she adored but from whom she had received so little warmth and affection in return. Prince Rainier tried his best to comfort her, but Grace withdrew into herself. She was disconsolate.

'She was over-sensitive to [the Kellys],' Rainier would say many years later. 'They mattered terribly much to her – more, it certainly seemed, than she mattered to them.'

Grace took her father's death very hard. She became uncharacteristically melancholy and emotional and would suddenly burst into tears at the slightest reminder of her father. And this despondence continued for months.

To add to her problems the palace was abuzz with rumours that Prince Rainier was having an affair. A well-meaning friend confided to Grace that, while she had been at her father's deathbed, Rainier had celebrated his thirty-seventh birthday with her new lady-in-waiting, the beautiful Zénaide Quinones de Léon.

When Grace confronted him with the story, Rainier denied any wrongdoing. He was backed up by other friends who had attended his birthday party and said it was all perfectly innocent. Grace took his word for it, but when she returned again from her father's funeral Monaco society was rife with new rumours of Rainier's unfaithfulness.

Embarrassed, and no longer convinced that Rainier was telling the truth, Grace acted decisively, dismissing Zénaide and banishing her from court.

Gwen Robyns believes Rainier cheated on Grace throughout their marriage.

'He wasn't a bit faithful,' said Robyns. 'Poor girl. There was no great love there. But there was a kind of fascination.'

Most Sundays, Rainier would leave the Palace, telling Grace he was off to watch a local soccer game. Instead he would go straight to the bed of his long-time French actress mistress for an afternoon of passion. The Prince had a close friend monitor the soccer games and brief him later to provide him with an alibi. Then he would return to the Palace and discuss the finer points of the game with Grace. This arrangement went on for years, until his mistress tired of Rainier and married a dentist.

The emotional stress over the death of her father – and her subsequent unhappiness at home – led to Princess Grace suffering two miscarriages in the early 1960s. As both she and Rainier desperately wanted more children to shore up their marriage, these were bitter blows. Grace's own sense of worth was badly shaken and she felt trapped as she began to miss her old Hollywood career and the creative outlet it had given her more than ever. Even Rainier began to worry about Grace's continuing melancholy, but was loth to let her return to Hollywood.

'I think first she regretted leaving her profession,' the Prince said in December 1996. 'And I think it was very difficult coming here and not managing the language too well. Coming to this small community where a lot of people were pushing either to meet, to see or to criticise. And she knew that.'

The couple frequently argued as Grace tearfully begged Rainier to allow her to resume her career. Finally, in 1962, her chance came when Alfred Hitchcock offered her the starring role opposite Sean Connery in his new thriller *Marnie*. Grace was delighted at the offer to play the beautiful, frigid woman who relieves sexual tension by stealing. For once Rainier agreed with the plan: Hitchcock was one of the few Hollywood people the Prince liked and trusted after getting to know him socially.

The contract would pay Grace $732,000 plus a percentage of the profits. And it was even arranged that Grace could shoot her scenes during the Grimaldis' forthcoming summer vacation in America, so the movie wouldn't interfere with any official responsibilities.

On March 19, 1962, a bombshell hit Monaco when the Palace issued a statement saying Princess Grace was returning to movie-making. The story was instant front-page news around the world, exciting millions of Grace Kelly fans.

But Grace and Rainier had not foreseen the uproar this would cause in Monaco. On hearing the news, Monégasques were aghast. How could their Princess demean herself by appearing in a movie? Surely a Princess must be above being a common actress? Besides, they asked, what would happen if she had to play a love scene and kiss another man apart from her husband? It was sacrilegious, beyond reason.

Local newspaper editorial writers speculated that Grace was 'bored and fed up' with her life in the principality and demanded to know why the Monégasques had not been consulted before she took such an audacious step. Some even surmised that the royal marriage was on the rocks and that this striking a blow for independence was Grace's first step to divorce.

As a result of the bitter public backlash, Grace had no alternative but to pull out of the movie. Prince Rainier called a press conference to explain her decision. It was one of the darkest days of Grace's life; her hopes of returning to acting were shattered. She found herself locked in a prison of her own making, without a key.

CHAPTER SEVEN

THE WONDER YEARS

ON FEBRUARY 1, 1965, Princes Grace finally gave birth to the healthy baby she and Rainier had so longed for. Their third child, Princess Stephanie Marie Elisabeth de Monaco, was seven years younger than Albert and eight years younger than Caroline. After the trauma of two miscarriages Grace was jubilant.

'Over the phone she marvelled . . . about being able to start over again with motherhood in almost a new generation,' said Judy Balaban Quine, who, like Grace, had just had a third child years after her two elder daughters.

Grace told her friend how she loved all her children, but admitted that she felt, 'Maybe a touch more for this one, though, because I was beginning to despair that I'd ever have another one, and now she's here.'

Although she considered herself a good mother, Grace was determined to avoid any previous mistakes, fussing over Stephanie far more than Albert and Caroline.

Remembers Gwen Robyns: 'Grace adored Stephanie. She used to

say: "My baby Stephanie is going to be the most interesting of my children. You wait and see."'

Grace threw herself into motherhood, realising that Stephanie would probably be her last opportunity to do so. She spent as much time as she could with her new baby, showering her with love and pampering her shamelessly.

That August Judy Balaban Quine visited Grace and Rainier in Monaco for the annual Red Cross Gala and spent some time with the ruling family. She found Grace 'aglow with motherhood'; the Princess had celebrated regaining her old figure by shortening all her skirts above the knee to emulate the newly fashionable mini-skirt craze.

One night, during dinner in a restaurant high up in the mountains above Monaco, Grace and Rainier told Quine their concern about nine-year-old Caroline, who had just started attending a local convent school near the Palace.

'She was a most demanding child,' says Quine. 'According to them, Caroline alternated between adoring her baby sister and wishing to dispose of her. About Albert she was not so equivocal. There her sibling rivalry raged. Grace insisted, "I've bent over backwards not to favour the younger child, hoping to avoid just such jealousies, even though Albie's much cuddlier than she is."'

Little Caroline's dislike of her brother was so intense that once she ripped her favourite cut-out book into shreds just because he'd touched it.

A couple of days later, at the Prince's traditional Red Cross Ball Sunday lunch, the adults retired inside the Palace, leaving the children unsupervised by the pool. At the end of lunch Grace and Judy went back outside and found all the children had disappeared – except Albert, who was playing by himself at the shallow end. When Grace asked him where the other children were, he solemnly pointed to a poolside bathroom.

As they approached they heard Judy's ten-year-old daughter Amy desperately shouting at her eight-year-old sister Victoria and Princess Caroline.

Judy Balaban Quine: 'Opening the door we found the two younger girls trying to lower baby Princess Stephanie upside down, head first, into the toilet bowl. Amy gave us an "I tried" look while Grace and I ran to rescue the baby. Grace huffed, "Caroline!" But before any question could arise as to who the culprit was, Caroline put her hands on her hips and, in the very image of self-justification, indignantly announced, "*She* was *annnoying* us!"'

As they grew up the two sisters did not get along any better. Caroline was jealous of Stephanie, believing that their parents gave her far more leeway than she had received at the same age. It was left to kind-hearted Albert to protect his younger sister. Stephanie in turn worshipped her brother, faithfully following him around the Palace like a puppy dog.

'I played with Stephanie a lot when we were kids,' recalls Albert, who regularly took his sister to soccer games.

'I was kind of fascinated by this little baby in the family. So we always got along great. We've always had a good relationship.'

By far the most spoiled of the Grimaldi children, at the age of four Stephanie was privately tutored. And when she was six, Grace would personally walk her daughter, wearing her navy and white uniform and her first *cartable* (book bag), to parochial school.

Judy Balaban Quine observed all three Grimaldi children during their formative years, fascinated by how they related to each other and the distinct roles they each played within the family.

'Caroline was clearly the hero-child,' says Quine. 'She was the oldest, and a very strong-willed little girl from the word go. Stephanie was the family clown. She was funny and amusing and one of those children that you laugh with. Albert was the lost child. He was book-ended on either side of siblings who are extremely strong-willed and self-assertive. He became the sweet little family mascot.'

Rainier and Grace's conflicting European and American roots were ever-present and the children were raised in both cultures. All the children are bilingual; Grace would talk to them in English while Rainier conversed in French. But whenever the children were left alone with each other they spoke French.

Each summer they went to the United States and joined their Kelly cousins at the same camps that Grace and Lizanne had gone to as young girls.

'The kids are very American,' said Lizanne. 'The girls went to Camp Omeka in the Poconos where my mother had been a counsellor many years before and Albert went to Camp Tecumseh.'

In 1966 Grace and Rainier celebrated their tenth wedding anniversary. When the Prince asked what she would like as a present Grace had, only half-jokingly, replied: 'A year off!'

It had been a particularly busy summer for Grace because of the official centenary celebrations for Monte-Carlo. There had been a host of special galas, concerts, ballets and firework displays, all of which Grace dutifully attended. The climax of the celebrations came on November 4, when Rainier ceremonially exhumed the bodies of all his Grimaldi ancestors and reburied them in the Cathedral with full pomp and ceremony.

One of the highlights of Grace's summer had been American Week, which she had organised as a public relations bid to boost tourism and attract new US business to the principality. Perhaps the most successful event had been a barbecue and softball game held at Prince Rainier's private golf course: T-bone steaks, sweetcorn and baked potatoes were flown over from New York for the occasion and an American Air Force band entertained.

Rainier, looking unusually relaxed in an undersized red baseball cap and khakis, greeted his guests with Grace, Caroline and Albert by his side. Eighteen-month-old Stephanie remained in the palace with her nurse Maureen King.

Princess Grace sported an 'American Week' T-shirt and shorts to lead her 'Ambassadors' softball team against one from the US Seventh Fleet.

English film star David Niven manned first base while various American ambassadors completed her team. For once the Princess let her hair down in public as she sprinted around the bases in the first ball game she had played since her Philadelphia childhood.

The following day it was a far more formal Princess Grace who sat by the Palace pool, fielding questions from American television interviewer, Barbara Walters. Looking decidedly uncomfortable throughout the interview, Grace nervously fidgeted, constantly pushing her cuticles back.

And when Waters questioned her about the state of her ten-year marriage, Grace was distinctly evasive.

'I think that the thing that has helped most in my marriage, and adjusting to life here, is the fact that the Prince and I share the same religion,' she said. 'It's been a great bond between us and I think that has helped us overcome any of the differences of our backgrounds and culture.'

Later in the interview Walters appeared to hit a raw nerve when she asked the Princess if she was happy in Monaco.

'I've had many happy moments in my life, yes,' began Grace slowly and deliberately as she carefully selected each word. 'I don't think happiness or being happy is a perpetual state that anyone can be in. But I suppose I have a certain peace of mind.'

A few weeks later one of Grace's old friends from her New York acting days, David Swift, visited the palace with his wife Micheline. David had found fame in 1960 when he wrote and directed the hit movie *Pollyanna*, starring Hayley Mills. One night, after a hearty meal in a Monte-Carlo restaurant, Grace persuaded Rainier to let her walk back to the Palace alone with Micheline as it was such a beautiful evening.

On the way home Grace surprised Micheline by admitting it was the very first time in her marriage that she had been allowed out on her own. Tears welled up in Grace's eyes as she became unusually emotional. 'He has me cornered,' she told a stunned Micheline. 'I can't move. I can't go anywhere. I have no freedom.'

★　★　★

Since the end of the 1950s Prince Rainier had paid far more attention to building up Monaco and his personal fortune than to satisfying the needs of his family. He took great pride in describing himself as Chief Executive Officer of a business called Monaco. Over the first few years of his reign, the Prince had taken some tough business decisions to turn Monaco away from total dependence on gambling and tourism and toward the far more lucrative and reliable areas of banking, investment and industry.

'In a way the principality has become a family business,' the Prince explained to author Jeffrey Robinson. 'I don't think it's really Grimaldi Inc. and I'm not certain it will ever turn into that. But it's much more businesslike now than it was years ago.'

When he came to the throne in 1949, Rainier immediately realised the necessity of expanding his realm to ensure the principality's future survival. His plan was to reclaim from the sea two areas at opposite ends of Monaco, making one a site for light industry and the other a beach resort. The landfill would come from a huge tunnel then being excavated to re-route the Paris–Menton railway line under Monte-Carlo; that in turn would free up more land for residential development.

Another string in Rainier's business bow was Monaco's unique status as a Mediterranean tax-free haven with minimal levies on corporations. As early as the late 1950s the principality had begun to attract businessmen and tax exiles who were keen to reap the advantages of its special status.

But if Monaco had once been international business's best-kept secret, the well-publicised wedding of Rainier and Grace opened it up to the world. Throughout the 1950s Monaco's annual business turnover increased four-fold to top $128 million in 1961; it was expected to reach the $200 million mark in 1962.

Realising his limitations, Prince Rainier quickly gathered a team of business advisors around him, led by an ambitious young American called Martin Dale. Assuming the title of the Prince's Privy Councillor, the high-flying twenty-nine-year-old, formerly the US Vice-Consul to

Nice, would be the key to Monaco's growing financial success. The Prince was also heavily reliant on his boyhood friend Jean-Louis Marsan, who became his trusted right-hand man and Minister of Finance.

'Rainier was very astute in his business arrangements – he chose the right people,' says Gwen Robyns. 'I don't think he had the brain himself but he had very clever advisors telling him what to do.'

Nicknamed the Prince's 'pocket Richelieu' by jealous Monégasques, Dale gathered a crack business team together. In the early 1960s he set up the Monaco Economic Development Corporation – MEDEC. Their brief was to attract new business investors into the principality.

Within two years MEDEC had been so effective that it had welcomed 103 new foreign corporations into Monaco, with almost twice as many waiting to be granted business permits. Almost overnight scores of gleaming new skyscrapers began obscuring the Monaco skyline as British, French and American companies began relocating to the principality, generating hundreds of new jobs locally.

Some international companies did not even bother to relocate. Under Monaco law, all a French, Italian or English company needed to set up a corporation and become tax-free was to buy office space in Monaco and obtain a business permit from MEDEC. With minimal disruption to his life the owner could continue living abroad while reaping all the principality's tax benefits. Some greedy companies even blatantly flouted the law by renting out their 'corporate headquarters' as living quarters for local families.

Most of the companies avoiding tax were French and President Charles de Gaulle was not amused by this huge loss of revenue to France. The situation between France and Monaco was potentially explosive and perhaps the only reason it didn't blow up until 1962 was the President's affection for Princess Grace.

In 1959 Grace and Rainier had paid a state visit to France. It would be the first time Grace had officially represented Monaco abroad as First Lady and she was extremely nervous. To prepare herself for the trip she pored through de Gaulle's recently published war memoirs and studied hundreds of years of French and Monégasque history.

'Like a senior in high school, she stayed up nights cramming as if for a critical exam,' remembers Judy Balaban Quine.

When the big day came Grace was suffering from a debilitating head cold and was not feeling well. And on their arrival at the Elysée Palace there were so many flashbulbs popping that Grace was temporarily blinded. Later she told Judy Quine that she had seriously feared walking into a wall and single-handedly wrecking Franco–Monégasque relations.

But ultimately, Princess Grace was a triumph, charming the notoriously anti-American General de Gaulle by talking to him in her fractured French and making him smile at her charming mistakes. The following morning *France-Dimanche* declared that Grace's meeting with the President was a 'victory', adding that she had helped to 'reaffirm the prestige of her Prince'.

'After de Gaulle, Grace felt as proud as a child who has performed well at her first recital,' said Quine.

But three years later, as more and more French corporations poured into Monaco, costing the French Government millions in lost tax revenue, de Gaulle decided that enough was enough.

The angry President finally took action after Prince Rainier suspended trading of Radio Monte-Carlo on the Paris stock exchange, following an attempt by State-owned French companies to gain control. It was a highly sensitive situation; the powerful Monaco-based station broadcast directly into North Africa, reaching thousands of French citizens who lived there.

De Gaulle was furious. He viewed Rainier's action as direct interference in French international policy, an infringement of the 1918 treaty. He responded by telling Emile Pelletier, Monaco's French Minister of State, to tell Rainier to relax the ban.

Enraged at having his absolute authority in Monaco questioned, Rainier refused point blank. In fact, he dismissed Pelletier immediately and literally throwing him out of his office. When a bitter Pelletier reported back to de Gaulle he described Rainier as 'dangerously anti-French'.

Three months later President de Gaulle gave Rainier an ultimatum: start charging French residents and corporations taxes, payable to France, within six months – or the Monaco/French border would be closed and the principality 'asphyxiated'.

The very future of Monaco was now in jeopardy. And Rainier was in serious danger of losing both his throne and the Grimaldi family's 665-year tenure of Monaco. Although precisely what de Gaulle had meant by 'asphyxiation' remained unspecified, local newspapers warned that the French might blockade the tiny principality, cutting off its essential supplies of gas, water and electricity.

'I don't know how the General thought he would get away with it,' Prince Rainier said in 1988. 'He couldn't have done it legally.'

The rest of the world treated the whole affair as something of a joke. The David and Goliath battle seemed a real-life version of the 1949 Ealing comedy *Passport To Pimlico*, in which a newly-discovered ancient treaty enables residents of the London district of Pimlico to declare their independence – with hilarious results. The only difference was that, whereas *Passport To Pimlico* took as its heroine Margaret Rutherford, Monaco had the world-famous Grace Kelly as its leading lady.

Events took a dramatic turn on the night of October 12, 1962, when a band of French customs officers marched up to the borders of Monaco at midnight and set up customs barriers. Then they began stopping every vehicle entering or leaving the principality and checking passports.

On hearing the news Rainier rushed back to Monaco from Paris and convened an emergency meeting of the National Council, which he had recently restored after abolishing it in a fit of pique three years earlier.

'They may enclose Monaco with barbed wire tomorrow,' an anxious Grace wrote to a friend.

The customs checks proved more of a nuisance than anything else, causing long traffic delays in and out of Monaco. With a long-established free trade agreement between both countries – who shared the French franc as their currency – the lengthy checks only inconvenienced motorists and sent tempers soaring.

The Franco–Monégasque stand-off was finally broken when France began boycotting Monaco-manufactured pharmaceuticals, putting 300 people out of work. A further threat to stop Monaco trucks driving into France would have spelled economic ruin for Monaco. Rainier was forced to capitulate.

The agreement hammered out in May 1963 was a clear victory for President de Gaulle. Not only did Rainier agree to dismantle MEDEC and allow the French to buy shares in Radio Monte-Carlo, but from now on French citizens could no longer enjoy tax exemption. But although the French would have to pay the full rates of tax to France, all other nationalities – Americans, English, Italians, and Germans – could carry on as before.

Ironically, Rainier's surrender would in the long term give him more power in France as the principality's vast financial holdings came under the French monetary system and directly benefited the French economy.

'There is no doubt that the tax-exile money in Monaco stabilises the rather weak French franc,' said a financial expert.

As a result of Rainier re-establishing the new National Council during the emergency, a new constitution was drawn up for Monaco. Thanks to Princess Grace, women were allowed to vote for the first time. It seemed that Monaco was, albeit slowly, making progress, and had moved from the 17th century into the 19th.

A year before the showdown with France, Rainier and Grace had taken a cruise with Aristotle Onassis and Maria Callas, who were in the midst of a passionate affair. The couples got on well as they cruised the Mediterranean on Onassis's luxury yacht the *Christina*, bound for

Mallorca. Grace was particularly happy; she felt an artistic bond with the world-famous opera diva.

But there was a growing tension between Rainier and Onassis over the future direction of Monaco. The Greek tycoon still owned a controlling fifty-two per cent share in the SBM; but Rainier, who owned a mere two per cent, had the power of veto over any decisions the SBM made. On this voyage – and in many business meetings in the years to come – the two men would bitterly argue over Monaco, their tempers often boiling over as they almost came to blows. But a few hours later they would be the best of friends again, hugging each other as if nothing had happened.

The two men had vastly different views over the future direction of Monaco. Onassis wanted Monaco to remain the exclusive enclave of the super-rich; Rainier wanted to expand, going down-market and building new hotels to attract middle-class American tourists.

Onassis had always revelled in the social cachet that the SBM gave him. He said at the time: 'Monaco will always be prosperous so long as there are 3,000 rich men in the world.'

Grace's cousin John Lehman – now the chairman of the Princess Grace Foundation USA – claimed Onassis did not want Monaco to grow.

'He wanted to keep the principality just the way it was,' says Lehman. 'As a grand old dame of Russian Princesses and the ultra-rich. And that was not the Prince's vision.'

In 1965 Prince Rainier outlined his dream of Monaco as a democratic tourist destination with its own Holiday Inn, where rooms cost no more than $15 a day.

'My own feeling is that the economic wealth of the principality would be greatly improved if we could start off with 2,000 modern hotel rooms of the kind at which the Americans are so good,' he proclaimed.

Rainier even approached the Holiday Inns group, suggesting that they build hotels in Monaco, in direct opposition to the SBM. As a direct affront to Rainier, Onassis then agreed to build two new hotels and a new luxury apartment block in Monte-Carlo, but insisted on guarantees that the development would exclude Holiday Inn or any of its rivals. Rainier vetoed the scheme and went on television to attack the SBM for 'lethargy and bad faith'.

In a letter to Rupert Allan, Prince Rainier confided his fears of Onassis. 'Dear Rupert . . . I'm going to have to have stern talks with "O" and try and avoid the continuation of this situation which only harms Monte-Carlo. I hope to get him to play on my team.'

Indeed people were now openly calling Monte-Carlo 'Monte Greco' and referring to Onassis as 'the other prince'. Rainier became increasingly convinced that the Greek saw the SBM and the principality as a personal plaything; that he did not truly have Monaco's interests at heart.

Princess Grace stepped in to the mêlée when she attacked Onassis in an interview with *Playboy* magazine, saying that the Greek's interest in Monte-Carlo was 'more for his own amusement than a serious business affair'.

In June 1966, Prince Rainier moved decisively to get rid of Aristotle Onassis once and for all. He persuaded his National Council to create 600,000 new SBM shares, to be bought and held solely by the government. In one stroke Rainier wiped out Onassis's control of the SBM. Furious at being out-manoeuvred by the Prince, Onassis tried – with little success – to sue in the unsympathetic courts of Monaco.

Eventually Onassis cashed in his chips. After the Monégasque Treasury paid him $10 million compensation for his SBM shares, he sailed out of Monaco forever on the *Christina*.

Rainier's victory heralded a new era in Monaco. The SBM now belonged to the state and after fourteen years of crisis and struggle, Prince Rainier was at last the undisputed ruler of Monaco. No one would ever stand in his way again.

★ ★ ★

On November 15, 1969, Grace turned forty. She turned to her favourite astrologer Carroll Righter to help her organise a party for her many celebrity friends who, like herself, were Scorpios. The Princess, a life-long believer in astrology, had fallen under the influence of Los Angeles-based astrologer Righter after he had predicted she would marry a Prince; this happened years before she met Rainier.

Every day she religiously read her horoscope. She would often call Righter in Hollywood for a personal daily horoscope, which would have direct bearing on her palace and official activities.

Grace's fortieth birthday invitations, prepared by Righter, were designed like horoscopes. They were mailed to famous friends all over the world, including Rock Hudson, Richard Burton, Elizabeth Taylor and David and Hjordis Niven.

Held in the *belle époque* dining room of the Hotel Hermitage, Grace's birthday party was the stuff of legend. In Monaco it is still talked about to this day. But although it was Princess Grace's birthday, the real star of the show was Elizabeth Taylor, who dazzled everyone with the first showing of the famous Krupp diamond that Richard Burton had recently bought her as a gift.

Grace would later describe the party in a letter to Judy Balaban Quine, who had been unable to attend.

'Grace said she found it hard to take her eyes off Elizabeth, whom she thought to be "almost unbearably beautiful,"' said Quine.

'Next to this comment was an asterisk. At the bottom of the letter, under her signature, Grace had added, "*Forty . . . Ugh! I almost cannot bear that either!"'

As Grace entered her fifth decade she suffered a mid-life crisis. Two years earlier, in July 1967, she had suffered her third miscarriage while visiting the World's Fair, Expo '67, in Montreal. Forced finally to accept she would never have another child, Grace conceived instead her most ambitious and far-reaching project yet.

'Her instincts toward the invention of "Grace Kelly, Movie Star" had been nearly infallible,' says Judy Balaban Quine. 'But once she committed herself to it wholeheartedly, the invention of "Grace, Princess of Monaco" was a far more complex and taxing matter.'

By the dawning of the 1970s Princess Grace had resigned herself at last to the restrictions of her life in Monaco. She tried to make the best of the situation, devoting herself to charity work and being a good mother to her three children. But she nonetheless felt stifled and frustrated with no creative outlets to express herself artistically.

Her never-ending treadmill of civic duties was exhausting; she often longed to escape to Roc Agel for a few precious hours of peace. But instead of cutting down on her punishing schedule, she increased it deliberately so she would have no time to become introspective. She told friends that being Princess Grace day-in and day-out made her feel like 'a one-armed paper hanger'. In short, she was burned out.

'Grace's greatest treat in life was to go to bed,' says Gwen Robyns. 'She'd just spend all day reading books and calling her girlfriends and she was at peace. It's sad that here's one of the world's most beautiful women and the one thing she wants is one day in bed alone.'

On a typical day Grace would drag herself out of bed at 7 AM, prepare breakfast for Rainier and the children and ready the kids for school. Then she would dress and walk from her private quarters to her office on the other side of the Palace. For the next hour she would review the Palace's daily schedule and consult her fifty-strong staff, which included her major domo and three personal maids as well as a small army of gardeners and laundresses.

'There's always a crisis or a problem,' the Princess complained to *The Philadelphia Evening Bulletin* in July 1971. 'I sometimes feel hemmed in – very hemmed in.'

Most days were spent attending meetings of the various organisations she was involved with. In addition to her other responsibilities Grace took on two pet projects in the mid-1960s – the Princess Grace Foundation and the Garden Club.

The Princess Grace Foundation was started in 1964 when the Princess noticed that local artisans were having a hard time selling their crafts. To give them a proper retail outlet she opened the Boutique on the Rock as a non-profit organisation. It was so successful that she opened a second shop in 1970, expanding it to benefit other cultural pursuits, such as ballet.

The Garden Club was born in 1968 out of Grace's lifetime love of flowers. For several hours each week Grace would hike through the hillside of Monaco studying local plant life and flowers and studiously learning their Latin names. She would be joined by the club's members – which included Monégasque housewives – and this led to several rewarding new friendships. In time the club became an internationally recognised centre for flower-arranging competitions; Prince Rainier would often compete, successfully, in the men's section.

In July 1974 the SBM unveiled a new $2 million casino and pleasure palace, to celebrate Prince Rainier's Silver Jubilee and launch a new era in Monte-Carlo nightlife. The old Sporting Club had been ripped down to make room for the new club – a bigger, better and more luxurious state-of-the-art building with a fully retractable roof.

For the first Red Cross Ball in the new Sporting Club, SBM chairman Prince Louis de Polignac invited 650 guests for a sit-down dinner. This was followed by the Ball.

Henry Ford, David Niven, Gregory Peck and the Begum Aga Khan made their grand entrances, filing into the new gaming rooms, where the tables were still covered in plastic. While they sipped Blue Sharks and Pinkies – two new cocktails especially created for the occasion – there was a gasp of exhilaration as Prince Louis ceremoniously pressed a button and the heavy ceiling slowly opened to reveal the stars above.

Then, as the Holiday for Strings orchestra of Monte-Carlo struck up 'True Love' from the old Grace Kelly movie *High Society*, their Serene Highnesses, Grace and Rainier, appeared to lead the procession into the dining room where *perles de* Sterlet grey caviar, consommé Monte-Carlo, *charolais* beef and peach surprise were served. Before the night was over the guests had managed to down 350 bottles and twenty magnums of Pommery and Greno Brut 1969 champagne.

The only damper on the evening came when Sammy Davis Jr refused to leave his yacht and perform at the Ball. The entertainer apparently felt slighted as Princess Grace had not invited him to the Palace cocktail party the night before.

Producer André Levasseur was in a panic when Davis failed to arrive and enlisted Bill Cosby and Burt Bacharach to perform instead. The legendary singer Josephine Baker closed the spectacular show.

'She was unbelievable,' remembers Levasseur. 'It was certainly the greatest performance that I've ever seen at the Red Cross Ball and I've rarely seen an audience applaud for anyone the way they did for her.'

At 1.30 AM the sky over Monte-Carlo was ablaze with fireworks. The guests watched the great electric arcs of colours exploding over Monaco, lighting up the towering new reinforced-concrete apartment buildings that had sprung up all over the principality.

Then the guests went downstairs to dance the rest of the night away in Jimmy'z – the new ultra-modern discotheque owned by the legendary queen of nightclubs, Régine.

'Everyone there felt that Monaco was at the height of its glory,' said R. Couri Hay. 'It was a night that would live forever and it was hard to see how it could ever be topped.'

CHAPTER EIGHT

———— ❧ ————

GROWING UP
IN PUBLIC

BY 1972 THE Grimaldi family seemed picture-perfect. To the outside world the fairytale continued as the beautiful Princess and her handsome Prince raised their three lovely children in their magic principality. It almost seemed too good to be true.

'Nothing is more important to me than a harmonious family life,' Grace wrote to her old friend Don Richardson, describing her children as 'my jewels'.

Caroline, now fifteen, already spoke four languages fluently and was getting excellent grades at high school. In September 1971 Grace enrolled her at St Mary's Convent in Ascot, England, an establishment that mixed religious austerity with the discipline of an English public school. The strong-willed Caroline found it difficult to conform to the strict regime.

Already a dark-haired beauty and sophisticated beyond her years, Caroline also found it hard to relate to the rather superficial daughters of socialites, who insisted on calling her 'Grimmy'.

'Caroline had Rainier's Latin temperament and some of his sense of entitlement to a divine right to rule,' says Judy Balaban Quine. 'That is not what most children grow up with.'

If the independent Princess Caroline was bursting with confidence, her brother Prince Albert was quite the opposite. Naturally shy and reticent, the young Prince was handicapped by his stammer, much preferring to remain in the background.

'Albie was shyer and more affectionate than Caroline,' says Quine. 'He was not as self-reliant, and was far more dependent on other people.'

As the baby of the family, Stephanie was already an overpowering presence. From an early age she had her father wrapped around her little finger and would play her parents off against each other.

When writer Curtis Bill Pepper spent a day with Princess Grace and the children at the Monaco Beach Club in 1974 he saw how manipulative Stephanie could be. While passing the beach pool on the way to lunch, the little Princess suddenly presented Princess Grace with a single yellow daisy.

'Here, Mommie – it's from that little girl,' said Stephanie pointing out a blonde-haired child walking away.

'How sweet,' said Grace. 'Where are your brother and sister?'

'I dunno. Can I have a hot dog?'

'We're going to eat lunch now. You'll have no appetite for lunch.'

'Yes, I will. I promise.'

As Princess Stephanie ran off triumphantly to get the hot dog, her mother smiled, confiding to Pepper: 'If I had to bet I'd say this [daisy] really came from Stephanie – to soften me up for that hot dog.'

The Grimaldi children's first cousin Baron Christian 'Buddy' de Massy – the son of Rainier's sister Tiny – then in his early twenties, was a frequent visitor to the palace. He remembers the nine-year-old Stephanie as an immature child who always sucked her thumb – a childish habit she would maintain well into her teens.

'She was spoiled and deeply dependent on her mother,' recalled de Massy. 'She argued frequently with [Aunt Grace] to the point of intransigence. As I came to know her better, though, I discovered her to be genuinely sweet and vulnerable.'

When Caroline graduated from St Mary's in 1973 with excellent grades, Princess Grace couldn't contain her pride in her elder daughter's academic achievements. But Caroline, thrilled to be free from the strict school environment, suddenly rebelled, directly challenging her mother's conservative standards.

'Caroline went a little crazy,' remembers her Aunt Lizanne. 'And Grace had a fit. She *really* had a fit, but there wasn't much she could do.'

After she graduated from the convent, Princess Caroline decided to follow in her father's footsteps and go to Paris to study at the *École Libre des Sciences Politiques*. Before she could be accepted, however, she would have to pass the French *Baccalauréat* and she persuaded her parents that it made sense for her to go to Paris and study for the examination.

Princess Grace had been hoping her elder daughter would have an American education at an Ivy League university, but she changed her mind after reading about the current drug epidemic in the States. Like so many other mothers in the thrill-seeking 1970s, Grace wanted to protect her daughters from the dangers of sex and drugs. But she was also well aware that being a teenage Princess posed far greater hazards.

'Grace was mortally terrified about raising her children in the world that raged about her,' says Judy Balaban Quine, whose own daughters were also in their late teens. 'The idea of drugs and the dangers of teenage life without limits made her all the more anxious to control.'

But Grace – who had been a rebellious teenager herself, leaving home at eighteen – found herself in a moral dilemma when she tried to control Caroline.

'I remember as a girl saying, "I'll never say that to my children,"' explained the Princess in 1974. 'But now I find myself echoing the same phrases.'

Torn by her loyalties to Rainier, her duties toward Monaco and her love for her children, Princess Grace's parenting decisions were often illogical and erratic. Alternating between excessive repressiveness and unbelievable permissiveness, she found it hard to find a middle ground.

The child that would suffer the most from Grace's mixed signals would be her eldest. For Caroline resented the fact that her mother was far stricter with her than with Albert and Stephanie, who always seemed to get away with murder.

But eventually Grace realised how desperate Caroline was to leave home and make her own way in life.

'She wants to fly, to be on her own,' Grace admitted in 1974. 'It's natural and normal. She's more mature than I was at that age.'

Tall and graceful, Princess Caroline's Mediterranean looks, with her dark blue deep-set eyes, owed more to the Grimaldis than to the light-skinned, fair-haired Philadelphia Kellys. She already bore a striking resemblance to her grandmother, Princess Charlotte, and had her fiery temperament and passion.

Once she arrived in Paris it didn't take long for the international press to discover Caroline and turn her into the world's first disco-dancing, topless Princess. By the time she was eighteen columnists were already busy linking her romantically with some of the world's most eligible bachelors, including Prince Charles. And with little knowledge of the real world outside the Palace and her convent school, Caroline suddenly found herself an international cover girl – much to the distress of both her and her parents.

'It was clear to Grace that her children were going to be subjected to the very invasions of their youthful privacy that she and Rainier had tried to prevent,' said Judy Balaban Quine.

To try and minimise the damage it was decided that Grace would chaperone Caroline to Paris and live with her at the family apartment on elegant Avenue Foch. Stephanie was to join them and go to school there, but Albert would stay in Monaco, making occasional visits to Paris with Prince Rainier. The family planned to divide their time between Monaco and Paris until Caroline was settled.

Caroline was furious when she heard her mother would be intruding on her new life. She accused her parents of not trusting her; she said she wanted to stay with her beloved grandmother, Mamou. Grace was horrified: Mamou's lifestyle was the talk of Paris. She employed only ex-convicts at her chateau in Marchais, outside Paris, and there was talk that she took many of them as lovers. The possible consequences of placing Caroline in her grandmother's care were unthinkable. Grace and Rainier finally compromised, agreeing to let the young Princess go to Paris under the watchful eye of a family friend.

The minute Caroline arrived at her new home at 26 Place de l'Avenue Foch, the French paparazzi set up camp outside. She was photographed relentlessly every time she went in and out of her front door. Within a few days she reached breaking-point, crying tearfully, 'Why do I have to be a princess? I hate it.'

The moment Princess Grace heard what was going on, she reactivated her original plan and moved to Paris with Stephanie. But the publicity machine she and Rainier had willingly fed twenty years earlier in order to jump-start modern Monaco was now threatening to take over her children's lives. Asked about why she had come to Paris with Caroline, Grace attempted to explain the problems of bringing up a modern-day princess:

'She is not a normal girl,' explained Princess Grace. 'Her father is a reigning prince, and because of this people will be watching, looking, seeking her out. It's happening already.'

Grace also had an ulterior motive to move to Paris: she had grown bored in Monaco and was looking forward to the freedom that Paris would give her. And she was eager to renew her old friendships and rediscover her love of life.

But the move to Paris backfired in every possible way. Instead of being able to protect her daughters from publicity, having three Princesses living under one roof only intensified the pressure from the paparazzi. Grace's children felt like hunted animals, with the press constantly in pursuit.

On one occasion paparazzi actually shattered the windscreen of a car to get a shot of nine-year-old Stephanie on her way to a ballet lesson.

'Stephanie was terrified,' said Judy Balaban Quine. 'The paparazzi were practically overturning the car on the street and she thought she was going to be killed. After that she used to hide in the trunk of the car to avoid them. It was horrible.'

Princess Caroline soon discovered Paris's late-night hot spots, such as Régine's and Castels. Now Caroline was finally ready to assert her independence, and she did it with a vengeance. Taking up small cigars in defiance of her mother's no-smoking ban was just one example.

After *Time* magazine put her on the cover she found herself one of the world's most famous and admired teenagers. Almost every day the newspapers of Europe published pictures of her late-night partying at Parisian discos. There was a string of headlines such as PRINCESS HEART-BREAKER and PLAYGIRL PRINCESS, linking her to a variety of eligible young bachelors including Henri Giscard d'Estaing, the son of the French President, and French rock star Philippe Lavelle.

The daily gossip and speculation on her daughter's 'romances' infuriated Grace, who denounced them all as 'imaginary'.

'The less said about those the better,' she told *McCall's* Curtis Bill Pepper.

'She's not interested in marriage to anybody . . . not now. Like most girls her age, she wants to be free to move on, to grow and develop her own identity.'

In an effort to set the record straight, Princess Caroline gave her first serious interview, to the *New York Times*, on the eve of her eighteenth birthday.

Under the headline PRINCESS CAROLINE AT 18: A SERIOUS STUDENT, CASUAL PARTYGOER, the story painted the picture of a studious, responsible girl who did three hours of homework every night, ten to thirteen hours on weekends, to the accompaniment of classical music.

'I would like to get this straight,' she began in her curious combination of Anglo-American English. 'I don't spend my life on the social scene and those romance stories annoy me. I have to do homework every moment I have free.'

But that certainly wasn't the case on the night she was at a Parisian disco dancing with Philippe Lavelle. In the middle of her gyrations a button on her tight, low-cut blouse burst, revealing a bare breast. A paparazzo caught the moment and the following day the picture of the half-naked Princess made newspaper front pages around the world.

'It was the first time she had been in any sort of adult scandal,' said Judy Balaban Quine. 'They were running stories implying that she was second only to a streetwalker and that there was something wrong with the family.'

When Prince Rainier heard he was furious and ordered Grace to reprimand Caroline for her immoral behaviour. But the young Princess had heard rumours of her mother's love affairs in New York and Hollywood and confronted her about them, calling her a hypocrite.

Realising that she was in no position to preach morality to her daughter, Grace found herself in a difficult position. As a mother she wanted to protect Caroline from the dangers that she believed were lying in wait; yet she had fallen prey to many of the same temptations herself in her youth, and knew that such behaviour was only natural.

Grace's frustrations became clear when she uncharacteristically criticised Caroline in a newspaper interview.

'She was careless,' said Grace of the bare-breasted incident. 'There was nothing wrong with the dress itself. It was just the way she wore it.'

At the end of her first term Caroline's active night life had taken its toll on her grades, which were the lowest she had ever received. The formerly hard-working student had lost interest in her studies and announced that she was quitting school at the end of the year to make her own way in the world.

This was totally unacceptable to the Grimaldis. A furious Grace brought Caroline back to Monaco so Prince Rainier could talk some sense into their rebellious daughter. Behind Palace doors Caroline argued vehemently with her father about her future. Finally, after a series of bitter confrontations, Rainier persuaded her to go to America to study at Princeton University, where the Kelly family could keep an eye on her.

Grace and Rainier felt they had reached the perfect solution; removing Caroline from the perils of sophisticated Paris by transferring her across the ocean to New Jersey. But a few weeks before Caroline was due to start classes her parents' worst fears were realised when she fell madly in love.

Chapter Nine

~

The Princess Bride

WHILE SHE WAS in Paris trying to contain 'the Caroline Problem', Grace found her own skeletons were in danger of coming out of the cupboard and into public view.

Throughout her career in Hollywood and subsequent marriage to Prince Rainier, Grace had carefully maintained her chaste public image. But one day, to her horror, she received a manuscript of an unauthorised biography which contained revelations about her steamy pre-marital love affairs with Ray Milland, Clark Gable, Jean-Pierre Aumont and William Holden. It had been written by respected new Zealand journalist Gwen Robyns, who had previously penned successful biographies of Agatha Christie and Margaret Rutherford. Just ten days before she was due to deliver the manuscript to her publisher, Robyns had become so concerned about the effect the book might have on Grace's marriage that she decided to send a copy to the Princess so she could prepare herself for the furore which would follow publication.

Two days later Grace's secretary called and summoned Robyns to

Paris to meet with the Princess to discuss the book. The following day Robyns arrived at the Avenue Foch house, a stone's throw away from the Arc de Triomphe. As she sat in the foyer, waiting, what appeared to be a schoolgirl burst through a door and passed her, wearing 'a pleated skirt, blazer and rather lank hair without make-up.'

It took several long, hard looks before Robyns realised to her astonishment that the apparition had been Princess Grace. A few minutes later the concierge summoned her upstairs and she was ushered into the pale blue salon for her audience with the Princess.

'She was terribly nervous,' remembers Robyns. 'She was behaving like a schoolgirl and looked extremely shy and anxious. She just sat there pushing the quicks back on her fingers, which was what she did when she felt very insecure.'

The now conservative Princess – who had recently begun sanctimoniously decrying the lowering of sexual standards, relaxed dress codes and nudity – was being confronted with her own youthful immorality. She was clearly finding it difficult to put her thoughts into words.

Finally, to break the silence, Robyns asked what she thought about the book. Grace looked up. 'Well, it's all true. I know I can't stop you publishing it but it will cause me some trouble.'

Gwen Robyns recalls: 'And so I said, what sort of problems? and she went, "Well, I'm trying to stop my daughter Caroline from going out with married men, and here I am seeing married men in the book. And Rainier also doesn't know about some of these things."'

Robyns found herself falling under Princess Grace's spell. The former actress reverted back to her childhood role of the vulnerable little girl who needed everyone's help and protection. Seduced by Grace's candour and frankness, Robyns told her to edit out anything she didn't want to see in the book.

'And she said, "That's going to spoil your book",' said Robyns. 'And I said, "It doesn't matter about my book – what really matters is your marriage."'

When the sanitised version of *Princess Grace* was published in the spring of 1976, Robyns immediately sent a copy to Monaco. A couple of weeks later she received a warm letter from the deeply-relieved Princess, saying she hadn't really believed the author would omit the steamy revelations.

Although Gwen Robyns' censored look at Princess Grace's life never did make the bestseller lists, it did win her a friendship with Grace that would last until the Princess's death. From their first meeting Robyns – who had proved herself trustworthy – was admitted to the select band of women who shared Grace's closest secrets.

In 1976 Princess Caroline was literally swept off her feet when she met international playboy Philippe Junot at a Parisian disco. It seemed to be a case of history repeating itself: Junot, physically, very much resembled Grace Kelly's old fiancé Oleg Cassini. And, just as Grace's family had thoroughly disapproved of Cassini, so did Grace and Rainier disapprove of Junot.

Seventeen years Caroline's senior, Junot was a notorious womaniser who oozed Continental charm and sophistication. Longing to get away from her parents' clutches, Caroline, then nineteen, saw the thirty-six-year-old Junot as her passport to freedom. It was never quite clear how the unconventionally attractive Junot, the well-heeled son of a deputy Mayor of Paris, made his living; he claimed to be a 'merchant banker'.

'He was very charming and he was a ladies' man,' said Lizanne Kelly LeVine. 'He snowed you like you wouldn't believe. You walk into a room, "Ah, Ma'am, how gorgeous you look." So she was snowed!'

With Junot's reputation as an international roué preceding him, Princess Grace was against the match from the beginning. Knowing from first-hand experience the dangers that worldly-wise older men can pose to an innocent young girl, she desperately appealed to Caroline to give up the relationship.

But the more Grace opposed Junot, the deeper became her

headstrong daughter's infatuation with him. Many of Caroline's friends believed she was confusing lust with love. Junot was an avowed hedonist who proudly boasted he owned the Princess: on one occasion, at the Beverly Hills Hotel in Los Angeles, he showed a friend a raunchy love letter that Caroline had written, offering to leave her parents and Monaco and become his slave.

When Junot pursued Caroline to New York during the 1976 American Bicentennial celebrations, her parents refused to let him see her. Rainier's bodyguards barred him from entering their hotel. In an effort to divert her love-struck daughter's attentions away from her lover, Grace called all her friends in New York and Los Angeles and asked them to suggest suitable young men for Caroline. One possibility was the handsome young Prince Ernst of Hanover, a godson of Queen Elizabeth II. Grace thought the Prince would be the perfect match – but Caroline found him boring. (Ironically, twenty years later, she would have an affair with him which contributed to the break-up of his marriage.)

By the time the Grimaldis reached California during the Bicentennial, Caroline was distraught.

'She cried most of the week she was in Los Angeles,' recalled Hollywood columnist Jack Martin.

Angry at her parents for not letting her see Junot, Caroline refused to attend any of the parties planned for her and had to be taken back to Monaco. Finally, Rainier and Grace surrendered. They couldn't bear to see their daughter so miserable. They invited Junot to the palace for a meeting – highly reminiscent of Oleg Cassini's visit to the Kelly family twenty-five years earlier.

To Grace and Rainier's astonishment Philippe Junot managed to charm them, especially impressing them with the authority he exerted over their spirited, self-willed daughter. Caroline refused to take orders from her parents; but when Junot told her to go home and change into something more suitable for a chic restaurant dinner, she obediently obliged. Yet she saw her situation differently.

'Philippe has given me the first freedom I have ever known in my life,' she told a girlfriend.

Grace and Rainier decided to drop their Princeton plan. They would let Caroline move back to Paris and continue her studies at the Sorbonne, hoping her affair with Junot would burn itself out, as young love often did.

'Caroline was mesmerised,' says Gwen Robyns, who was a frequent visitor to Avenue Foch at that time.

'Grace made this rule that Junot would have to come and collect her if they were going out on a date. We'd all be together having a drink and Junot would come in wearing the tightest pants and they would start rubbing up against each other in the most physical way. It would be so embarrassing.

'When they'd left I asked Grace how she could allow this behaviour and she said, "This is young love, Gwen. I can't stop it."'

Once, in a taxi on a shopping trip to the London department store Harrods, Grace asked Gwen Robyns outright why she didn't like Philippe Junot.

Recalls Robyns: 'And without thinking I said, "His remarks are too trite, his teeth are too bright and his crotch is too tight." Well, Grace laughed so much that she fell off the seat. And as we arrived at Harrods, a man opens the door and there is Her Serene Highness on the floor, absolutely killing herself with laughter.'

Caroline and Junot's unrestrained displays of sexual affection caused a sensation when the couple were photographed by paparazzi aboard a yacht. These explicit photographs showed a naked Caroline reclining on deck with Junot kissing her bare breasts.

Furious that his daughter had achieved the dubious distinction of becoming – for the second time – 'the topless princess', Rainier called Junot and Caroline into his study and 'gave them hell'.

But in January 1977 Junot proposed to Caroline. The ecstatic young Princess bounded into the bedroom of her cousin and best friend Grace LeVine at 2 AM, shouting, 'Guess what, guess what! Philippe has proposed!'

When Junot arrived at the Palace to ask officially for Caroline's hand in marriage the Grimaldis balked.

Grace's cousin Buddy de Massy says that Rainier and Grace initially wanted to use their sovereign authority to forbid the marriage, but were afraid that Caroline would break away from the family and marry abroad.

'Uncle Rainier thought Philippe was a seducer and a fortune-hunter,' said de Massy. 'They were puzzled and embarrassed by the scandal surrounding Caroline's behaviour, which contrasted with the flawless image of the family Grace had always projected.'

Grace and Rainier decided to stall for time. They asked the young couple to postpone marriage for at least a year so Caroline could continue her studies at the Sorbonne and get her degree. But that gamble failed when only nine months later the couple again requested permission to wed.

Grace was now totally opposed to the marriage, believing that Junot would be unfaithful and break her daughter's heart. She implored Rainier to deny permission, but the Prince was afraid of losing his beloved daughter forever. When he threatened to ban the marriage, Caroline put a metaphorical gun to his head, saying she and Junot would live in sin instead. Although it was the 1970s, and quite acceptable for young couples to live together prior to marriage, Caroline knew that this would be totally unacceptable for a Roman Catholic Princess of Monaco.

'There were strong principles that you didn't leave home until you were married,' explained Caroline in 1996. 'So having been told that I wasn't going to leave home unmarried by the time I was twenty-one, I thought [marriage] was a way of independence. Which it wasn't. And it's a foolish thing to think.'

Given Caroline's ultimatum, Grace and Rainier had no alternative but to capitulate and give their reluctant permission for Caroline and Junot to have a church wedding in Monaco.

Remembered Princess Caroline: 'Mommy said, "Of course he's the

wrong man and you shouldn't marry him – but now you've been compromised. You've been dating him for too long, so either get engaged
officially or stop seeing him.'''

Although Caroline was ecstatic as she showed off her giant new
engagement ring – a sapphire surrounded by diamonds – her parents
were in a state of shock. On the night before the official engagement
announcement Gwen Robyns was at Roc Agel for a small private
celebration with Caroline and Junot.

On her arrival Rainier ushered her to one side and asked her into his
den for a quiet word.

'He asked me what I thought of Junot,' remembers Robyns. 'I said,
"Sir, I think he's a playboy." And I asked Rainier what he knew about
Junot. And he said, "Not much." I was amazed. I said, "Sir, how can you
not know what he does for a living? What's he doing in America with
all this money?"'

Then the Prince asked Robyns to take Junot into the garden for a
stroll and try to find out what line of business he was in.

'I said, "Sir. She's engaged to him, so couldn't you use your Secret
Service investigation team to find out?" He hadn't thought of that.'

Although she publicly put a brave face on the situation, Grace was
terribly unhappy about the marriage. She was willing to risk anything
to avoid a scandal in Monaco and she could only hope that Caroline's
common sense and strength of character would carry her through the
inevitable marital crises.

Grace had resigned herself to the fact that the marriage was doomed
before it had even reached the altar. She told Gwen Robyns it would
last just two years and on the very night before the nuptials reasoned to
Rainier: 'Well, perhaps it's for the better. This way she'll have a successful second marriage.'

Whereas his strong-willed sisters were both a constant cause of anxiety
for Grace, Albert presented few problems to his adoring parents. More

like the Kellys than the tempestuous Grimaldis, Albert was quieter and more easy-going than his bombastic siblings. As a result he was disciplined less; he was also a boy, which meant that in any case he was given a far looser rein.

Although both his sisters had been spanked by Grace when they were little, the well-behaved Albert usually managed to escape any physical punishment.

'It's different with each child,' Princess Grace told *McCall's* magazine in 1974. 'When Caroline was little, it seemed as if I spanked her every other minute; Albert didn't need so much. A sharp word to him was enough. Stephanie . . . I should have beat her like a gong long ago. You get a little tired with the third one and give in to keep the peace.'

Grace felt closest to Albert, who, like her, was the middle child. She related to the difficulties he faced sandwiched between two domineering sisters; she also understood his clinging need for affection. Though Rainier saw Albert's inherent gentleness as a handicap and deliberately tried to toughen him up, Grace responded to his sweetness with love and sympathy.

'Albie was a piece of Grace's true American soul,' says Judy Balaban Quine. 'He had a very sensitive nature.'

Prince Albert had spent his formative years at special private classes in the Palace, taught alongside a hand-picked group of local children. His parents had done this primarily to shield their shy son from the outside world, but Albert, who was a friendly child, resented not going to a proper school like his sister Caroline. He craved the rough and tumble of 'normal' education. Finally, at the age of eight, his wish came true and he was sent to public school in Monaco. Here he blossomed as he discovered a passion for competitive sports that allowed him to prove himself on equal terms with the other boys. He began studying judo at the age of eleven and went on to become a black belt.

It was through sports that the Prince developed his self-confidence; through hard work and resolution in his middle teens he finally lost his stammer.

'He was quiet and subdued,' said Buddy de Massy of the young Prince. 'Almost as if the duties and obligations he would one day inherit were beginning to weigh upon him.'

Prince Rainier's single-minded determination to prepare his son for eventual rule could verge on cruelty and Albert feared his father. David Swift – Grace's old friend from New York drama school days – once played a game of tennis with Rainier and his teenage son during a visit to the Palace.

'It was embarrassing when he was playing with Albert as his partner,' recalled Swift. 'If the boy played bad – and he was only a kid – Rainier went mad, shouting at him.'

At one point in the game Rainier became so incensed that he threw his racket at Albert, who managed to duck just in time.

In 1996 Albert admitted that when he was growing up his father would explode at the least provocation:

'He had a temper that he showed us very clearly when we annoyed him. But it would die down as quickly as it had flared.'

Although Grace, as a concerned mother, had kept a watchful, puritanical eye on Caroline when she started to become interested in boys, she took a far more liberal approach where Albert and the opposite sex were concerned. Keeping up appearances was paramount to Grace; it would cause a major scandal in Monaco if her daughters were seen bedding young men. But it was an entirely different story for a boy, who needed to prove his manhood; it was even something to take pride in.

When Albert started dating at fifteen Grace actively encouraged him to sow his wild oats. She and Rainier carefully explained the mechanics of birth control to Albert and she gave him *carte blanche* to experiment with the rich young ladies of his own social circle.

'Grace never worried about Albie,' said Judy Balaban Quine. 'Instead, she encouraged him to "do whatever you have to do".'

From early childhood Grace had taken Albert to America, where he'd spend the summer with his Kelly cousins at the Jersey shore and go off to camp. The young Prince loved America, other children were less deferential to him than they were in Monaco and he could feel just like anyone else. Albert was always determined to succeed in life on his own merits – not just because he had been born a Prince of Monaco.

As the years went on he would become far more American than European in speech and outlook, enjoying the ease and informality that his father deplored.

So it was only natural that, when Albert graduated from high school, he should go to an American university. He chose Amherst College in Massachusetts to finish his education. Princess Grace escorted her nineteen-year-old son to register as a freshman at the beginning of September, 1977. After buying him a mattress, pillows and bed-linen for his dormitory room, Grace met his professors and made it clear that she didn't want her son to get special treatment from the other 385 freshmen.

Introducing himself as 'Al Grimaldi' the young Prince was an immediate hit with the fellow students, many of whom did not even recognise him. He soon settled into college life, delighting in being an all-American boy.

'He took to American college life like a character out of a Fitzgerald novel,' says his fellow Amherst student Tony Peck, the screenwriter-son of movie star Gregory Peck. 'I kind of shepherded him into his freshman year, but he didn't need a lot of help. He has that ability to connect.'

Another Amherst classmate, Jesse Rucker, described the Prince as 'affable' and 'modest', adding that, if pressed about what his father did for a living 'Al will say: "he's involved in government."'

Despite placing a 'No Soliciting' sign on his dormitory door, the student Prince was always receiving unsolicited visits from curious girls in the co-ed college, who kept banging on the door until he let them in.

'He is friendly and talks to all of them,' said dormmate Dee Brown. 'But if they are pretty he is much more likely to invite them in.'

At weekends Albert would visit the Kellys in Philadelphia or drive to

Manhattan, where he would often be denied entry into some of the city's hottest nightclubs.

'He would never use his name to get in,' says Albert's long-time friend Anton Katz, also at Amherst with him. 'I remember we got turned away from quite a few places in those days.'

Soon after coming to Amherst the press began linking Albert with a string of beautiful young women. After he was pictured in New York with Louise Rambo – the seventeen-year-old daughter of Princess Grace's friend and bridesmaid Maree – the newspapers declared it to be a 'hot romance'.

'Albert is much too young to be getting involved in anything serious,' said his Aunt Lizanne at the time.

Like Caroline, the Prince became a target for the paparazzi; but he was far more adept than his sister at keeping his private life private. His student days at Amherst gave him a better grounding in reality than his sisters, who were constantly shuttling between world capitals in the bright glare of publicity.

Albert's first cousin, Chris LeVine, recalls the cavalier way he and the young Prince would deal with chasing paparazzi in those days:

'I would be driving a car behind him. When we stopped at a red light I'd get out of the car and leave my car blocking the paparazzi. And I'd jump in with Albert and off we'd go, leaving behind a honking group of photographers.'

In 1981 Albert quietly graduated from Amherst with a degree in Political Science. He distinguished himself only by singing with the Glee Club and becoming an American jock, enthusiastically participating in tennis, swimming and football.

'Quite frankly I wouldn't be who I am today if I hadn't been involved in sports and [become] competitive,' said Prince Albert. 'There was no way.'

Rainier and Grace's veteran PR man Rupert Allan – whose nephew Todd was at Amherst with Albert – warned that the Prince was almost too trusting and friendly to rule Monaco.

'He's very accommodating – almost too much so,' Allan told *People* magazine in November 1982.

'He bends over backwards to hold people's chairs. The Monégasques want a leader who is strong. Albert is going to have to develop some toughness if he wants to take over the leadership of Monaco.'

After leaving Amherst Albert joined the French Navy, spending six months serving as an ensign aboard *La Jeanne d'Arc*. By this time his sister Caroline's romantic adventures had taken centre stage, allowing Albert to keep a low profile. He created few ripples during his time in America – where, in fact, he had lost his virginity and fallen in love.

'He created a certain kind of little bubble to protect him,' says Judy Balaban Quine, of Albert's student days. 'It gave him the notion that he could control [his life].'

But the same could not be said of Princess Stephanie, whose lack of self-control would soon send shockwaves through Monaco.

The night before Princess Caroline married Philippe Junot, a lavish pre-wedding ball was held at the Palace. The 800-strong guest list included the cream of European aristocracy and minor royalty; the representatives of the English, Dutch, Belgian, Danish and Swedish monarchies had declined to attend. Palace press spokeswoman Nadia LaCoste explained that they had 'prior commitments', pointing out it was not a state wedding. But a strong Hollywood contingent showed up, including Frank and Barbara Sinatra, David Niven, Cary Grant and Gregory Peck.

One notable figure who stayed away was thirteen-year-old Princess Stephanie, who was deliberately boycotting the sumptuous affair.

'I bought her a wonderful dress,' her exasperated mother told Judy Balaban Quine, who had inquired where Grace's youngest daughter was hiding, 'but she said she would only come to the ball if I allowed her to wear pants or jeans. I had enough to think about and do, so I just said if she got dressed correctly she could come and if she didn't, she could stay out.'

With or without the rebellious teen, the Ball was a great success. Princess Caroline, on the arm of her father, opened the ball to the strains of Neil Diamond's 'Sweet Caroline'. The Princess looked spectacular, wearing a white tulle Marc Bohan gown and a glittering diamond necklace belonging to the family. The next couple to take the floor was Prince Albert and his mother. The guests danced to the music of Aimé Barelli and the Youngsters Incorporated until 4 AM. And on the following day Jeanne Kelly van Remoortel hosted a cocktail party for the American wedding guests at her apartment. Grace's Monaco friend was in sparkling form as she served Tex-Mex delicacies to her guests: dishes that she would one day dish up at her Le Texan restaurant, later to open in Monte-Carlo.

In an attempt to prevent their daughter's wedding from turning into the same fiasco that their's had twenty-two years earlier, Rainier had banned helicopters over Monaco airspace for the four days over the wedding. All wedding souvenirs were outlawed; only Palace-appointed photographers were allowed at the ceremony.

Even now the invited wedding guests were arguing over exactly what Junot did for a living: a recent story in *Paris Soir* repeated rumours that Junot was being backed financially by Saudi Arabian millionaire Adnan Khashoggi, who wanted to gain influence in Monaco. An official Palace press release, however, described Junot as a financial and investment advisor to international banking establishments with offices in Paris and Montreal. It was a mystery.

Frank Sinatra hit the perfect note for the controversial wedding when he serenaded the happy couple with 'My Way' at a pre-wedding lunch thrown by David Niven.

On June 28, 1978, thirty members of Caroline and Philippe's immediate families attended the civil ceremony in the palace Throne Room. The following day the Bishop of Monaco, Monsignor Gilles Barthe –

who had married Grace and Rainier – performed the religious ceremony in the Palace courtyard.

Prince Rainier's official wedding speech to the Monégasque popu-
lation, who were invited to the Palace to celebrate with the happy couple, carefully hid the forebodings both he and Grace felt about the
union. Thanking his people for their 'precious comfort' in his days of
'often heavy duty', the Prince said Caroline and Junot's wedding united
Monaco.

'I invite you to unite with the Princess, with myself and my children
in the affectionate wishes that we make for the young couple. In a
moment we will lift our glasses to their happiness: that they build a
solid and happy family under the protection of Sainte Dévote.'

Princess Grace was once asked whether she believed in the notorious
Curse of the Grimaldis. 'No, no,' she replied; 'I believe in Sainte
Dévote.'

The Grimaldis marital record is littered with divorce, separation and
infidelity. Rainier's own parents had a tragically unhappy union that
tortured him as a child. Although Prince Rainier claims to have beaten
the curse himself – though many would argue that point – the same
cannot be said for his children. And even Sainte Dévote – the patron
saint of Monaco outside whose Monte-Carlo church the superstitious
Princess Grace placed her own wedding bouquet for good luck – could
not save them.

Even on her Tahiti honeymoon Princess Caroline began to wonder
whether she had made the right decision in marrying Junot. Her doubts
began when she discovered that her new husband had lined up a photographer friend to take their honeymoon pictures and sell them to the
press. Caroline was furious.

'That's when it started to click,' she said in 1989. 'That was terrible.
The end started right there. But it took me a year and a half to finish it.
A long time.'

Within months of the wedding, rumours that Junot had resumed his playboy habits filtered back to Caroline. And in January 1979 paparazzi caught Junot in New York's Studio 54 dancing with his old girlfriend, Countess Agneta von Furstenberg; he had told Caroline he was going on a one-day business trip to Montreal.

When the Princess saw the picture she broke down in tears, feeling scorned and betrayed. Deciding to teach Junot a lesson she retaliated by spending time with Roberto Rossellini, Ingrid Bergman's love child.

From then on the marriage quickly disintegrated. During its collapse Caroline's cousin Grace LeVine, who was living in Monaco, became an advisor and confidante.

'She loved him – she really did,' Grace LeVine told author James Spada in 1986. 'And she was a wreck when the marriage broke up. Philippe was a *very* charming man and he did change his ways before the marriage. But after that it was all downhill.'

Caroline and Grace LeVine spent long nights analysing the marriage, sifting through every aspect of the relationship, searching for a solution. Grace and Rainier had no idea of the misery their daughter was going through; Caroline's pride wouldn't allow her to admit they'd been right about Junot all along.

Finally the Junots' private problems became all too obvious when they had a major row in public at the official ball following the 1980 Monaco Grand Prix. Caroline stormed out in a fury. After that, she finally confessed to her parents that her marriage was on the rocks.

In a letter to Rupert Allan, Rainier wrote: 'Poor Caroline's marriage is not going well. She's been hurt, and – God be blessed – she came to mum and dad and told them of her unhappiness.'

Two weeks before the final break-up Gwen Robyns went to interview Caroline and Junot for a cover story in *Ladies' Home Journal*. She was appalled to see that Caroline had been crying and was clearly very miserable. At one point Junot offered to pay Robyns to write that the marriage was happy but she refused, saying she would do it anyway for free as a family friend. After the interview Robyns was so concerned about Caroline that she telephoned Princess Grace, who was in New York.

'I said, "Listen, this child is so unhappy,"' remembers Robyns. '"It's dreadful."'

Two weeks later Robyns was staying with Grace in Paris when Caroline phoned up in tears saying she'd had enough.

'It was Princess Grace who went over to the flat and confronted Junot and got her out of the flat,' says Gwen. 'She packed her bags and said, "That's it – you're coming home." Grace took care of everything because Rainier wouldn't have done. He left it up to Grace to do the tough jobs.'

When Princess Grace told her daughter she had to get a divorce Caroline was amazed. Her mother was a devout Roman Catholic — it seemed totally out of character. Grace said that religion should have a positive effect on people and not prolong human misery, bravely declaring that she would rather risk scandal and censure from the religious Monégasques than see her daughter unhappy.

Junot blamed Grace and Rainier for breaking up the marriage, accusing them of constantly meddling in his and Caroline's affairs. He declared that his wife's parents had never approved of him.

'There were problems,' he told reporters. 'Her parents interfered . . . the whole thing became impossible.'

In August 1980 the Palace announced that Caroline and Junot had separated. By October the divorce had become final. But it would take many years of bitter battles with the Vatican to get the marriage annulled.

CHAPTER TEN

HONG KONG
ON THE
RIVIERA

PRINCE RAINIER'S ACKNOWLEDGED wish to be remembered as the 'builder prince' of Monaco is not a self-aggrandising one. But such a designation may be less than flattering: during his reign the Prince has transformed the once-charming small Mediterranean cove, with its old pastel villas and glorious gardens, into a dull consolidation of reinforced concrete resembling a mini-Hong Kong.

After forcing Aristotle Onassis out of Monaco in the mid-sixties, Rainier and his advisors launched a two-pronged development approach: to expand tourism and attract new foreign businesses that would use Monaco as a tax shelter.

'First of all he gave a very strong boost to what you would call upper-class tourism,' says Andrew Jack, the Paris-based correspondent of the *Financial Times*.

'Marrying Grace and making [Monaco] *the* place to be seen clearly had all sorts of spin-offs in terms of giving a new lease of life to the luxury hotels and restaurants. But Rainier also did quite a lot to diversify the economy.

'He tried to encourage the development of light industry in the service sector. And of course he oversaw a period when there was enormous property development in the area. That was very important to the economy.'

This unrestrained building programme changed the face of Monaco beyond recognition and brought the Prince and his principality riches beyond their wildest dreams. Throughout the 1970s and 1980s the tiny principality became one big building site, with concrete mixers and cranes becoming more prominent than palm trees. And with the government collecting twenty-five per cent AVT (value-added tax) on all building costs, the development provided a huge source of revenue.

The 30,000 residents became so used to the ground shaking from controlled explosions blasting through bedrock to prepare the way for new tunnels, walkways and parking lots, that when a real earthquake hit Monaco, nobody noticed.

But although, visually, Monte-Carlo has been ruined beyond repair, few would criticise Prince Rainier's ongoing building programme. For the 5,000 native Monégasques are the most pampered ethnic group in the world; having their once-perfect views blocked by towering skyscrapers is a small price to pay for their ease of living. They pay no tax and receive generous state subsidies for living in government-owned buildings, where rents are kept artificially low.

The Monégasques are given priority in employment; in January 1997 there were just thirty-five without jobs. Rainier's unquestioned absolute rule in the country is ensured, as only Monégasques can vote to elect the eighteen-member National Council. Long-term residents may in theory become Monégasques, but the honour – which is extremely rare – must be personally bestowed by Prince Rainier. The remaining 25,000 residents have no say in their government whatsoever.

Monaco is Europe's last remaining dictatorship; Prince Rainier the last absolute ruler. He formally appoints the four-person cabinet and proposes all legislation on which the National Council votes. But, unquestionably, the sweeping changes the Prince has made during his forty-eight year rein have greatly benefited his people, who will not – publicly at least – say a bad word against him.

'It was a sacrifice that had to be made,' explains Rainier's second cousin, Lionel Noghes, who watched the Monaco landscape change over the years.

'At one time there was no building at all and it was all very beautiful but now there is a lot of concrete. I think it was the only way to build up Monaco.'

After Rainier's 1962 run-in with General de Gaulle, French citizens who arrived after October 1957 could no longer reap the tax advantages of living in Monaco. To make up for the losses, Rainier started wooing other foreign businesses, pop stars and celebrities who wanted to dodge paying heavy taxes in their own countries.

Although other tax havens, such as Liechtenstein or the Isle of Sark, required only a simple brass door plate to establish presence and thus ensure freedom from taxes, Monaco demanded a slightly more tangible presence. Resident status in the principality required the buying or renting of an apartment; this led to the erection of scores of luxury high-rise blocks all over Monaco. These were so numerous they obscured the sun for much of the day.

'Monaco is heavily over-developed,' says Andrew Jack. 'There's hardly any spare land for building or anything else.'

With no room left in Monaco for new development the fifty-four acre Fontvielle district, which had been reclaimed from the sea, opened in 1974 to loud fanfares.

'We expanded our borders peacefully,' boasted Rainier. 'A rare thing these days, no?'

But Fontvielle was soon chock-a-block with light industrial factories, a three-star hotel and an American-style shopping mall, complete with the principality's first McDonald's fast-food restaurant and a 20,000-seat sports stadium. Ten years later, when large cracks started appearing in some of the apartment buildings along with untraceable sulphuric odours, it was found that the new quarter was slowly sinking back into the sea. Urgent action needed to be taken.

Prince Rainier's long-cherished dream of building an affordable Holiday Inn in Monte-Carlo was also not the success he had envisaged. When it finally opened in 1972 it failed to turn a profit; it closed nine years later to become yet another high-rise apartment complex.

In the early 1970s Prince Rainier realised he needed another financial white knight to help fund his ambitious projects in Monaco. The scaled-down model of what would become Loews's Monte-Carlo had long been the Prince's favorite toy, with its helicopter pad, traffic tunnel, modern casino, and ultra-modern convention centre. He loved explaining it to visitors like a little boy showing off a favourite Christmas present.

Rainier came to America and successfully wooed the ultra-wealthy Tisch brothers – Larry and Bob. The Tisch family already operated a string of successful hotels, casinos and convention centres, stretching from Atlantic City to California. And in addition they presided over an international empire including hotels, cigarette manufacturing plants, insurance, and oil-drilling, with an estimated worth in today's terms of $60 billion.

In 1971 Rainier was instrumental in setting up a partnership between Loews, the SBM, the government of Monaco and a syndicate of French and German investors. They agreed to construct and operate the massive Loews complex on the site of the old pigeon shoot, right below the old casino.

Straddling the harbour on concrete pillars, like a beached Martian in *The War of the Worlds*, the hotel is an architectural concrete nightmare. It is perhaps best known as part of the Monte-Carlo Grand Prix circuit, which passes directly underneath; in fact every year Bob Tisch hosts an annual Grand Prix party from his suite for his friends so they can watch the race in style.

'When Onassis pulled out of Monaco, Loews moved in,' said a

financial expert who monitors the principality. 'It was with Loews that Rainier made his first serious money.'

While Prince Rainier was working flat-out developing and enriching Monaco, he had little time for Grace. In the final years of her life Princess Grace led what was virtually a separate life from her husband. She felt Rainier took her for granted, often treating her interests and pursuits with disdain.

In an effort to recharge her batteries, Grace decided she needed a new project. In 1978 she agreed to collaborate with Gwen Robyns on *My Book of Flowers*. The women shared a love of flowers and the deal with publishers Doubleday was sealed over a champagne lunch at Robyns' idyllic sixteenth-century cottage, a short drive away from Oxford in England.

The Princess invited Gwen to make an extended visit to Monaco so they could work on the book together. Robyns was duly installed in the Hermitage Hotel in Monte-Carlo and she would drive up the Corniche to Roc Agel at 8 AM every morning. The two women spent hours talking in the glass-roofed conservatory surrounded by the old telephone books Grace used to press the flowers she collected on the mountains around Monaco.

During her time at Roc Agel Robyns got to know the Grimaldi family over long dinners that stretched late into the night. Prince Rainier liked Gwen and the two were soon in cahoots, sneakily mixing dry martinis behind Grace's back.

'He was a very cosy, nice, ordinary man,' she says. 'He loves football and cowboy films but he wasn't interested in ballet or poetry like Grace. He wasn't at all sophisticated.'

As Gwen got to know the couple better she realised they had drifted apart long ago. The only thing they now had in common were the children, whom they both adored. One day, as the two friends strolled through the rose garden, Grace broke down, admitting her terrible loneliness to Gwen. She was no longer the world's most admired wife and mother, but a middle-aged woman facing the fact that her marriage was no longer a source of happiness.

'You know, I have come to feel very sad in this marriage,' Grace said mournfully. 'He's not really interested in me. He doesn't care about me.'

As the Prince's hectic business schedule intensified over the years, his temper had worsened; the smallest irritation could now cause him to snap. During the early years of their marriage Grace had stoically bitten her tongue when Rainier vented his anger on her without cause, believing time would mellow him. But that had not proved to be the case.

'Instead, under the pressures of the enormous tasks he had undertaken, Rainier grew moodier than ever,' noted Judy Balaban Quine.

Princess Grace's life in Monaco was now anything but idyllic.

'I don't wake up in the morning thinking I'm living in a fairytale,' she told an American interviewer in March 1982. 'I have the job to be done, children to raise and a lot of responsibilities and obligations that perhaps are more tiring than a lot of people have.'

While staying at Roc Agel Gwen Robyns witnessed Grace's sheer professionalism and dedication to duty as she transformed herself into her life's role of the mythical Princess of Monaco over the course of the day. She'd emerge each day at 9 AM looking 'pathetic', with no make-up, very puffy around the eyes from her bad sinuses, and with her thin hair braided into two little plaits.

At about 11.30 AM Grace would have her daily swim and then disappear. And it would be a totally different woman who returned an hour later to greet her luncheon guests.

Said Gwen Robyns: 'She would look absolutely lovely, with her clear, natural face and a turban on to cover her hair, and a kaftan. She looked wonderful.'

After lunch everyone would retire for a siesta; when the Princess returned at about 5 PM she would have added another hairpiece and would be one step nearer to being the legendary Princess Grace. At 6.30 she'd retreat upstairs for the next stage of her metamorphosis.

When she returned to greet a new crop of guests who had arrived for evening drinks she would look magnificent.

'She had changed and perhaps put on another hairpiece,' said Robyns. 'She was so vivacious, so pretty and so charming and feminine. All the things that made a woman a woman.'

There would be one more trip upstairs and then finally, at 8 PM, Grace was ready to make her grandest entrance yet.

'When she appeared this time there could be no doubt that she was the most beautiful woman in the world. She'd put on another hairpiece and a little more of what I called her 'no make-up make-up'. I was mesmerised. This cycle she did every day was fabulous. She manufactured herself. And that's what she did for Rainier. That's what she did for Monaco.'

Grace considered it all part of the job of being the Princess of Monaco. In many ways the dramatic transformation was just the same as it had been when she put on stage make-up as a young woman and hit the boards for the summer season.

Six months before her death, when she was asked what she would most like people to know about Princess Grace, she replied: 'I like to think they would consider me a professional at my job, no matter what it would be.'

Ironically her husband was the one person in the world not to appreciate Grace. He would not learn to do so until it was too late, until he was forced painfully to realise that Grace had been the glue that held both Monaco and the Grimaldi family together. And when Grace died, everything would fall apart.

In April 1981, Grace and Rainier celebrated their twenty-fifth wedding anniversary at a quiet dinner with their children and close friends like Cary Grant and Frank Sinatra. During the dinner Prince Albert stood up and made the toast, telling the guests what a great team his parents made, and what they had achieved together for Monaco.

'My mom and dad did more for the principality than anyone else in history,' the Prince would say.

'They did it together. They gave Monaco a prestige that no one else ever did or probably ever could have. It's hard for me to put into words.'

Then an emotional Prince Rainier toasted Grace and tried to articulate what she meant to him and their children. It was a moving public performance by the man who usually had few good words to say for his wife and her accomplishments.

'I'll wager there are a lot of people who thought we'd never get there,' the Prince had joked five years earlier at their twentieth wedding anniversary. And they might well not have done if Rainier hadn't allowed Princess Grace to return to the stage at the 1976 Edinburgh Festival. Her new career – from which she would derive so much satisfaction – began with a telephone call to Gwen Robyns from producer John Carroll, who was organising the festival's poetry recital. Carroll was looking for an 'American' name who could headline the recital.

Robyns suggested Princess Grace and immediately telephoned her about the project, arguing that it was the perfect vehicle for the Princess of Monaco to express herself creatively outside Hollywood.

'She said she might not be able to read properly,' remembers Gwen. 'I said, "Well then, find out." And she was excellent.'

Princess Grace's poetry debut at the Edinburgh Festival was a sensation. She recited the moving Elinor Lylie poem 'Wild Peaches' in a lilting Southern accent. The performance was chosen by the BBC's 'Pick of the Year' as the best poetry reading of 1976.

It was a new, rewarding career for the Princess. Over the next six years she would perform all over the world. But although her performances received considerable critical acclaim, on the only occasion that Prince Rainier bothered to attend a performance, in London in 1978, he fell asleep during her reading.

Her husband's lack of attention caused Grace to gravitate toward younger men who were only too willing to squire her around town. A film-maker called Robert Dornhelm entered her life in 1976 when he came to Monaco to film the Princess delivering the introduction to a Russian ballet documentary, *The Children of Theatre Street*. Soon afterwards she befriended a handsome Irish–American businessman, Jeffrey FitzGerald, after they'd sat next to each other on a transatlantic Concorde flight and he'd failed to recognise her. Another close male confidante was New York restaurateur and former model Jim McMullen.

There has been much speculation that Grace embarked on a string of affairs as she entered middle age, but Gwen Robyns believes the relationships were platonic and refutes the allegations.

'These were charming young men who came into her life,' said Robyns. 'They were enormous flirts and Grace loved their company. It made her feel young again. I don't think for one second she had a physical relationship with any of them.'

The immaculately-groomed, handsome young men loved to be seen out on the town with Princess Grace and Prince Rainier didn't seem to mind when Robert Dornhelm visited the Palace on several occasions.

'There was a great deal of flirting going on,' says Robyns, who had regular girl-to-girl talks with the Princess almost every night at this point in Grace's life. 'The kissing of hands and cheeks. But at this stage in her life she was putting on weight and would have been ashamed for any young man to see her naked.'

Away from Monaco Grace seemed to sprout wings. For the first time since she had married she felt a sense of freedom: that anything was possible. She travelled all over the world giving poetry recitals, seeing old friends, shopping and enjoying herself as she had before her marriage. She seemed to become her old, happy self. Friends noticed that she was visibly more relaxed than she had been for years.

In March 1981 Grace delivered a poetry recital at Goldsmiths' Hall in London. The night was a memorable one: the guest of honour was Prince Charles, who was accompanied by his new fiancée Lady Diana Spencer, making her very first official public appearance.

Lady Diana was extremely nervous at her first formal engagement.

To make things worse, her dress for the evening had not arrived so she'd had to resort to a low-cut strapless black taffeta gown, several sizes too small.

'Her bosoms were spilling out all over the place and she was so embarrassed,' said Gwen Robyns, who was accompanying Grace that evening.

Diana's entrance caused a sensation. She got her very first taste of the paparazzi who were to become the bane of her life – and haunt her to her death. That night Diana realised the enormity of what she was about to undertake by marrying Prince Charles. She saw for the first time how her life would be irrevocably changed.

'She realised that she would never be a private person again,' said Judy Balaban Quine, who was later told about the night by Princess Grace.

'The thought frightened her beyond comprehension. At one moment she felt quite panicked. Grace – whom she'd met only a few minutes earlier – appeared by her side to ask if she would like to go to the ladies' room. Once the two women were inside at the mirror, something about Grace prompted Diana to open her heart.

'She couldn't stand it, she told Grace, the way people yelled things at her, spied on her, invaded her every waking moment and even her nightmares. Grace, too, Diana realised, had been subjected to that kind of public scrutiny all her adult life. "What could she do?" the fledgling Princess, near despair, asked of her senior counterpart. When she had finished blurting it all out and was in tears, Grace put her arms around Diana, held her and patted her on the shoulder like a mother comforting a child. After a moment Grace backed away a bit, raised her hands and cupped them around Diana's tear-stained face. Grace had a way of cooing reassuring words that were among the most comforting sounds ever to emanate from a human voice.

'"Don't worry, dear," she cooed to the soon-to-be Princess of Wales. Then, in the same tone, she added quietly, "It'll get worse." The candour, the kindness and the wit put Diana straight back on her required course.'

Princess Diana felt an almost psychic kinship with Grace that night. She explained her feelings to English journalist Andrew Morton some years later.

'I remember meeting Princess Grace and how wonderful and serene she was,' said Diana. 'But there was troubled water under her. I saw that.'

Grace and Rainier had reached an amicable accommodation with regard to their marriage. But in the fall of 1981 newspapers around the world began to question whether they had lost all control of their children. After a troubled childhood, Stephanie openly revolted against being a princess as soon as she turned sixteen.

She stubbornly refused to obey any authority. She was ordered to repeat her sophomore year at the Institute St Dominique in Paris after getting extremely poor grades. She defied all school rules by smoking in her room and sneaking off to late-night discos and parties.

'Stephanie's academic results were very mediocre,' wrote her headmistress Christine Alavoine in a report. When Grace tackled her daughter about her poor results a series of bitter arguments ensued. Violently rejecting her upbringing and the official duties she was expected to perform as a Grimaldi, Stephanie would throw screaming tantrums, telling her parents that she hated being a princess.

Many of the worst fights between mother and daughter were over the typical teenage issues of clothes and boys. Stephanie hated the elegant gowns her mother wanted her to wear, much preferring casual T-shirts and bleached jeans.

At the 1981 Red Cross Ball Grace put her daughter under 'house arrest', just as she had been forced to do at Caroline's pre-wedding ball. The stubborn Princess refused to wear the designer dress her mother had selected and spent the evening crying alone in her room.

A year earlier, again at the Red Cross Ball, R. Couri Hay had witnessed a heated public argument between the two in the early hours of the morning after Grace had forbidden her young daughter to go nightclubbing at Jimmy'z.

'Princess Stephanie was standing in the passageway between the Sporting Club and Régine's yelling at her mother, "I'm going to stay out,"' remembers Hay.

'Stephanie then stormed off into Régine's and all Grace could do was throw up her hands in exasperation and go home. I mean, it was so embarrassing for Grace.'

Stephanie seemed to calm down temporarily when she persuaded Grace to transfer her to Cours Charles de Foucauld, a more liberal co-ed school in Paris. She managed to graduate from there in the spring of 1982.

Princess Grace was, however, extremely concerned about the string of relationships Stephanie had embarked on with what she considered highly unsuitable men. At the age of only fifteen she ran away from boarding school to Deauville to spend a weekend with twenty-three-year-old Spanish rock singer Miguel Bose; when her parents heard what she had done they were furious and ordered her back to school, forbidding her to see Bose again. Her next romance, with Urbano Barberini, the twenty-one-year-old son of an Italian nobleman, was also short-lived as a result of Grace's angry intervention.

The media began concentrating their attentions on Stephanie, branding her the new black sheep of the Grimaldi family. In March 1982 Grace was asked how she felt about having her daughters' romances played out in the gossip columns.

'It's very difficult for children to grow up in a goldfish bowl and have the spotlight on them,' she said. 'Certainly children are going to do silly things growing up and make mistakes.'

The Princess then singled out 'the yellow press', blaming them for hounding Stephanie and following her to school.

'It is a big problem,' said the Princess. 'They've been after my youngest daughter now, who's seventeen. I think they should at least let her finish her schooling quietly and not bother her.'

Although Grace had successfully thwarted Stephanie's previous relationship she would not be so lucky with Paul Belmondo, the seventeen-year-old son of rugged French actor Jean-Paul Belmondo. Over
the summer of 1982 the two became inseparable; when Grace ordered
Stephanie to see less of Belmondo there were violent confrontations
between mother and daughter. And the more Princess Stephanie
asserted her iron will and independence, the more beaten-down and
depressed her mother grew.

That summer, Grace battled with her weight gain and the hormonal
mood swings caused by the menopause. Her physical problems, combined with frustrations over Stephanie, made Grace feel increasingly
unhappy and redundant. She would, only half-jokingly, refer to herself
as 'Blimposaurus Rex':

'Have you ever felt permanently bloated in the head?' she asked Judy
Balaban Quine. On another occasion she said sadly, 'The menopause
with its "angry jaws" is catching up with me.'

A few weeks before she and Stephanie made their fateful drive from
Roc Agel, Grace told Judy Quine she was planning to move on to a
new phase of her life. In the last conversation they would ever have,
Grace said she wanted to spend more time in America, pursuing various new projects. She told Judy about her dreams for the future and the
problems she anticipated if she were to break away from Monaco.

'I'm seriously thinking about taking a small apartment [in New
York],' she said. 'So everyone is going to say I'm leaving Rainier, and
abandoning my children.'

Then, as if shocked by the audacity of her own plans for the future,
Grace began giggling, telling her friend that she no longer intended to
be 'between gigs'.

Judy Balaban Quine: 'I started to speak, but I could hear her laughing to herself about something, so I remained silent. "Between Gigs",
she reflected, reciting it as if it were a title of a movie and still giggling
in spite of herself. "The Life Story of Grace Kelly . . . oops . . . Princess
Grace of Monaco." They were the last words I ever heard her utter.'

CHAPTER ELEVEN

──── ❧ ────

AFTER THE
FALL

IN THE DAYS following Princess Grace's death on September 13, 1982 the shattered Grimaldi family drew together to begin the long healing process of mourning. It was Prince Albert, the shy twenty-four-year-old who had always avoided the spotlight, who was forced to shoulder much of the burden; initially, Prince Rainier was so distraught that he withdrew into himself, spending long days alone on his yacht, unable to face the world. He felt a deep guilt that he had taken Grace for granted during the final years of her life. He began to understand just how much she had done for him and for the principality. He was also devastated by the loss of his best friend and advisor Jean-Louis (Loulou) Marsan, who had died just three weeks before Grace.

The many condolence calls from Grace's friends were fielded by Prince Albert, who put plans to start a job at the Morgan Guaranty Bank in New York on indefinite hold.

'This was a time of great sorrow,' Prince Albert later said. 'We just pulled together as a family and leaned on one another. And not only the strict immediate family, but cousins and aunts . . . call them whatever. We found tremendous support for us.'

In the aftermath of the tragedy Princess Caroline found the strength to take over her mother's nurturing role, devoting herself to 'minding' her father and taking care of him. She ordered his meals, oversaw the palace housekeeping and became Monaco's acting First Lady.

As a form of therapy, Caroline spent the days after her mother's death carefully cataloguing Grace's staggering collection of hundreds of dresses dating from her days in Hollywood to her years as the Princess of Monaco. She personally placed them in special covers, storing them in chronological order in the huge wardrobes that take up entire rooms in the Palace.

From then on Princess Caroline would find a brief escape from her darkest days by taking out Grace's favourite dresses and trying them on in front of the huge ceiling-high mirrors. She told friends it brought her closer to her mother, it made her remember the excitement she felt as a little girl when she saw her mother dressed up for a grand ball.

But it was the physically-injured and emotionally-traumatised Stephanie who was the most vulnerable, as she slowly recovered from the effects of her fractured neck vertebra. Already shaken to the core with sorrow and guilt, the Princess became a target of increasing press speculation that she was to blame for Grace's death. The rumours that she had been driving the car, although under age – or that she had tried to wrest the wheel from her mother during a raging argument – would haunt her for years.

'In other words, "you killed your mother,"' said the Princess in 1997, speaking for the first time about the accident. 'It's hard enough losing your mother and then being blamed for it. I'd like them to try and put themselves in my skin. Can't you just leave people in their pain?'

Helen Veret, the Paris-based correspondent for *Life* magazine, says Stephanie was deeply affected by the accident.

'No psycho-analyst or psychiatrist would be able to help that extraordinary classical drama that she went through,' said Veret. 'So maybe she transformed these anxieties by this kind of nervous energy that she will always [have].'

Grace's sister Lizanne played a vital part in the family grieving process, staying in daily contact from her New Jersey home. Always positive and upbeat, Lizanne reminisced about the good times with Grace, dispensing advice and encouragement to both Prince Rainier and his children.

During the private mourning period the Grimaldis slipped away from Monaco for a fifteen-day recuperative vacation at the exclusive Lyford Cay Club on Nassau in the Bahamas. They re-bonded as a family, taking daily cruises on a yacht, swimming and playing tennis.

'I think it was very difficult for Rainier because Grace took care of the children,' said Lizanne. 'She raised them and he let her have her way. You know, "Whatever your mother says, goes."'

And it wasn't long before Rainier had his first serious clash with Stephanie, who now refused to go to the Paris School of Couture Fashion, where her mother had wanted her to study. Newspaper reports suggested that Stephanie was 'blackmailing' Rainier, threatening to elope and marry Paul Belmondo if her father forced her to go to fashion school.

With Grace no longer there as a mediator and the voice of good sense, Rainier caved in to Stephanie's demands. From now on the wilful youngest Grimaldi would always get her own way. When older sister Caroline finally intervened, attempting to exert some parental influence over Stephanie, a bitter row ensued.

'It's a hard passage to go from the mother's authority to the sister's,' a frustrated Prince Rainier explained at the time. 'When you're eighteen, like Stephanie, you don't want to take advice from anybody. You sort of think you know it all.'

If Princess Stephanie had been difficult before Grace's untimely death, witnessing her mother's fatal accident only served to harden her rebellious streak. For a long time she questioned why her life had been spared and her mother's had not; it was a terrible weight for such fragile shoulders.

'She changed after her mother's death and became a little rebel,' said the Countess of Lombardy. 'She felt guilty and became a little aggressive. She revolted against Rainier and would accept no authority.'

Feeling that the whole world was against her, Stephanie suddenly announced that she had decided not to be a Princess any more. She did not want to undertake any sovereign duties.

Judy Balaban Quine says the effects of her mother's death on Stephanie were 'unfathomable. It had an extremely profound impact. I don't even know how to measure it.'

In the wake of Grace's death Rainier gamely tried to shore up Monaco's fortunes, amidst much speculation that the loss of its main attraction would adversely affect tourism. He broke his silence early in 1983 to give a rare interview with *Life* magazine's managing editor Richard B Stolley. Hoping to set the record straight, he said that Monaco had existed for 700 years and would survive Princess Grace's passing.

'She was of course a great attraction for tourists,' he hastened to add. 'She did a lot for the glamour and prestige of the principality, but I don't think her disappearance means that people are not going to come. They didn't come only for that. They came for the whole atmosphere, which we will try to carry on.'

Rainier revealed that he had already drafted in Caroline and Albert to assume their late mother's official duties. Caroline would take over Grace's cultural responsibilities; Albert would handle the Red Cross. As for Stephanie, Rainier remained tactfully non-committal.

'She has to stop and think. It's very hard to advise her,' said Rainier. 'She has to show that she wants to be active, but she doesn't know yet what or how and I can't push her into too much.'

In late February 1983 Prince Rainier and Stephanie flew into New York for a series of business meetings with Bob Tisch and other Loews board members, who were concerned about the future of their huge Monaco investment. Rainier took the opportunity to visit Prince Albert, who had finally moved to New York to study international finance at the Morgan Guaranty Bank, taking the internship he had postponed after his mother's death.

The Grimaldis stayed at the Loews-owned Regency Hotel in Manhattan. Rainier seemed irritable and on-edge throughout the trip, his first visit to America since Grace had died. He was particularly annoyed that Stephanie had insisted on bringing Paul Belmondo along as her escort. The strain of the last few months clearly showed on the Prince's face; he seemed to have become an old man overnight.

Rainier had always disliked the American paparazzi – he still blamed them for disrupting his wedding twenty-seven years earlier. Now, without Grace to defuse his explosive temper, the Prince went on the attack, physically lashing out at pressmen. When veteran New York photographer Hy Simon tried to snap the Prince and his escort – Texan socialite Lynn Wyatt – as they stepped out of the Regency to their limousine, Rainier punched him to the ground. And less than twenty-four hours later the Prince hit photographer Vinnie Zuffante in the face outside a Broadway Theatre calling him a 'little bitch bastard'.

The next day one of the Prince's bodyguards threatened two New York photographers with 'a gun' in an underground garage in Manhattan. The ensuing New York Post front page, showing Prince Albert angrily giving photographers the finger next to a seething Rainier, carried the banner headline: PRINCE OF FURY. It was certainly not a good advertisement for Monaco tourism.

Lizanne Kelly LeVine defends her brother-in-law's behaviour in the States.

'He goes to New York and the people in the press are pushing and shoving,' she said. 'They think it's their God-given right to be there in your face. It's just terrible.'

On January 26, 1983, Princess Caroline made her first official appearance as First Lady when she appeared at the Monaco national celebration of the Feast of Sainte Dévote. Wearing exactly the same outfit

Princess Grace had previously worn to the same event – right down to a 1940s-style turban – Monégasques were delighted to see Caroline confidently at the helm of her first state occasion. The image of the ubiquitous party girl and the world's first topless princess had been replaced by a sombre, more responsible one.

'After Grace died Caroline changed, because before she was very wild,' said the Countess of Lombardy. 'She knew she had to take her mother's place and put her country first.'

In April Princess Caroline became engaged to her long-term lover Robertino Rossellini, and began planning a September wedding. The pair, who had been together since Caroline divorced Philippe Junot in October 1980, had been brought closer together by tragedy; Rossellini's mother Ingrid Bergman had died of cancer in August 1982, just fifteen days before Princess Grace's accident. Later that year Caroline travelled to the tiny Swedish fishing village of Fjallbacka and solemnly watched Rosellini scatter the ashes of his mother.

But the engagement was to be short-lived. Reports in European newspapers stated that the impulsive and passionate Caroline had thrown caution to the winds to have a romantic weekend in Paris with German actor Mathieu Carriere, while Rossellini was away on business. When Rossellini countered this infidelity by romancing Italian starlet Isabella Ferrari, the couple broke off the engagement and scrapped plans for a month-long vacation on the Greek island of Paxoi. Instead, Caroline joined some Italian friends on their yacht to cruise the Mediterranean to Sardinia. And met a man who would change her life.

Stefano Casiraghi, the handsome twenty-three-year-old heir to a Milanese oil-refining and construction fortune, had first met Caroline a year earlier at Jimmy'z nightclub in Monaco. Although Caroline was with Rossellini at the time, their companions noticed she and Stefano had a great rapport.

'I felt right away there was something in the air,' said Casiraghi's then-girlfriend Pinuccia Macheda.

Well-known in Riviera society circles as a rake and spoiled playboy,

Casiraghi loved to lavish money on his conquests. His friends had nick-named him 'Fancazzista – meaning 'he doesn't do a fucking thing'. His official line of business was said to be importing shoes and sweaters into the United States, though he also had a part-share in a Milan nightclub.

When the six-foot tall blond Casiraghi next met up with Caroline while sailing his yacht off the coast of Corsica, the Princess was smitten. She immediately jumped ship and spent the next five days making passionate love to Casiraghi aboard his yacht as it aimlessly cruised the Mediterranean. By the time they landed in Sardinia, Caroline was hopelessly in love and she didn't care who knew it.

Tempestuous by nature, Caroline – as she would do on so many other occasions – abandoned all propriety as she and Casiraghi flew to Milan, installing themselves in a suite at the Hotel Principe. By this time the paparazzi were in hot pursuit of the couple, who spent the week shopping and having late-night romantic dinners together.

Casiraghi's former girlfriend Pinuccia Macheda – whom he left for Caroline – said Stefano knew how to make a woman feel special. A typical date might start with an invitation from Stefano to fly to Paris for a candle-lit dinner.

'And if I agreed,' said Macheda, 'we would catch a plane, and a couple of hours later we'd be sitting in the latest "in" restaurant ordering oysters and champagne.'

The lovestruck couple split their time between the Grimaldis' Paris residence and Stefano's bachelor apartment in Monaco. Friends of the Princess became increasingly concerned that she was falling too hard for Casiraghi and, as she had done so disastrously in the past, confusing good sex with true love.

When Princess Caroline became pregnant in the fall of 1983, and decided she wanted to marry Casiraghi, both her family and friends heard alarm-bells ringing. To all intents and purposes Casiraghi was just another Philippe Junot.

'He's fine for a flirt, for an affair,' a friend of Casiraghi's told *People* magazine at the time, 'but not to marry when you are Princess of Monaco.'

In September a worried Prince Rainier summoned Stefano to his seventeenth-century Chateau de Marchais outside Paris to find out exactly what his intentions were. During a man-to-man talk while the two men were out pheasant-shooting, Casiraghi requested Caroline's hand in marriage. As his daughter was pregnant, and wanting to prevent another scandal at any price, the Prince grudgingly agreed.

News of the marriage was kept quiet; Princess Caroline was still hoping that the Vatican would annul her first marriage by the end of the year. Although Princess Grace had had an audience with Pope John Paul II before her death to lobby for an annulment, the pontiff had refused to commit himself. However, the case remained 'fully active'.

But the Pope was in a difficult position: Philippe Junot had vowed to cause a major uproar if the annulment was granted. He was furious that Caroline had been allowed to cite 'sexual incompatibility' as the reason why the marriage should be annulled.

'The Pope has a respect for the sacrament of marriage,' he told reporters. 'I scarcely conceive of him giving his blessing [to this] without causing a major scandal.'

Ironically, just as the Grimaldis were pressing the case for annulment, there was a move to elevate Princess Grace to sainthood. One year after her death, Father Piero Pintus held a mass and declared he was proposing her as a candidate for sainthood.

'As an actress I preferred Ingrid Bergman,' announced Father Pintus from his pulpit in Rome. 'But Grace of Monaco was a faithful wife and an impeccable mother. She was rich in temperament and rare in potential. She had the gift of grace — and not only in name.'

Princess Caroline, who could no longer take Holy Communion herself because of her divorced status, was delighted at the prospect. But she knew the chances that her mother, who had undergone an abortion and had many affairs in her movie star days, would ever be declared a saint were slim indeed.

'I'm afraid we're a little short on documented miracles,' admitted Caroline.

In early December Stefano Casiraghi made his first official appearance with the ruling Grimaldi family in their box at Monte-Carlo's annual Circus Festival, sparking speculation about an impending marriage. On December 19, 1983 – just four days after the end of the official mourning period for Princess Grace – the Palace issued a terse, two-sentence announcement of the imminent wedding. Grace's brother Kell, who was not invited to the ceremony, said the Philadelphia Kellys first heard about the wedding in the US press.

Monégasques were stunned by the haste of the announcement and horrified by the scandal of Caroline having to marry outside the Catholic Church. Some questioned whether it was a shotgun marriage: of course, the Princess was in fact carrying Casiraghi's child. A cynical editorial in the Paris newspaper, *Le Monde*, even went so far as to bet a bottle of whisky that Caroline was pregnant – and a bottle of champagne that the marriage would be over within eighteen months.

There were none of the lavish celebrations which had accompanied her first wedding when Princess Caroline wed Stefano Casiraghi on December 29 in a private, twenty-minute civil ceremony at the Palace. Twenty guests attended the ceremony, presided over by Monaco's new Director of Judicial Affairs, Noel Museaux. The marriage took place in the Chamber of Mirrors, in full view of a life-sized portrait of Princess Grace.

The ceremony was dignified and noticeably restrained; there were no peeling bells as Prince Rainier led Caroline, in her simple beige satin dress, and Stefano out on to the balcony of the Palace. There, they were enthusiastically applauded by hundreds of tourists in the square below.

'It was a great occasion,' remembered Museaux many years later. 'It really seemed that laughter and happiness had returned to this family which had endured so much tragedy.'

★ ★ ★

Two months earlier Princess Caroline had made her first American appearance as Monaco's First Lady at a celebrity fundraising ball for the Princess Grace Foundation in Los Angeles. But when the Princess glided into the ballroom at the Beverly Wilshire Hotel almost an hour late on the arm of Cary Grant, she decidedly underwhelmed the black-tied Hollywood crowd, who had paid up to $500 each to mingle with her.

Throughout the aptly named 'An Evening in Monaco' Caroline looked bored. She chain-smoked, continually taking out a gold compact to check her make-up. The only people she talked to were Cary Grant and actor Robert Wagner, with whom she reluctantly took a short spin on the dancefloor.

'It was a very emotional night [for the princess],' a spokesperson for the event later said tactfully; 'because she is standing in for her mother.'

Princess Grace had always been the consummate professional at all her public events, assiduously seeking out people to talk to and using her magnetic charm to win goodwill for Monaco. Her daughter took no such pains. It was obvious that Caroline felt official functions were a chore to be endured and her resentment showed.

'The discipline that Grace had had all through her life was never installed in her children,' said Oleg Cassini, who had helped Grace through her early awkwardness and taught her how to project herself on important social occasions.

'Look, the difference is this. They were born with a silver spoon in their mouths. They didn't have to work hard, they didn't have to train for a career, they didn't have to be disciplined. They had it all made. Grace had to make herself. Invent herself.'

In February 1984 the Grimaldi family turned out *en masse* to inaugurate the newly-organised American branch of the Princess Grace Foundation. A snow-white-bearded Prince Rainier – now aged sixty – seemed in better spirits than on his last troubled New York visit when he met reporters in his suite at Loews' Regency Hotel. Tourist revenue in Monaco had plunged since Princess Grace's death; there was a huge void in the principality that no living member of the Grimaldi family seemed able to fill. The Princess Grace Foundation USA was an attempt to reinvigorate Monaco's fast-fading image using Grace's name.

The highlight of the trip was a weekend of public appearances in Washington DC. President Ronald Reagan and his wife Nancy hosted a small White House reception and dinner for the Grimaldi clan and Stefano Casiraghi. On the following night the Reagans also attended a special fund-raising gala for the Princess Grace Foundation. The *crème de la crème* of American society paid $5,000 to attend the Ball, which featured a duet by the Spanish singer Julio Iglesias and Placido Domingo.

The Grimaldis had resorted to corporate sponsorship to underwrite the event. The Piaget watch company and the Italian fashion house, Genny, had each donated undisclosed amounts for the privilege of displaying their logos and products.

Now almost six months pregnant, Princess Caroline was beginning to show, despite all her efforts to hide her pregnancy with a long, loose Marc Bohan blouse over wide pajama pants.

'Everyone was asking the same question over the Washington weekend,' reported society columnist Eugenia Sheppard. 'They all wanted to know if Princess Caroline was pregnant.'

On the way to Washington Caroline had secretly visited Rome to plead her case for an annulment from Philippe Junot so that her baby might be legitimised in the eyes of the Church. After testifying before the Sacra Rota she was granted a personal audience with the Pope, who bluntly told her he was extremely disappointed in her and did not approve of her superficiality.

'Did you ever make a sacrifice to save your marriage?' he asked her, refusing to grant the annulment.

Judy Balaban Quine saw Prince Rainier for the first time in months at the White House reception. She was shocked by how sad and out of place he looked. When Quine asked him what was wrong the Prince replied: 'I feel old. Old and tired all the time.' The Prince seemed tortured as Quine wondered if he ever found any relief from the responsibilities of his life. 'I wish it did, but it doesn't,' he told her cryptically.

During his press interviews Prince Rainier concentrated on soliciting funds for the new Foundation, which was aiming to raise $1 million dollars to assist the arts. And the Prince asked everyone – rich or poor – to contribute.

'The foundation in Monaco is supported not only by corporations and the very wealthy,' he explained to Enid Nemy of the *New York Times*, 'but even by very simple people, who often give contributions after an occasion like a wedding.'

He hastened to add that people shouldn't be 'shy or embarrassed' to send in their donations.

On the key question – when his son Prince Albert would succeed him as ruler of Monaco – Rainier was less forthright. Before Grace's death Albert's succession had not been an issue; but now the situation had changed. At twenty-five, Albert was now almost the same age as Rainier had been when he'd come to power – but, according to his father, he still had a long way to go.

'I don't believe in making him wait until I die off,' said Rainier. 'We talk about it. We have a mutual agreement that when he feels ready and sufficiently informed – and I feel he is – he will take over. I would like to be around to help him in the first years.'

After Grace's death Prince Albert had embarked on a series of apprenticeships to give him the business grounding he would need to rule a country like Monaco. He worked in New York, first as an intern for the Morgan Guaranty Trust and then as a paralegal at the Rogers and Wells law firm. Next he moved to Paris to study public relations at Moet-Hennessy, a prestigious drinks company.

'That was actually a marvellous experience,' said the Prince. 'I wish I could have spent more time there. It's really a fascinating business. Fast-paced.'

Prince Rainier was personally supervising his son by making him attend business meetings in Monaco to learn the mechanics of the principality's administration. He tried to encourage him to overcome his shyness and express his ideas.

But in fact Albert was now enjoying his independent lifestyle too much to want to give up his freedom for the awesome, overwhelming task of ruling Monaco. When asked by writer Christopher Buckley in 1986 if ruling Monaco was a responsibility he would rather not have, Albert replied, 'Much.'

As what the media had styled the world's most eligible bachelor, by 1984 Albert had already been linked romantically with a string of eligible society women and film stars, including Brooke Shields, Catherine Oxenberg and Lady Helen Windsor. In Monaco and abroad he maintained a hectic party schedule, often drinking and dancing in nightclubs with his friends until 4 AM.

'Rainier doesn't like [Albert's] friends, by and large,' an unnamed friend told *Interview* magazine in January 1986.

But Albert's gift for subterfuge has served him well through the years and has allowed him to keep an unusually low profile.

'You almost have to use secret agent tactics to elude the press,' explains the Prince.

'He has a lot of dates but he's very discreet,' says his cousin Grace LeVine. 'He doesn't get nearly the kind of publicity Stephanie and Caroline get.'

Prince Albert's placidity and good nature have also served to keep him out of the gossip columns. After being photographed in New York giving a photographer the finger he developed a non-confrontational policy, which paid good dividends.

'At an opening we were swarmed by the cameras,' a friend of the Prince's told journalist Christopher Buckley. 'He just stood very still, let them take their pictures, then turned on his heel and said, "Thank you very much," and walked away. You're not going to print a photo of someone who just stands there and says, "Thank you," are you? But one of Caroline or Stephanie fighting or sticking their neck out is different.'

CHAPTER TWELVE

꧁꧂

PRINCESS PUNK

T HE EDITORS OF *Le Monde* won their bet on June 8, 1984 when Princess Caroline gave birth to a healthy six-pound ten-ounce baby boy at the Princess Grace Clinic in Monaco. Reported to be 'overcome with joy' Prince Rainier dashed to the hospital to see his first grandchild, the newest link of the Grimaldi dynasty who was now fourth in line to the throne. Caroline named him Andrea Albert.

The Palace downplayed the birth, coming as it did only five months and two days after the marriage, with a terse three-line official announcement. And the Monégasques tactfully chose to ignore the factor of the Princess's pre-wedding pregnancy, just as they would increasingly turn a blind eye to the ruling daughters' modern morality.

'That's something that concerns the Grimaldis and not the Monégasques,' explained the Countess of Lombardy. 'When you are a real Monégasque you don't gossip about the family and disturb them.'

But Madame Jean Busnard, a frequent visitor to Monaco from Paris, was more outspoken. She told *People* magazine: 'Princess Grace was a wonderful woman. But her daughters – ugh!'

Although Prince Rainier tried to put a brave face on Andrea's birth, he had still not accepted Casiraghi as his son-in-law.

'I am happy to announce that I'm the grandfather of a little boy,' Rainier proudly telegrammed to friends and relatives after the birth. 'Caroline and the baby are doing well,' he added, making Casiraghi highly conspicuous by his absence.

After the marriage Casiraghi, who had not been given a title or any official duty, tried to adapt to his new life at the Palace, but seemed awkward and out of place. He devoted his energies to exploiting his new princely connections to his financial advantage; in partnership with two Italian friends he invested in Monaco's two Christian Dior franchises and bought a car dealership to sell imported American cars.

But by March, ten weeks after the wedding, there were reports that the fun-loving Italian was beginning to stray in the manner of Philippe Junot. While Caroline was away in England, Casiraghi set off on a ski-ing trip to St Moritz with friends. But he still couldn't resist the attraction of pretty young girls. The paparazzi soon caught up with them, photographing Casiraghi on the slopes with beautiful twenty-year-old Christine van Schrabel. Casiraghi then loaded her skis into his white Land-Rover and drove her to a friend's chateau.

When Princess Caroline saw the pictures, the couple had their first serious argument. Casiraghi denied any wrongdoing, but the angry Princess told him to stop being a playboy and start facing up to his new family responsibilities.

An accident-prone daredevil, Stefano Casiraghi was addicted to the adrenaline thrill of racing fast cars and powerboats. In early May he competed in the Atlas Rally, a dangerous cross-country race from Lyon, France to Agadir, Morocco. While he was speeding through the southern Morocco desert his Suburu hit a pothole and overturned; pursuing paparazzi rescued the shaken Stefano and drove him to safety. In return Casiraghi took their film of his crash back to Paris and delivered it to their publication with his compliments.

Just two weeks later Casiraghi had another narrow escape while racing his powerboat in the second annual Grand Prix Offshore Riccaronna Trophy in Monaco. A very pregnant Princess Caroline watched the start of the race with binoculars from her palace window and was horrified to see her husband's boat disappear from sight in a thick cloud of black smoke after blowing an engine at top speed.

'Stefano has read too many comic books,' quipped one of his friends. 'He gets behind the wheel of a fast boat or car and lives out his hero fantasies without really knowing what he's doing.'

That summer Judy Balaban Quine returned to Monaco for the first time since Grace's death. She found that it was, slowly, coming back to life. She spent time with Caroline and baby Andrea, noticing that the Princess was far less 'gooey' about motherhood than Grace had been. Prince Rainier seemed to dote on his new grandchild and Prince Albert was busy preparing to go to the Summer Olympics in Los Angeles.

The only Grimaldi who didn't seem to have found a new purpose in life was Princess Stephanie. When Judy Quine had last seen her at the Princess Grace Foundation reception in the White House she had been horrified by the change in the young girl.

'Steph had way too much fear in her eyes in Washington,' Quine wrote at the time. 'And I think it's going to take a long while for her to lose that – poor darling.'

Now working as an apprentice to designer Marc Bohan at Dior in Paris, nineteen-year-old Stephanie had become the number one target of the French paparazzi. Since her sister Caroline had given up her wild days and settled down to married life and motherhood, the press had turned its full attention to Stephanie. And the beautiful, doe-eyed Princess was doing anything but keep a low profile.

After ditching Paul Belmondo and moving on to nineteen-year-old Anthony Delon – the troubled son of the French tough-guy actor Alain Delon – the Princess began running with a fast and dangerous party crowd.

Judy Balaban Quine, whose own daughter Vicki was fighting a

crippling cocaine and alcohol addiction, began to suspect that Stephanie was taking the same route.

'I worry when I see her photos,' wrote Judy Quine. 'Her eyes look terrified, and it's a sign I've come to dread. For one reason or another, too many of our children have lived in their own private hells way too young.'

Although they were both the sons of famous French movie stars, Paul Belmondo and Anthony Delon were as different as night and day. Belmondo, the quiet, caring young man who had selflessly nursed Stephanie through her darkest days after Grace's death, had – with his father's backing – successfully worked his way up the professional motor-racing ladder to Formula Three. Anthony Delon, on the other hand, who had been described as a 'moody nightclub fixture', had recently been sentenced to an eight-month suspended sentence for stealing a BMW car and carrying a pistol without a permit. His father had disowned him and had even taken legal action to stop his son using the initials 'AD' on a line of leather clothing he was marketing.

When Princess Stephanie was photographed by the long lens of the paparazzi locked in a passionate embrace with curly-haired Delon on a public beach outside Monaco, the Palace tried to take out an injunction against *Paris-Match* to stop publication on the grounds that it was an invasion of privacy. The photograph of a bikini-clad Princess Stephanie – captioned 'torn between passion and good sense' – was certainly not the image of post-Grace Monaco that Rainier wanted to project to the world.

But the court refused the injunction, saying that the Princess and Delon had been photographed in a public place. And this decision would have far-reaching consequences, not only for the Monaco ruling family, but for celebrities the world over.

The media had an insatiable appetite for anything concerning the Monaco ruling family and its increasingly bizarre exploits. In the first eight months of 1984 *Paris-Match* had run nine Monaco-related covers compared to a single one about the French President Francois

Mitterand. The wildly glamorous Princesses from Monte-Carlo boosted circulation; the controversial cover photo of Stephanie in a bikini improved sales of *Paris-Match* by five per cent.

Rainier and Grace's plan to use publicity to shine a spotlight on the principality had been far more successful than they ever dreamed – or, indeed, wanted. And there was a cruel irony: the Grimaldis had unwittingly turned themselves as well as their principality into a product, making millions for the moguls of international publishing rather than for Monaco.

'Look, it is our *Dallas*, our serial,' explained Roger Thérond editor-in-chief of *Paris-Match*, to the *New York Times* in August 1984. 'They are our Kennedys, and we didn't invent any of it. The scenario is beyond belief, but do you think someone at *Paris-Match* told Grace Kelly's daughter to dump Belmondo's son and throw her arms around Delon's son, who just happens to have been convicted for car theft and having a pistol? No – we just publish the pictures.

'Before it was Caroline – now it's Stephanie. The public has invested in this story. It participates, it judges, it condemns, it pities. It's a second life for a lot of people. And then the Palace says we're invading their privacy. Hah!'

Loyal palace spokesperson Nadia Lacoste countered the attack, saying the attentions of the paparazzi had become intolerable, with their pictures often being taken out of context to suit the publisher's purposes.

'The problem is that when you appear so often,' said Lacoste, 'the public starts thinking you love the publicity. They can't realise the family has nothing to do with it. So you lose on both ends.'

But Stephane Bern, royal reporter of the French newspaper *Figaro*, said publicity was the lifeblood of Monaco.

'The image is what, principally, the family is for,' he said. 'It's a country with 30,000 people in work and they want to make money. More and more money. They have no taxes and they want to be flourishing for the next few years. So they need to have a promotional campaign all the time and they have just one agent – the Ruling Family of Monaco.'

Prince Albert has acknowledged the advantages of free publicity, but pointed out that the ever-present paparazzi make life very hard for his family.

'There are circumstances where we are pretty open to the demands of the press,' said the Prince in June 1997. 'But then when we try and lead a normal life outside the palace it's very difficult when you are being followed by fifteen or twenty paparazzi who infringe on your privacy. It's very difficult to accept.'

Albert also admitted that his 'fragile' younger sister went through a very difficult period after the trauma of her mother's death.

'I think Stephanie was the one who suffered the most,' he said. 'But it was very hard for my father to still work and to cope with all the pressures of: one, being head of state; and two, being a confidante for his daughter, who was going through the growing pains of being a young adult.'

In September 1984 the *National Enquirer* carried a story headlined: RAINIER SAVES STEPHANIE FROM NIGHTMARE WORLD OF COCAINE. It claimed that word of the Princess's increasingly public use of the drug at Jimmy'z nightclub had reached Prince Rainier, who had forced her on a family cruise that summer so she could clean up her act. Certainly as soon as the Princess left Monaco there was a police crackdown on Jimmy'z; several of Stephanie's friends were arrested and thrown in jail.

Shortly afterwards Régine was forced out of Monaco. She moved her operation to the rival resort of St Tropez.

'Princess Grace always thought Jimmy'z was dreadful – cheap and distasteful,' said R. Couri Hay. 'Plus she felt the place ruined the girls because it was like their club hangout and they were there every night drinking, smoking and cahooting. Grace always felt Régine brought the whole place down.'

One night during the cruise the three Grimaldi children and Stefano Casiraghi went ashore in Sardinia to visit a nightclub. At 1 AM, when the rest of the party wanted to leave, Stephanie refused, saying she was having too good a time. When she threw a tantrum in the middle of the dancefloor Caroline stalked out, sending a bodyguard back in to physically remove Stephanie.

A month later the Princess returned to Paris to resume her apprenticeship with Dior. But she seemed hell-bent on self-destruction. She broke up with Anthony Delon and began dating so furiously that the French press started to refer to each new boyfriend as Stephanie's '*Nouvel élu*', her 'new chosen one'.

Every night the leather-clad Princess went out to trendy Paris clubs with what even a friend described as 'not a nice crowd'. Magazines reported that she'd frequently disappear into the ladies' rooms where cocaine was openly passed around, and then dance euphorically into the early hours.

'Everything Stephanie has done recently has been stamped with defiance,' reported *Redbook* magazine; 'as if daring someone to stop her race toward self-destruction.'

For a couple more months Stephanie stayed at Dior, but her increasingly erratic behaviour alarmed the conservative fashion house. Once she arrived for work with punkish streaks of red dye in her hair and was sent home to remove it. Furious at being told what to do, the rebellious Stephanie reacted by spraying it bright green. Then she began to show up late and miss appointments.

Her cousin Buddy de Massy said that although Caroline bore a striking physical resemblance to their unconventional grandmother Mamou, it was Stephanie who had inherited her wild streak – in spades.

'[Stephanie's] totally defiant of convention and determined to do "her thing",' said de Massy. 'She dares to try everything and mocks everything.'

On October 29 Stephanie was at the centre of a bizarre kidnap attempt. She claimed that a couple tried to kidnap her at gunpoint as she drove her Italian sports car into the underground garage of her Father's Paris apartment in the elegant Avenue Georges Mandel.

'A guy put a gun to my head,' the Princess later told author Jeffrey Robinson. 'My body was like jelly but my mind was functioning. I kept trying to squirm around in the car. I kept thinking, if he's going to shoot it's better to get it in the arm or the leg and not in the head.'

A girl suddenly appeared, shouting, 'Shoot her! shoot her!'

Stephanie said to the pair, "Look, my father is upstairs. If you want to speak to him, let's all go up there and talk it out. Because nobody is going to pay for a dead body." At that point the man and his accomplice turned and ran.

But according to the police version the attack took place outside the garage of the building. When the man ordered her back into the car she began screaming, running toward her apartment. The attackers fled in a red Volkswagen.

Later, amidst press speculation that the 'kidnap' might be linked to undesirable elements Stephanie had encountered during her nocturnal forays, Parisian detectives wrote in the official report of the incident: 'There were no witnesses. The Princess was shocked and gave a report that is completely subjective.'

That Christmas Prince Rainier's attempts to control Stephanie by cutting her allowance were met with open rebellion. Telling her father she didn't need his money and could earn her own, Stephanie quit Dior in January to sign up with a Paris modelling agency, earning a reported $10,000 a day.

Although her boyish-looking five-foot-eight, 120-pound body and newly-cropped punk hair were hardly conventional for a model, news that she had signed the contract on her twentieth birthday caused a sensation. Paul Hagnauer of the Paris-based First Agency told *People* magazine that Princess Stephanie's androgyny was right at the forefront of fashion — as was her desire to earn a living.

'We're in the twentieth century,' he announced. 'You can be a princess, you can be beautiful — and you can still have a job.'

Stephanie was immediately welcomed to the modelling ranks by the *grande dame* of American model agencies, Eileen Ford, who declared it would be great for the business.

'I think it's wonderful to have a career,' said the Ford Agency founder, as she put in a bid to represent the Princess in America.

Agencies were eager to capitalise on Stephanie's international fame and her status as a Princess; she was deluged with offers. Almost overnight she seemed to be plastered on the glossy front cover of every fashion magazine. She shot fashion spreads for *Elle*, German *Vogue*, the Italian magazine *Moda* and the English *Company*, which carried the banner headline SCOOP ROYAL.

Vanity Fair chronicled Princess Stephanie's short-lived modelling career in a cover story in July 1985:

'There . . . was Stephanie, looking plump and slightly hydrocephalic, on the front and back covers of a magazine called *Company*. And there she was in a bathing suit on the cover of *Elle*. By the standards of American fashion, the *Company* cover did little to help the Princess. The *Elle* cover could have launched a career.'

Princess Stephanie brought her rebellious attitude straight on to the pages of the world's top fashion magazines. Although her unprecedented commercial modelling potential owed everything to her mystique as a Princess, she was photographed as a streetwise urchin. She was seen drinking from a bottle of beer, or scowling at the camera with a cigarette defiantly dangling from her lips. Pomp and punk were a winning combination.

At the beginning of March 1985, Stephanie signed with the top American model agency Wilhelmina for a reported rate of $1,200 an hour, in direct defiance of Prince Rainier's orders.

'It was a rebellious act against the family's wishes,' said Frances Grill, owner of New York's Click agency.

Princess Stephanie would now join the rank of top supermodels such as Jerry Hall and Christie Brinkley. The Wilhelmina Agency appointed its top agent, Karen Hilton, to organise a full-scale American tour for Stephanie in April. There she would shoot covers for *Vogue*, *Mademoiselle*, *Rolling Stone* and *New York*.

Hilton gushed to the press: 'She's handsomely pretty, she has an extraordinary body – and, of course, quite a story.'

But the pressure of being an instant supermodel proved too much for Stephanie. Just ten days after signing with Wilhelmina she was rushed to a private clinic outside Paris. Amidst rumours that the Princess had collapsed after a four-day cocaine and alcohol binge, Prince Rainier and Caroline rushed to the Belvedere Clinic in Boulogne as Stephanie entered detox.

The official line from the palace was that the Princess was 'suffering from gastroenteritis and had been hospitalised as a precaution'. The First Agency cancelled her modelling engagements for the following week.

'Were she any other twenty-year-old, Stephanie's behaviour during the last few months would be considered flighty,' wrote diarist Ross Benson in the *Daily Express*. 'For a princess to behave in such a way is nothing less than scandalous, as Rainier is painfully aware.'

Soon after Princess Stephanie's release from the clinic – as she was making the final preparations for her forthcoming two-and-a-half-week American tour – she was summoned to the Monaco consulate in Paris to see her father. Behind closed doors the Prince read her the riot act, threatening to seize her passport if she didn't abandon her modelling career. Princess Stephanie had no choice but to obey.

On April 21, two days before Stephanie was due to arrive in America, the palace called the Wilhelmina Agency to tell them the news. The media hype for the tour had been unprecedented; advance stories already filled the New York gossip columns. With millions of dollars of advertising revenue at stake, embarrassed Wilhelmina blamed the cancellation on 'women's problems', promising that it would be rescheduled in the near future.

Vogue fashion editor Polly Mellen said she was still looking forward to her planned fashion shoot with Princess Stephanie.

'She's very shy,' said Mellen, who added that the Princess definitely had what it takes to be a top model.

'We were very disappointed when she didn't show. We were going to do the most beautiful series of pictures of her. I didn't want to shoot her as a jock, but in wonderful, modern clothes, with a dress that was almost falling off her, just covering her boobies. But the palace said no. I got a letter with a lovely apology.'

Princess Stephanie may have been down but she was certainly not out. After a recuperative skiing vacation with a new 'chosen one', who raced her down the slopes of fashionable Courchevel, she returned to Monaco for the annual Grand Prix as the prodigal daughter. Delighted by Stephanie's promise to turn over a new leaf, Prince Rainier bought her a baby-blue Rolls-Royce and offered to buy her a house in Monte-Carlo so he could keep an eye on her.

For a while Stephanie did her best to lose her image as Monaco's 'bad girl'. She developed a routine, getting up at 9 AM and having breakfast with her father, then going to the beach to spend the day with Caroline and her one-year-old son, Andrea. After dinner she might drop into Jimmy'z with her new boyfriend, Geoffrey Moore – the scion of the current James Bond, Roger Moore – for a nightcap. She was usually in bed by midnight.

She was also determined to get back into the world of fashion, as a designer instead of a model. She formed a partnership with Alix de la Comble, a young woman who apprenticed at Dior with her. Although de la Comble was ten years older than Stephanie, the two became inseparable, spending the summer in Monaco drafting a start-up plan for a swimsuit-design company called Pool Position.

Princess Stephanie agreed to finance the company with the money she had already earned modelling. She seemed to be moving in the right direction at last. But many questioned the strong influence that de la Comble seemed to exert on the impressionable Princess.

'My only real girlfriend is Alix,' the Princess told *Boston Herald* writer Christa Worthington. 'We're like sisters.'

They even moved in together, sharing an apartment in Paris's upscale sixteenth arrondisement. Prince Rainier, Caroline and Albert all met de la Comble and welcomed her as a sobering influence on the wayward Princess.

'I've grown up a lot,' said the Princess, declaring that her wild-child nightclubbing days were over. 'I saw that people were just interested in my name, but now I have friends that I know care for me, for my personality and myself.'

After picking the Nautic swimsuit manufacturer out of the telephone book the Princess sat down to design her first 'sexy but not vulgar' swimwear collection.

'It's like designing a collection is the only way to express yourself,' she enthused. 'I don't know; it's weird.'

In August 1985 150 members of the world's fashion elite gathered around the pool at Monte-Carlo's exclusive health spa California Terrace. They were there to see the launch of Princess Stephanie's Pool Position swimsuit collection. Although the Princess wasn't modelling herself, there were plenty of revealing publicity photos of her on view.

The entire Grimaldi family were there to lend support, as well as Monaco-based designer Karl Lagerfeld and photographer Helmut Newton. 'Okay, girls – let's go,' said Stephanie, launching a host of swimsuited models who sashayed along the pool to the enthusiastic applause of Princes Rainier and Albert.

At the climax of the show, to the strains of rocker David Lee Roth's 'Just a Gigolo', Stephanie appeared with the last model and they dramatically plunged into the pool together, bringing the crowd to its feet.

'A very good collection,' said Lagerfeld after the show. 'She's kind of a sporty version of Madonna.'

Again, as she had done with her short-lived modelling career, the Princess had started at the top with nowhere to go but down. After the show Pool Position was immediately swamped with massive orders from the likes of Harrods, Bloomingdales and Macy's, who believed that the Princess's image was highly commercial.

But when she came to New York in October to publicise Pool Position, the publicity surrounding the launch of the new collection backfired when Stephanie and Prince Albert – who was in the States for the first Monaco–New York boat race – went nightclubbing. When a photographer took a picture of the Princess guzzling beer out of a bottle she flew into a rage and threatened to knock his teeth out; Prince Albert had to physically restrain her and lead her from the club to avoid further trouble. But, predictably, next morning's New York papers carried the whole story, along with pictures showing a haunted-looking Stephanie desperately putting her hands up to the camera like a trapped animal.

'I still see photos of Stephanie that concern me,' wrote Judith Balaban Quine in August 1985.

'Still a lot of fear in her eyes. God, but it was tough for her to lose [her mother] so suddenly at that particular juncture in her life.'

CHAPTER THIRTEEN

A NEW COAT
OF PAINT

WITH TOURISM IN decline after Princess Grace's death, and a steep fall in the value of the American dollar in the mid-1980s, Prince Rainier realised that drastic action was needed to revitalise his tarnished principality. And, just as he had done thirty years before, the Prince looked to Hollywood to save Monaco.

At that time the two highest-rated programmes on British and American television were *Dallas* and *Dynasty*. The Prince spotted the huge potential of linking Monaco to one of these shows. Not only would it ensure exposure to millions of viewers worldwide, but the producers could foot the bill. The Grimaldis licked their lips in anticipation, thinking of the marketing potential of JR Ewing (Larry Hagman) leaving South Fork for Monte-Carlo to pull off a spectacular tax-free oil deal; or Alexis Carrington (Joan Collins) staging a grand seduction at the Hotel de Paris after a spectacular appearance at the Red Cross Ball with the sovereign family.

In January 1985 Prince Rainier secretly contacted the producers of both shows, inviting them to film three episodes in Monaco; in return he and his family would make cameo appearances.

'In a shrewd move that would make JR Ewing proud, Rainier told neither of the fiercely competitive shows that he [was] negotiating with the other,' said the *Boston Herald*'s showbusiness columnist Paul Sullivan. 'This was the Prince's plan: to get worldwide publicity at minimum cost for Monaco.'

After the initial approach Prince Albert personally visited the producer of *Dallas* in Los Angeles, promising that a couple of Grimaldis would come to the US to film two episodes of the series 'at home with the Ewing family'. The producers loved the idea and enthusiastically began developing potential storylines based around Monaco.

At the same time *Dynasty* producer Aaron Spelling – who was in Europe scouting locations for a new movie – was invited to an audience with Rainier at the Hotel de Paris. At the meeting Rainier repeated his offer, inviting Spelling to film key scenes in the Palace. Spelling told Rainier he would probably give the green light to the idea, but that he first needed to do a cost analysis in Los Angeles. When Spelling returned he discovered, through the Hollywood grapevine, that Rainier had made an identical offer to his chief rivals. He was incensed. Ultimately both shows decided to reject the Grimaldis' offer.

To add insult to injury, Spelling went ahead with the royal project without Rainier, using a storyline about a small, European tax-haven kingdom called Moldavia. Needless to say, it bore an uncanny resemblance to Monaco. The Moldavian crown prince had married a beautiful, well-to-do American heiress. In the story Moldavia came under siege, and the ruling family had to flee in terror. Would this be Monaco's sorry fate?

Prince Rainier ultimately decided that Monaco needed a *new* Grace Kelly and carefully considered the possibility of remarriage. Besides the allure and glamour a new First Lady would offer the principality, the unsophisticated Rainier was desperately in need of a partner who could help him cope with awkward social occasions. Several fashion magazines had already noted Rainier's dinner-party stiffness without the reassuring presence of Princess Grace by his side.

'He somehow lacks *savoir faire*,' observed Bob Colacello in *Vanity Fair*. To illustrate his point, Colacello recounted the story of how Rainier had once been kept waiting at a Houston restaurant before finally being seated at a table:

'He entertained his party of high-powered business people by whistling,' said Colacello.

In preparation for courtship – and prodded by Princess Caroline – Rainier underwent plastic surgery in Paris to remove his unsightly double chins and excess skin on his neck. He was now ready once more to search for a new Monaco Princess.

His opportunity came at the Rose Ball which opened the 1985 Monaco season. He was seated next to the beautifully voluptuous Princess Ira von Furstenberg, whom he had known socially for many years but towards whom he had never been romantically inclined. Well over six-feet tall in her high heels, the forty-five-year-old Princess was an imposing woman. A former B-movie actress who – unlike Grace Kelly – *had* taken her clothes off for the camera, she had recently posed naked for a citrus fruit advert. Now she was seeking a third husband and had Rainier firmly in her sights.

Princess Ira engaged the shy widower's attention at the Ball. The pair seemed to 'click' as they laughed and joked. Friends who saw them there noted that Princess Ira was the first person to bring a sparkle back to Rainier's eyes since Grace's passing.

The twice-divorced German Princess, who had appeared in more than twenty eminently forgettable movies in the 1960s, was a well-known fixture in European and American high society. The niece of the Italian billionaire chairman of Fiat, Gianni Agnelli, Ira had had a colourful past. At the age of only fifteen, a year before Rainier married Grace, Ira tied the knot with Austrian Prince Alfonso von Hohenlohe in what was, like the Grimaldi marriage, billed as 'the wedding of the year'. After the ceremony the couple glided down Venice's Grand Canal in a gondola, waving to the adoring crowds.

But the marriage was short-lived and at the age of twenty-one she moved on to marry Brazilian copper millionaire Francesco 'Baby' Pignatari. Three years later she divorced him, receiving a generous settlement.

In the late 1970s Princess Ira briefly romanced the young Libyan Colonel Qaddafi, who then owned fourteen per cent of her uncle's Fiat company. Now she was moving on to another absolute dictator – only this time it was one who could take her to the very pinnacle of status and society.

That summer Rainier accompanied Ira on a private Mediterranean cruise on Agnelli's yacht, followed by a weeklong 'cure' at the Hotel Miramar in Biarritz. After that they became constant companions. In August Ira was the Prince's guest of honour at the Red Cross Ball, seated on his left where Princess Grace used to be. Rainier seemed enchanted by Princess Ira, visibly lighting up in her presence.

The only obstacle in Ira's path appeared to be Princess Caroline, who had taken an instant dislike to Ira and had snubbed her at the Red Cross Ball, considering her to be a direct threat to her own position as acting First Lady.

By the fall newspapers were forecasting an imminent engagement announcement, especially after the third anniversary of Grace's death on September 14. On hearing the news that Rainier and Ira might marry, Britain's Princess Margaret summed up the situation in her own inimitable way: 'Ira marry Rainier? Such a *big* girl for a *small* country.'

Princess Ira von Furstenberg was nowhere to be seen when the Grimaldis flew to Beverly Hills on Halloween night for the second Princess Grace Foundation, USA Weekend. It was a chance for the family to try and compensate for some of Princess Stephanie's recent bad publicity – and raise $1 million for the Foundation at the same time.

The busy weekend began at the Hard Rock Cafe with a party thrown for Stephanie by a Swiss skincare company to celebrate a new advertising campaign created around her. The campaign was themed 'Beauty is Not Only Skin Deep'. The Princess arrived wearing one of her own creations – a revealing turquoise lycra dress which Stephanie described as a 'bathing suit with a little skirt'.

As the party began she seemed unusually relaxed and friendly. But all that changed when the Princess was introduced to a handsome young Mexican called Miguel Nunoz. Suddenly she seemed to have eyes only for Miguel, losing all interest in the other guests who had come especially to see her. A few minutes later Stephanie and Nunoz left together; when paparazzi surrounded them on their way out she physically lashed out at the cameras.

After a few hours of intimate dancing at Tramps nightclub, the couple retreated to her hotel to spend the night. The following day they reappeared to head a conga line at a party given by Jerry Buss, the owner of the Los Angeles Lakers. Later that night, after making a brief appearance at the Princess Grace Foundation gala dinner, Stephanie met Nunoz at Tramps and danced a second night away. The next morning the newspapers printed pictures of the Princess and her new boyfriend together: it was also reported that Prince Rainier had given her a dressing-down, ordering her to behave with more dignity on official occasions.

The Grimaldis finally managed to present a united front at the weekend's main fundraising gala, which took place at the Beverly Wilshire Hotel. Sitting on the stage with his three children around him, Prince Rainier benevolently handed out awards to winning artists for their work. But beneath all the smiles and bonhomie there was tension as Princess Stephanie, appropriately clad for once in an elegant black dress, gritted her teeth and stayed on her best behaviour. It was a brief calm before the storm for the much-troubled Princess.

★　★　★

As usual, Prince Albert was being quite the opposite from his unpredictable sisters. Understated and polite, Albert was quietly getting on with his life. He maintained his uncanny knack of avoiding press attention, even though he had recently been dating well-known actresses – all blonde-haired and blue-eyed – including Catherine Oxenberg and Donna Mills.

'He is very playful,' says Mills, star of *Knot's Landing*, who shared a romantic night out with the Prince in Monte-Carlo. 'He loves to go out and dance and party and all that. He has a good time.'

Now in his late twenties, with anxious Monégasques wondering when the heir to the throne would marry, the Prince showed no signs of settling down. Although he had a number of casual relationships with women – and one serious love affair while at Amherst – unlike his sisters he skilfully managed to keep his amours out of the press. His self-proclaimed strategy for avoiding the paparazzi was simple: plan ahead, don't ask for trouble and 'train with the Secret Service – spy manuals and all'.

'It's kind of funny for me to try and lead the press in different directions,' the Prince confided in June 1997.

'You do everything possible to maintain a decent private life so you almost have to use secret-agent tactics to elude the press for a while to have a secret or peaceful vacation somewhere.

'I don't usually do it on purpose but it just happens that way. I know that even if I go out with a friend, who I know I'll never be involved with, I'm pretty sure that some pictures are going to appear. It's kind of fun to see what the captions will be.'

One particular photograph that would come back to haunt him some years later was the result of a brief affair he had had with American *Playboy* model Teri Weigel. The Prince had first spotted the shapely brunette when he saw her perform with the *Playboy* 'Girls of Rock 'n' Roll' revue in the Monte-Carlo Casino in the mid-1980s.

After the show Albert sought out twenty-nine-year-old Weigel – who had posed nude for *Playboy* two months previously – and asked her out on a date. Weigel says she had to fight off the balding Prince's amorous advances on their second date.

'We chased each other around the apartment,' recalled Weigel. 'He was, like, trying to get my clothes off. He wanted something quick. Until he got it, he wasn't going to quit seeing me.'

Weigel deliberately refused to let the Prince – nicknamed 'Dirty Bertie' by the English press – have his way until her final night in Monaco, when she finally capitulated. She figured: 'Well, I've put him through enough torture now. It's time to make him happy.'

Unfortunately for Prince Albert that night was immortalised when a friend took a photograph of him nuzzling into Teri's chest, smiling angelically.

Over the next few years Teri descended into explicit X-rated movies, starring in more than a dozen, including *Raunch III* and *Centerfold Fever*. When she fell on hard times in 1991 she sold her photograph of Prince Albert to the American tabloid show *Hard Copy*, and gave them a full interview on her time with the Prince. Admitting that she hadn't spoken to Albert since their night together, Teri felt sure he would appreciate her movies. 'He's a pervert,' she claimed.

But it was a more serious Prince Albert who travelled to Los Angeles on official business in November 1985. There he did a major interview with *Los Angeles Times* society editor Jody Jacobs. Asked about his recent on-the-job training in various professions in New York, Albert said he most enjoyed working in advertising, which he found 'fascinating and high pressure'. He also made a point of detailing his current responsibilities:

'Now I'm back in Monaco helping my father out,' he explained. 'I'm in charge of the Red Cross and different sports programmes. I'm in charge – as my mother was.'

The Prince also told Jacobs that he had been responsible for the first Monaco–New York yacht race which was presently in progress.

'I'm also in charge of the yacht club,' he explained. 'And this year I organised the transatlantic Monaco to New York race. The winning ship should reach New York on Sunday, but unfortunately, I won't be there. But I will be in New York on Friday, and Mayor Koch has declared it Monaco Day.'

Asked about his love of sports the Prince said he was sailing a lot at the moment and considered himself a 'fair tennis player. I did win the last [Monte-Carlo] pro-amateur tournament.'

And the Prince revealed that he no longer had to worry about his father throwing a tennis racquet at him in a fit of temper. 'Dad doesn't play so much any more. He's into golf.'

When Jacobs asked Prince Albert about his sovereign duties and whether he was ready to rule Monaco, the Prince acknowledged that he had been aware of his looming responsibilities since the age of two, adding: 'Actually, it's always been in the back of my mind, but I never let it bother me.'

As to being a Prince, Albert said he was enjoying it. 'I get to meet interesting people, and I go to interesting places. But sometimes it's tough. But my father is really marvellous about giving me advice.'

The hardest part of his job, from the Prince's point of view, was the social side, which he admitted he could live without:

'Sometimes we have a very busy schedule,' he said. 'And a lot of the times you just don't want to go out. You face a very busy schedule, with more and more events in Monaco where someone from the family must show up – and it's very taxing.'

Princess Caroline too, although she clearly enjoyed her role as First Lady, disliked some of the duties it involved.

'It's like a dog biting its tail,' she explained in 1996. 'The more you do for people then the more you have to do it and the more they demand of you. And if you say maybe, "I don't feel up to it," they say, "What! You can't let us down!"'

The Grimaldi children's apparent reluctance to serve Monaco was in marked contrast to their mother's willing professionalism. Grace understood the vital importance of being seen at every public event in the principality.

Said Bob Colacello: 'Grace worked hard for a quarter of a century on the *balls* and *fêtes*, the *musicales* and *soirées* that kept the *beau monde* coming long after the *belle époque* mansions had been converted into lobbies for concrete towers. She knew that Monaco needed tycoons and titles to lure tourists – just as New York nightclubs need open-bar stars to attract cash-carrying kids.'

And as early as 1987 Colacello foresaw how Albert's weaknesses could make him vulnerable if his stronger elder sister ever made a bid for power in time-honoured Grimaldi fashion.

'Some of Albert's partisans are concerned that he is leaving the door open for a power-play by his older sister, just as Rainier had to fight off the ambitions of *his* older sister, Princess Antoinette,' said Colacello.

Now expecting their second child, Princess Caroline and Stefano Casiraghi presented a much more solid and acceptable family image than the unmarried dilettante Prince Albert. The assured and self-confident Caroline, as the first-born of the Grimaldi children, had far more leadership potential than Albert. And she was well aware that, under Monaco Law, Prince Rainier was perfectly free to name a daughter to succeed him.

Indeed, when a local English-language newspaper, the *Riviera Reporter*, carried a story saying that the principality would revert back to France if a male heir did not inherit the throne, Princess Caroline asked her personal secretary Judith Mann to write to the editor to set him straight.

'I want to point out that no mention is made of succession passing only through a male heir,' said the letter. 'Essentially, in both the Franco–Monégasque Treaty of 1918 and the Constitution of 1962 the succession to the throne of Monaco can be ensured by an adopted child, of either sex, should the Reigning Prince have no legitimate issue.

'You will also note that succession is ensured through primogeniture (with priority given to males), thus the line can be continued through the female descendants.'

If Prince Albert was choosing to stamp his mark in Monaco through sporting achievements, then his elder sister was concentrating on the arts. Following in her mother's footsteps, Caroline was determined to make Monaco the ballet capital of the world.

After Grace's death she supervised the restoration of Monaco's opera house, spending three years championing her mother's long-cherished dream of recreating the legendary turn-of-the-century *Ballets de Monte-Carlo*. The Princess lobbied the government, persuading them to fund the ambitious project and hiring an artistic director and choreographer to lick the forty-member company into shape. She even personally oversaw the restoration of the original Diaghilev rehearsal studios.

'Without Princess Caroline the arts would die in Monaco,' says Andre Peyregne, the music critic of *Nice-Matin*. 'Prince Rainier and Albert have no interest in the arts and don't think they are important, but Caroline is quite incredible. She loves the arts – especially dance.'

Caroline also headed the Princess Grace Foundation and the Garden Club and was honorary president of the Monaco Girl Guides and the Ladies' Needle and Thread Society.

During her spare time at the villa Clos St Pierre – the home just three minutes away from the Palace that Rainier had given her on her marriage to Junot – Caroline would spend hours alone playing the flute and piano, or writing poetry in a little book. Twice a year she and a friend still publish a privately-circulated paper called *The Egoist*.

Always appearing calm and composed in her Karl Lagerfeld-designed outfits, Caroline's only visible sign of nerves was her habit of chain-smoking American cigarettes, which had led to her being nicknamed 'the puffing princess' in some quarters.

Her fierce streak of independence and need for privacy sometimes made Caroline appear aloof; even her mother had called her '*insulaire*'.

'Some people need friends more than others,' she stated. 'I have never felt the need to confide in anybody. I've always felt that when I had a problem I could find a solution within myself.'

In early 1985, during a turbulent period in her marriage to Stefano Casiraghi when he was reportedly seeing other women, Caroline invited her old beau Robertino Rossellini to Monaco. She made sure that they were photographed together at a public pool with little Andrea. A few weeks later Rossellini had disappeared and Caroline and Stefano were enjoying a 'second honeymoon'. Her ploy had worked.

In January 1986 the palace announced that the twenty-nine-year-old Princess was pregnant again, denying speculation that the baby would be named Grace if it was a girl. The only dark cloud left hanging over the Princess was the troublesome problem of her annulment, which looked no nearer to being resolved. The Pope still refused to give his approval.

Roger-Louis Bianchini of *Nice-Matin* claimed in his 1992 book *Monaco: Une Affair Qui Tourne* that Monaco's highest-ranking churchman Archbishop Joseph Sardou had sabotaged the annulment, fearing that her second marriage to Casiraghi would also end in divorce and embarrass the Church even further. A top-secret report from the Archbishop of Monaco to the Vatican put the annulment on indefinite hold.

On August 3, Caroline gave birth to a six-pound, eight-ounce baby girl. She was named Charlotte, after her unconventional great-grandmother. Just two hours after the birth a delighted Prince Rainier took his son-in-law out to celebrate at a championship boxing bout.

Stefano Casiraghi's second child was born only days after the Italian Army announced it was investigating him for fraud: he had claimed to be impotent in 1979 to avoid army service. Perhaps even more sinister were reports that Franco Ufilugello, an Italian military prosecutor in Turin, was probing a link between Casiraghi and an organised-crime ring, which was reputed to sell medical exemptions on the black market.

But the possibility that he might have to face a tribunal and explain how his 'impotency' had so obviously been cured did not put the brakes on Stefano's devil-may-care lifestyle. The day after his new daughter's birth he competed in the Monaco–St Tropez powerboat race, finishing fifth behind the winner – Prince Albert.

Although Prince Rainier had recently appointed him a Duke of Monaco, Casiraghi had still not adapted to his official duties at the Palace. During Caroline's engagements as First Lady she was usually escorted by her father or brother; Casiraghi was noticeable for his absence from many state occasions. He now spent most of his time running his construction company, which had been awarded lucrative government contracts for some of the principality's biggest building projects. That, and his powerboat racing, meant he was away from home for much of the time. So, like Grace and Rainier, Caroline and Stefano led separate lives.

'Their marriage has always been rather strange,' a close friend of theirs told *People* magazine.

In late August Princess Caroline was driving along the Corniche from Monaco to Roc Agel, returning from a party at 5 AM in the morning. Suddenly she was blinded by the bright lights of an oncoming vehicle. She pulled sharply to the right, side-swiping a rock wall and almost wrecking her car. Had the car gone just a few feet further it would have plunged 100 feet over the edge to the road below. Miraculously uninjured, Caroline calmly got out of the car and walked up to Roc Agel.

The accident happened a mere 600 feet from the site of Princess Grace's fatal crash four years earlier. For once a member of the Grimaldi family had managed to beat the Curse of the Grimaldis. But the family would be granted no more than a short breathing space until its next appearance.

If there were any doubts remaining that the Grimaldis had 'gone downmarket', these were banished in March 1986 when Princess Stephanie set off on a tour of suburban shopping malls to promote her new Pool Position swimwear line to middle America. She was accompanied by her best friend and partner, Alix de la Comble, and business manager Jean-Francois Marchand, who had reportedly cut a half-million dollar deal with a store for exclusive rights on her swimsuits and in-store appearances by the Princess. Since Stephanie had launched Pool Position nine months ago it had sold 28,000 suits in the $80 to $150 price range. The company was highly profitable.

The publicity tour wound through the Deep South and Mid-West, where Stephanie cheerfully met housewives and high-school girls who had turned out in droves to see a real-life princess.

'I've seen every one of her mother's movies,' explained seventeen-year-old Chris Brackett, who waited for hours in Rich's Store in Atlanta to get Stephanie's autograph. 'And if she comes from Princess Grace, that's good enough for me.'

After keeping the crowd waiting for almost an hour, an MC walked to the front of the store to proudly announce, 'Rich's is proud to present Stephanie of Monaco . . .'

The audience burst into applause, rushing forward as the smiling Princess made her grand entrance to the click of instamatic cameras. Then Stephanie signed publicity photographs for the next thirty minutes as she chatted to her fans.

The invited press and television crews were told they could only ask Stephanie about Pool Position – no personal questions about her family were allowed. Stephanie happily discussed keeping in shape – by 'running her dog and water-skiing' – and even served up some home-spun fashion philosophy of her own for the housewives:

'Women have much better bodies [now] and they want to show them off,' she said. 'They want to be sexy.'

Asked why she had left her easy life in the Riviera to travel the length and breadth of America as a working girl, Stephanie replied: 'I just decided to work and do my own thing, instead of sitting back and enjoying life.'

A few months later she would tell author Jeffrey Robinson just how much she resented the constant questioning.

'It was driving me crazy,' she complained. 'People kept asking me why I was working. They kept telling me I was taking something away from someone who deserved success more than I did.'

At the beginning of April Princess Stephanie flew into Los Angeles for the West Coast launch. She had now been on the road for a month promoting her swimsuits — including a week-long tour of European cities. Dressed in a green leather jacket, a tight-fitting pair of Levi Jeans and black cowboy boots, the only hint that she was a Princess came from the six Louis Vuitton suitcases trailing in her wake. But even after twenty-seven hours of flying and waiting around in airports, the Princess managed to find the energy to do a little impromptu dance at LAX when she heard a boombox blaring.

Two days later the Princess faced a 350-strong crowd at Bullocks in the Beverly Center. Despite the usual pushing and shoving to get a glimpse of Monaco's Princess, Stephanie seemed thoroughly unfazed.

Posing for the cameras, Stephanie laughingly recalled her very first swimming costume. 'I hated it! It was my sister Caroline's suit, a hand-me-down. That happens a lot when you have an older sister.'

When asked about their business relationship, Alix de la Comble said that Stephanie, being ten years younger, designed 'the more plugged-in styles' while she concentrated on the 'sophisticated looks'.

'The partnership works very well," she added.

But within a few months Stephanie had tired of Pool Position. After a bitter row with de la Comble — who was fed up with the spoiled Princess's behaviour — Pool Position went on an extended break.

Stephanie would later complain she felt "betrayed" by de la Comble, saying she had thought of her as more of a friend than a business associate.

★ ★ ★

On her way back to Monaco Stephanie visited Harrods department store who had acquired exclusive English rights to Pool Position swimwear. While there she had dinner with the store's owner Mohammed Al Fayed and was introduced to his handsome thirty-year-old playboy son Dodi. The charming young Egyptian swept Stephanie off her feet; they spent the night together clubbing and arranged to meet in Paris the following weekend.

Back in Paris, Princess Stephanie celebrated her twenty-first birthday by becoming a pop star. A few months earlier she had signed a lucrative recording contract, going into a Paris studio to record her first pop single, 'Irresistible'.

The record company had astutely realised that Stephanie had become a huge phenomenon in Europe. Her image as a 'bad girl', combined with her status as a Princess, had captured the imagination of millions of young girls, who saw her as their role model.

American producer Jack Robinson was hired to write her a hit song. He soon came up with 'Irresistible' – a racy pop song with explicit lyrics in both French and English to give it international appeal.

'She's an idol already for millions of teenage girls across Europe,' explained Robinson, adding with a great deal of hyperbole, 'and she has a really beautiful voice.'

Unfortunately Stephanie's scratchy singing voice was in reality rather thin. It took hours of mastering in the studio to get the recording up to par. But when 'Irresistible' was released on March 1, it was a sensation. Within one month it had sold more than 200,000 copies; it topped the French charts and within three months had 'gone platinum', racking up sales of 1.3 million.

The Princess city-hopped Europe publicising her new pop career, appearing on television shows lip-synching to 'Irresistible'. The song had highly suggestive lyrics: 'He's in my system, though I try to resist him. I can't fight him anymore. Irresistible. Irreversible. I can't fight the temptation. Call it physical – call it illogical, still I want a sensation.'

She recorded a sexy video version of the song in an attempt to break into the US market via MTV.

'You can't sell a record here without a video,' the Princess explained cynically.

When asked about her father's reaction to her career as a pop star – and what her mother would have made of it – Stephanie sidestepped the issue, pointing out that she had always been the 'headstrong' child in the family. Then she said: 'My mother always told me I would be an artist. I think she would be very happy.'

But Stephanie's attempts to follow Grace into acting were less successful. When the aspiring young actress auditioned for the part of Maggie in a Geneva production of Tennessee Williams' *Cat on a Hot Tin Roof* in April '86 she was politely turned down.

That summer Princess Stephanie seemed to be everywhere. She followed up 'Irresistible' with an album; it too became an immediate hit, reaching number one across Europe. (The album included a track called 'Flowers of Evil', dedicated to Paul Belmondo.) The Princess declared that she would be donating all proceeds from the record's sales to the Princess Grace Foundation. She had a short-lived but well-publicised romance with actor Christopher Lambert; the enigmatic American rock sensation Prince expressed interest in working with her. Her life seemed to be firmly back on track.

But Princess Stephanie's meteoric singing career crashed to the ground after she appeared on a live German television special, reportedly high on cocaine. More than twelve million viewers were stunned to see the Princess stumbling around on stage, appearing disoriented as she attempted to sing her latest hit, 'One Love to Give'.

'She was completely unprofessional,' said German TV host Dieter Thomas Heck. 'But when you use such things before the show, you can't do any better.'

When Stephanie returned to Monaco she announced that she was sick of Europe. She was moving to Los Angeles where she could 'be herself'. Dismissing reports that her father had threatened to commit her to a psychiatric hospital for drug treatment, Stephanie launched a bitter attack on her would-be detractors who, she claimed, were jealous of her success.

Stephanie had decided the nastiness of Europe was too much. She complained that she constantly heard there that her musical success was due to nothing more than her royal birth. Her answer to such critics was terse: ' "Selling five million records can't be because it's me — it's because people like the music." '

She even accused a rival female singer of deliberately tripping her up and breaking her ankle as she was going on stage to perform.

But Princess Stephanie's real problem was her inability to come to terms with the death of her mother. The circumstances of the accident still haunted her. She tried to escape the guilt she felt — but she became increasingly paranoid, and convinced that people were talking about her behind her back.

'There was so much magic that surrounded Mom,' she would later say in a revealing interview. 'She almost stopped being human. People figured I must have caused [the accident] because she was too perfect to do something like that. After a while you can't help feeling guilty. Everybody looks at you and you know they're thinking — how come she's still around and Grace is dead? No one ever said it to me like that, but I knew that's what they were thinking.' Feeling abandoned, Stephanie just went off to do her "own thing."

CHAPTER FOURTEEN

--- ❧ ---

THE
DISNEYLAND
DICTATORSHIP

WHILE THE REST of the world was able to read all about Princess Stephanie's exploits, most Monégasques were blissfully unaware of her scandalous behaviour. Since the beginning of his rule Prince Rainier had carefully built an iron wall of censorship around the principality. Anything considered remotely offensive to the ruling family would be seized by the police.

'Yes, the police do come in and check on certain publications,' explained Jane France, who moved to Monaco thirty years ago and runs the principality's only English bookshop, Scruples.

'They have removed certain magazines like the *Le Canard Enchaie*, [which is the French equivalent of *Private Eye*] if there's anything critical about the family.'

For example, when James Spada's biography on Princess Grace – *Grace: The Secret Lives of a Princess* – was released (to critical acclaim) in 1986, it was conspicuously absent on Monaco bookshelves.

'The family weren't very happy about it so we didn't stock it for very long,' said France. 'Being foreigners one has to mind one's Ps and Qs.'

As an absolute monarch, Prince Rainier can do as he pleases, despite the presence of a constitution and an elected parliament. The Prince has the power to exile anyone he chooses and he will not tolerate any opposition. When a group of Monégasque intellectuals set up an association called CEPAM in 1976 to discuss the problems facing the principality, it was outlawed by the Palace.

'The Palace controls all information completely,' explains the former head of the Monaco Secret Service, Michel Vivien. 'There is the face of Monaco that the public sees – and another secret one that no one ever hears about.'

Monaco is part police state and part Disneyland, with its glamorous facade and squeaky clean environment. Everything in the principality is tightly controlled so it runs with the precision of a Swiss watch. Each morning a team of gardeners gather in the garden in the casino square to pluck out any wilting petals that might spoil the immaculate flowerbeds; at night a tape-recording of a bird of prey plays through discreetly-hidden speakers to stop sparrows from landing and soiling the park with bird droppings.

Prince Rainier had introduced a tough policing policy, drafting in 500 French policemen – one to every 100 Monégasques. He claims virtually to have rid the principality of all crime. According to official figures there is, on average, one murder in Monaco every ten years and too few robberies to talk about. But locals claim that unofficially some police discreetly drop any unexplained bodies over the border in France and leave their police to deal with the problem.

Monaco and French police are also said to have an understanding that if an Interpol fugitive is spotted in Monaco he won't be arrested.

'They first let him spend all his money in the casino,' said a well-informed source, 'and then, mysteriously, there's a roadblock once he's left Monaco on the way to the airport. He'll be picked up for apparently unconnected reasons and arrested by the French.'

The perception of Monaco as a crime-free society allows wealthy residents to feel comfortable and secure. And it is a common boast in

Monaco that ladies can walk the streets at 3 AM in their furs and jewels without risk.

'Of course Monaco is a police state,' says Jane France. 'And I think it's a very good thing. Obviously, if you are nefarious and underhanded it's not so good for you. But the whole essence of the principality is that it is a safe, clean place to live. That's what makes Monaco so desirable.'

Whenever one goes out in public in Monaco, the chances are the police will be watching. Since 1982 the Monaco police force – which is made up of French non-residents – have spent millions of dollars installing the world's most comprehensive electronic surveillance system, including 130 cameras and loud-speakers.

The nerve centre of the huge security operation – which Rainier sees as central to Monaco's survival – is located in a well-guarded room inside police headquarters in the Rue Louis Notari, near the old port. Police security men monitor the thirty colour-television screens spreading across one wall twenty-four hours a day, 365 days a year. The screens provide snapshots of almost every aspect of local life, showing every single car, cyclist and pedestrian in Monaco.

Using the latest fibre-optic technology, the state observers can instantly rotate any of the cameras placed over all banks, chemists' shops and jewellers through nearly 360 degrees. Back at HQ the watchers can even zoom in to see what newspapers are being read. The electronic eye observes every major road, reading car numberplates as all vehicles are checked entering Monaco. Identity checks are commonplace, either on the street or aided by hotel managers who routinely provide police with details of new arrivals.

Security is so tight that some do not even make it out of the Monaco train station. Many a weary, bedraggled backpacker has been stopped at the station and put on the next train out, deemed an unwanted eyesore. And the authorities proudly boast that they can seal up their borders in less than a minute to prevent any criminal escape.

'Our system is preventative,' insists Adrian Vivani, director of the administrative police which run the surveillance operation. 'Our role is, uniquely, to ensure public safety.'

But there is reason to believe there are abuses of the system by the state. There are widespread claims that telephones are regularly tapped in the name of state security, and mail searched.

'They've got a system of phone bugging that even the residents don't know about,' said Patrick Middleton, the English-born editor of the Nice-based *Riviera Reporter*, who has covered Monaco for more than a decade. 'I was once shown the control room by a police chief, whom I won't name. It's done on a word-trigger basis as they obviously can't record every telephone call. But there's a list of things that will activate the recording. If you said something derogatory about a Grimaldi it would undoubtedly hit the trigger.'

As in George Orwell's repressively sinister world of *1984*, Monégasques are encouraged to spy on outsiders and report anything untoward. And there are eighty plainclothes police officers (known as *'Police de Bruits'* or 'listening police') who are ever-present, pounding the streets and observing unnoticed in Monte-Carlo's many bars and restaurants. Their job is to keep their ears open for any rumours and gossip which are later filed at police headquarters. On one occasion a French schoolteacher was fired from his job in Monaco after he was overheard making a rude comment about the Grimaldis in a bar.

'You just never know who's listening,' said Middleton. 'You've got to be very careful if you live in Monaco. Luckily, I can say what I like because I live in Nice.'

American film director Robert Dornhelm had a painful run-in with the Monaco police in the late 1970s during a visit to his friend Princess Grace.

'I was just sitting peacefully in the grass,' he recalled. 'I was asked to show my papers. My revolutionary side kicked in and I said, 'Get lost.' After which they asked me to follow them and come to the police station. If not voluntarily, then by force.'

When Dornhelm finally managed to persuade the police that he was an official guest of the Palace he was allowed to go.

'I was really angry and I said to Princess Grace, "Listen, something terrible happened to me.They wanted to arrest me just for sitting in the grass. What kind of country is this?" She said, "Okay. I'm going to call them up and they are going to get a promotion; one should be very suspicious of characters like you.They did their job very well."'

Yet, ironically, one of Monaco's top policemen was a paid informant for the American tabloid *National Enquirer* right through the 1980s. He even visited the newspaper's headquarters in Lantana, Florida, during a summer vacation.

And directly after the publication of one 1988 *Enquirer* story accusing Monaco of being 'one of the drugs capitals of the world', Prince Rainier ordered a full-scale drug clean-up in the principality.

Paranoia is rife in Monaco – with some justification. Any visiting journalists daring to ask probing questions about the authorities are stonewalled. One Monaco businessman told the author that he didn't dare be interviewed on the record; he might be arrested and put in jail, and lose his business. Another declined to speak at all, saying he didn't want any repercussions from the police.

'Monaco is just like Russia in a sense,' says Patrick Middleton, who used to train police in England for the prison service.

'You just cannot survive here if you are against the government.'

Although Rainier has now cracked down severely on drugs and prostitution, there are persistent rumours that money-laundering continues through the casinos, allowing organised crime to gain a foothold in the late 1980s. But it would take the collapse of Monaco's biggest bank, and the subsequent scandal, to persuade the Prince to take action.

On a sunny February morning in 1990 the body of Jean Ferry, an official of the Industrial Bank of Monaco (BIM), was found in the bushes near his home in Menton. The respected employee had shot himself in the head: it was an obvious suicide.

But a police investigation discovered that one of Ferry's clients had set up an elaborate fraud involving the BIM. The investigation also revealed that dubious banking practices encouraging foreign tax evasion were widespread throughout Monaco banking.

Until then, under Monaco banking law, it had been perfectly legal for foreign investors to open accounts using the names of Monégasque citizens, who were paid for the privilege. As Monégasque banks did not question where any money came from, this system could easily launder dirty money, with the banks making a healthy profit.

Prince Rainier was so alarmed by the crash of the BIM, and concerned about the principality's international image, that he used a little-known law to tighten up banking regulations. And in a subsequent purge many bank officials were arrested and jailed.

'Banking in Monaco has developed almost by default, in the absence of a clear regulatory system,' says Andrew Jack of the *Financial Times*.

After the BIM scandal the banks were forced to clean up their act, but it was still relatively easy to deposit huge amounts of money with no questions asked. Using Monégasque companies or SAMs (*Sociétes Anonymes Monégasques*), foreign investors could legally create 'empty shell' companies which existed in name only. The banks would match investors with Monégasque citizens who were willing to lend their name to a SAM, thus protecting the investor from paying tax. Both the bank and the 'name' would then reap a percentage of the invested capital and a monthly stipend. It was alleged that organised-crime rings used SAMs to launder their dirty money.

'The whole system is well known to the initiated,' says *Nice-Matin*'s Roger Bianchini. 'But when underground deals begin to surface and scandal breaks through, Prince Rainier becomes concerned that the image of the principality could be tarnished and it could affect relations with France.'

In late 1994 the French Banking Commission set up an organisation to guard against money laundering through Monaco. It later published a report suggesting drug-money laundering was rife in Monaco.

'Because everything in Monaco is small, everything is exaggerated,'

The classically beautiful
Grace Kelly at the height
of her film career.
(Oleg Cassini)

Fashion designer
Oleg Cassini was briefly
engaged to Grace Kelly
before her parents stepped
in to halt the relationship.
(Oleg Cassini)

Prince Rainier and Grace held the world spellbound in
the marriage of the decade that put Monaco on the map.
(Rex Features)

Grace and Rainier presented the picture of the
perfect family during carefully orchestrated photo
opportunities. *(Rex Features)*

Princess Grace and her close friend Jeanne Kelly were the belles of the Monaco balls throughout the 1960s. *(Jeanne Kelly)*

Princess Grace met a highly nervous Diana Spencer during her
first public appearance and took her under her wing.
(Rex Features)

When Princess Caroline and Philippe Junot married in 1978 Grace accurately forecast the marriage would last just two years. *(Rex Features)*

Princess Caroline's second husband Stefano Casiraghi and their children. *(Rex Features)*

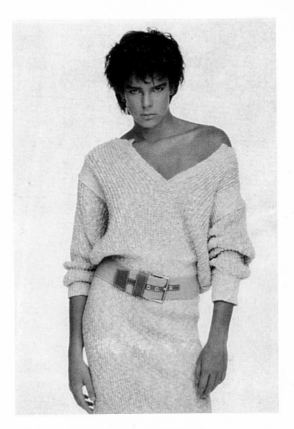

Princess Stephanie's modelling days were cut
short after Rainier stopped American tour in
the mid 1980s. *(Rex Features)*

Impulsive Princess Stephanie fell head over heels in love with convicted sex offender Mario Oliver. *(Rex Features)*

A night on the town
for Princess Stephanie
during her wild partying
days in Los Angeles.
(Phil Ramey)

Stephanie with her
record producer
boyfriend Ron Bloom
during the making of
her album in Los
Angeles. *(All Action)*

Princess Caroline
and Prince Albert
preside over an
official ball in the
early 1990s.
(Rex Features)

There was a huge
media speculation about
Albert's relationship with
supermodel Claudia Schiffer,
his constant companion
during the mid-1990s.
(Rex Features)

VE LEFT German
ess Bea Fielder had
ng with Prince Albert
then served him with a
ernity suit. A subsequent
od test cleared him of
onsibility.
orge Clare)

VE RIGHT Albert and
ie after their first night
Barcelona hotel.
ohanie Parker)

A signed photograph
from Prince Albert to
memorate his time with
ie and Christina Cox at
s secret Texas love nest.
(Stephanie Parker)

Princess Stephanie was blissfully happy with her bodyguard lover Daniel Ducruet at the start of their relationship. *(Rex Features)*

Stephanie bravely picked up the pieces of her life after Ducruet's betrayal by working out and going to the beach. *(Rex Features)*

When Princess Caroline's hair fell out due to stress she donned a turban and turned it into a startling fashion statement.
(Rex Features)

Princess Caroline and Prince Ernst of Hanover share a romantic moment during a cruise in Summer 1997.
(Rex Features)

Prince Albert and Tamara Rotolo during their whirlwind three week love affair in Monaco. *(Phil Ramey)*

Tamara Rotolo in court during her paternity hearing in California where she sought financial support from Prince Albert for little Jazmin Grace Grimaldi. The case was dismissed when the judge ruled he had no jurisdiction over the matter. *(Phil Ramey)*

Prince Rainier is still reluctant to relinquish the reins of power to Albert as the future of Monaco looks uncertain. *(Rex Features)*

A tragic dynasty—the Grimaldis at their 700th anniversary celebrations. *(Rex Features)*

says Gérard Cohen, chairman of the Monaco branch of the Republican National Bank of New York. 'Laundering can happen anywhere, but here one instance takes on huge proportions.'

After the collapse of the Italian lira, the wealthy Italian businessmen who had poured into the principality in the 1980s with Stefano Casiraghi found their money did not go as far as it used to in Monaco. They disappeared to seek pastures new; in their place came far more sinister wealthy Italians, members of the Sicilian Mafia who had been driven out of Italy.

'In the mid-1990s, podgy figures sucking on cigars were seen sticking large sums of money into Monaco's "no questions asked" banks,' explains Darius Sanai, of the *Guardian*.

According to Sanai, Prince Rainier was so concerned about the situation that in 1995 he appointed French civil servant Paul Dijourd to Monaco's previously strictly ceremonial post of Prime Minister. Dijourd's brief was to kick out the Mafia and crack down on money laundering.

'The government of Monaco didn't go about this with half-measures,' said Dijourd, who expelled forty people suspected of money laundering before setting about an overhaul of the casinos, which had recently suffered a spate of thefts by employees.

But Dijourd was too successful for his own good. He made enemies with some powerful conservative elements in the principality, who felt he was going too far, rocking their lucrative boat. So in January 1997 Rainier sent him back to Paris, replacing him with a less controversial (and perhaps less effective) Prime Minister.

'The problem is that the chapter of Monaco being a fiscal paradise and tax haven is closing,' says Roger Bianchini. 'And nobody, including Rainier, seems sure about what to do next.'

Prince Rainier is evasive on the subject of the Mafia. When asked directly if the Mafia were still operating in Monaco, he shrugged his shoulders.

'The Mafia's all over the place. [Monaco] is not particularly favourable to money laundering. It's small, it's very controlled, it's very well watched.'

When pressed further as to whether the Mafia had ever infiltrated the principality, Rainier was forced to concede: 'No, I can't say that it's not happening.'

Over the last few years Monaco has become very careful about granting applications for residency and about vetting requests for permission to set up a business in the principality. A complex government bureaucracy processes each application meticulously, demanding banking references and checking criminal records.

English publican John Haley, who runs the Ship and Castle Pub in Fontville, had to furnish a letter from Bristol licensing justices and give a full account of his finances before he was allowed to open for business.

'Everyone leaves you alone as long as you pay your dues to the government and keep your business affairs correct,' he explained.

'If you run your business properly, it's a lovely environment.'

CHAPTER FIFTEEN

——— ✤ ———

HOLLYWOOD
REVISITED

SHORTLY BEFORE HER mother's death, a deeply introspective Princess Caroline wrote in her journal: 'I do not think I'm the ideal woman for a man – with my tormented past, my uncertain present and perhaps my melancholy future.'

As she turned thirty, in January 1987, Caroline seemed to have buried her ghosts and found joy as a wife and mother. Although there were persistent rumours about the state of her marriage to Stefano Casiraghi, the Palace announced that the couple were expecting their third child in March. Publicly, at least, they seemed the picture of happiness.

The young rebel who had provided the prototype for her younger sister's 'naughty princess' was no more – 'la grande dame' had taken her place.

'She is the First Lady of Monaco and likes it,' said her cousin Buddy de Massy.

And de Massy, who was brought up in the midst of Grimaldi plotting and intrigue, was only too well aware of the present similarities between Caroline and his own mother Antoinette, who had conspired to seize power from her brother Rainier.

'Caroline will be in the same position as my mother,' said de Massy. 'Pushed out in favour of the new Princess when Albert marries – or if Rainier remarries. For the time being, she is the most powerful person in Monaco, after her father. She has a lot of influence over him.'

The consensus in Monaco was that Caroline was not doing a very good job as First Lady. Lacking her mother's gift of charming the press, she was widely perceived as moody and erratic. Caroline ran hot and cold, constantly exiling people from her inner circle for no apparent reason.

In June, Rainier and Princess Ira von Furstenburg seemed inseparable. It seemed likely that they were about to move to the next stage of their relationship and announce their engagement. The beneficial changes Ira had made in Rainier were obvious: the once-lonely ruler had relaxed considerably and no longer seemed to have a perpetual black cloud of gloom hanging over his head. So Princess Ira was eagerly anticipating a proposal that would place her at the very head of European society.

When her son Christoff (Kiko) Hohenlohe told the *Daily Mail* that his mother would definitely marry Prince Rainier by the end of the year, it seemed like the dawning of a new era in Monaco. But to Ira's embarrassment, her son Christoff had jumped the gun and there was no engagement.

The pink Palace immediately issued a denial of Hohenlohe's statement, saying that Rainier would 'absolutely not' marry. Desperate to repair the damage, Ira issued her own statement through *Paris-Match*, distancing herself from Christoff and saying: 'I reject the irresponsible declarations made by my son ... with whom I have been forced, painfully, to sever all links.'

But two days later a depressed Princess Ira told *Vanity Fair*'s Bob Colacello that her hopes of marrying Rainier were in tatters.

'I don't know,' Ira said, when asked if there was any chance of her becoming the Princess of Monaco. 'I mean, at the moment the whole thing is rather jeopardised. But you can never tell what happens in life, what?'

The romance between Rainier and Ira soon fizzled out, leaving a highly-relieved Princess Caroline safe as First Lady. But within weeks there was speculation that Caroline and Albert were locked in a bitter power struggle over who would rule Monaco if, and when, their father stepped down.

After she gave birth to a seven-pound, five-ounce baby boy, Pierre, on September 5, Caroline seemed ready to seize the initiative and wrest power from her weaker younger brother.

'Her character is stronger than Albert's [with] her regal posture and air of authority,' said her first cousin, Buddy de Massy.

Since their earliest days growing up in the palace, Caroline had been bitterly jealous of the placid, lovable Albert. But as Albert grew older and less vulnerable he began to stand his ground.

'He and I used to fight like cats and dogs while we were growing up,' admitted Princess Caroline.

'I mean, we'd fight with the determined intention of causing vast amounts of pain.'

Caroline finally had to admit physical defeat when Albert began to take judo classes.

'She was bugging me one day,' recalled the Prince in 1986, 'so she went after me and I threw her off-balance. She didn't appreciate it.'

Now Caroline – the girl who had once torn up her picture book because her brother dared to touch it – believed that her three-year-old son Andrea should one day become the ruling Prince instead of Albert.

'Caroline had some of Rainier's temperament and some of his sense of having a divine right to rule the country,' said Judy Balaban Quine. 'I think Rainier understood Caroline more instinctively than any of his other children. That made them very close.'

★　★　★

While Caroline was plotting to increase her power in Monaco, her sister Stephanie was doing everything possible to sever her ties with the principality. Now living in Los Angeles, the flamboyant young Princess soon made her mark on the town by joining the Brat Pack and having a whirlwind romance with actor Rob Lowe.

The Princess first met the twenty-two-year-old star of *About Last Night* and *Oxford Blues* after he had told comedienne Joan Rivers that she was his fantasy date. When Stephanie heard that, she let it be known she thought he was cute too and a meeting was arranged at the Deauville Film Festival in September 1986, as Stephanie was making the final preparations for her move to Los Angeles.

After spending ten passionate days together in Paris they met up again in Hollywood; the handsome young film star helped the Princess settle into her new home. A concerned Prince Rainier wrote to his old friend Rupert Allan, the veteran Hollywood PR man, asking for any information on the young movie star – whose film career would be severely damaged several years later in the wake of an under age, videotaped sex scandal.

Soon Princess Stephanie and Rob Lowe were appearing nightly at Hollywood's trendiest clubs and restaurants wearing each other's rings. Their friends forecast they would soon marry.

People magazine writer Lee Aitken captured one particularly wild night out when Stephanie and Lowe attended a small dinner party given in their honour at the Ivy restaurant in Hollywood.

'Presumably drunk with love, the two spent much of their time locked in long, passionate, tongue-baring kisses,' wrote Aitken.

And during the rare instances when her tongue wasn't occupied the Princess stunned fellow diners at the restaurant by screaming obscenities at her dining companion, actor Judd Nelson. The evening finished with the lovers groping around under the table searching for Lowe's glasses before they staggered off into the night – without paying the bill. (After they broke up Lowe would unchivalrously – and curiously – tell friends that Stephanie kissed like a boy.)

A week later Stephanie brought Rob Lowe along as her companion for the third Princess Grace Foundation USA gala in Dallas, Texas. After arriving more than ninety minutes late for the junior gala, attended by other members of her family, Princess Stephanie spent all her time in deep conversation with Lowe, refusing to mingle with the Dallas society crowd, who had paid $125 a head to meet the Grimaldis.

'But if the season's hottest couple flunked etiquette – they lead the class in star appeal,' Aitken wrote. 'Not since Mick [Jagger] and Bianca first took a plane has romantic fortune, jet-set division, coughed up such a news-making intercontinental pair as the handsome Princess and the pretty Hollywood kid.'

During the trip to Texas Stephanie showed off the ring Lowe had given her, telling friends she planned a December engagement with a large Palace wedding in the summer.

'It is obvious that, at twenty-one, Stephanie is going through a bad and difficult period,' an anxious Rainier wrote to Rupert Allan after the embarrassing weekend in Dallas.

'But I am confident, as she is an intelligent girl, that she will pull herself together soon. [Keeping] the door wide open is painful and worrying as her human environment is so awful and really trash-bad.'

But by the beginning of November, Rob Lowe was nowhere in sight. The fickle Princess had transferred her affections to Mario Oliver, the French-born co-owner of fashionable LA nightclub Vertigo. With his rugged good looks and long, shaggy, blond hair, Oliver – who was twelve years older than Stephanie – had a hint of danger about him that thrilled the impressionable young Princess.

As an ambitious waiter from Marseilles, Oliver had gone to New York to seek his fame and fortune in 1982. He first worked as a bartender in the notorious Studio 54 before moving to Los Angeles to wait on tables at La Bistingo and then Bono's, owned by the late 1960s pop star-turned-politician, Sonny Bono.

'He's a good waiter, a *great* waiter,' said Sonny Bono at the time. 'But it cracks me up that he's dating Princess Stephanie. He's the last person. But that's Hollywood.'

Princess Stephanie was besotted by the bleach-blond Oliver with his rakish diamond ear-stud. She publicly declared her love for him to a London tabloid.

'I am proud to show our happiness to the world,' gushed the Princess, revealing that Mario had helped her stop biting her nails. 'And I announce that we intend to be together for a long time.'

Prince Rainier had every reason to be alarmed about the twice-married new man in his youngest daughter's life. For in June 1982 Oliver and a friend had been arrested by the Los Angeles police and charged with raping nineteen-year-old Deana Nance. The girl alleged that she had met Oliver and the other man at a party in Bel-Air, and that they had lured her into the bedroom where she was raped.

'I live with it every day of my life,' said Nance. 'It is something I will never get over.'

After pleading No Contest to a lesser charge of sexual battery, Oliver was sentenced to ninety days in prison. The sentence was suspended, and he was placed on three years' probation. Although Oliver later described the incident as 'nothing special', the victim's mother publicly warned Prince Rainier that Stephanie was at risk.

'My advice to her father is, "Stop at nothing to keep her away from this dangerous man."'

Rainier was livid at his daughter's new live-in boyfriend. But he was powerless to act. The world's longest-surviving dictator, whose word was absolute in Monaco, had little or no control over his own daughter.

'I pray to God that she will drift away from this dreadful Mario,' wrote Prince Rainier to Rupert Allan in early 1987.

Rainier also asked Judy Balaban Quine, who lived in Los Angeles, to keep a discreet eye on Stephanie's welfare.

'She was in love with this terrible man,' remembers Quine. 'I met him a few times and he was obviously a difficult and dangerous guy. It was really a very troublesome and bad phase.'

Stephanie's cousin, Megan van Arkel, realised the Princess's deep unhappiness and desperate search for some peace of mind.

'She was just going through some difficult times,' recalled Van Arkel.

' This new boyfriend, that old boyfriend – I think her ultimate goal was just to be happy, and I don't think she was for a long time. I think it had to do with the loss of her mother.'

It was a tortuous period for sixty-three-year-old Prince Rainier. He was forced to confront magazine pictures of his topless daughter brazenly kissing Oliver in Mauritius, where they had gone in January 1987 on 'a trial honeymoon'.

Helen Veret, who covers Monaco from Paris for *Life* magazine, witnessed Stephanie and Oliver arriving at the Sygma photo agency in Paris to view the paparazzi's Mauritius photographs.

'It was extraordinary,' said Veret. 'She walked like a little soldier . . . and behind her, Monsieur Gitane, who was this rich blond gentleman who had a past – a very, very black past. He was behind in a long coat, with his two hands in the pockets. Stephanie wanted to look at the contact sheets of the pictures that had been taken of her and Mr Gitane when they were sunning themselves on some island. And I dare say she was very strict about the choice.'

Stephanie was well aware that photographs of the two of them together could fetch up to $100,000 on the open market. She stage-managed several photo opportunities: a friend would take pictures and then divide the proceeds with her.

'There was a series of long-lens paparazzi-type pictures of her and Mario at the swimming pool of the house they shared in Beverly Hills,' says the British-born Los Angeles-based photographer Alec Burn.

'When we saw the photographs everyone in the business knew something was not quite right. The quality was just too good and we realised that they were obviously, blatantly setup.'

Although Stephanie was already a *bona fide* pop star in Europe, she was determined to break into the American market. Soon after her arrival in Los Angeles the rock star Prince took her under his wing, offering to guide her career. She had first met Prince eighteen months earlier when he was filming *Under The Cherry Moon* in the south of France. Originally the Purple One had wanted to film in Monaco – but Rainier had refused, saying the X-rated rock star did not project the right image for respectable Monaco.

Minneapolis-born Prince – whose real name is Prince Roger Nelson – caused a sensation in 1981 when he released a song called 'Controversy', which asked, 'Am I black or am I white? Am I gay or am I straight?'

For his outrageous stage shows Prince dressed in a long raincoat, silk briefs and stockings, combining the provocative images of male and female, pimp and whore. He raunchily blended musical styles and in 1984 his hit album and movie *Purple Rain* took him mainstream, outselling Bruce Springsteen's latest album.

During the making of *Under The Cherry Moon*, Stephanie had hung around the film set and got to know Prince. He had suggested she sign with his manager Joseph Ruffalo. As rock's new Svengali, Prince had already successfully progressed the careers of Sheena Easton, Sheila E and Sinéad O'Connor; now Stephanie hoped he could perform the same magic for her. As Stephanie and Mario Oliver began planning a 'trial honeymoon', the diminutive pop star's publicity machine began leaking erroneous stories of a romance between the Prince of Pop and his Princess'.

But the Princess's real dream was to become a film star like her mother. She enrolled in a six-month drama course with Nina Foch, who was a contemporary of Grace Kelly's.

'I saw her occasionally during this time,' said Judy Balaban Quine. 'She was trying to make her career. It was interesting how Stephanie had come to LA after having great success with the album in Europe and she was now trying to make a career in music here – which was logical. But she also wanted to study acting and that was the most important thing for her.'

As with everything else she did, the Princess started at the top. She was immediately offered a guest-starring role as a fashion designer in the top-rated TV show *Miami Vice*; the show's producers even agreed to play her latest single on the show to promote it.

In March Stephanie and Mario Oliver declared their love for each other by renting a $10,000 a month mansion in Benedict Canyon, shared with Oliver's friend Roger Lagneau and three dogs. They lived in the lap of luxury: there was a four-poster with mirrors on the canopy in their master bedroom, and a dining room that *Paris-Match* described as resembling the Versailles 'hall of mirrors redecorated by the Aztecs'.

Even for a Princess of Monaco, Stephanie was living well beyond her means. Though she still received a £30,000 annual stipend from Monaco – and though she had, in addition, her lucrative swimwear design business and singing career – these funds combined did not go very far in financing her and Oliver's expensive tastes.

'[My income is] much less than those of my father, sister Caroline, or brother Albert,' she would answer those who criticised her spending habits. 'In any case, this official income does not cover the huge cost of all the things I want to do.'

But having been brought up in the lap of luxury, never having had to worry about money, Stephanie had absolutely no idea of its value. She spent freely, as befitted a Princess of the gambling capital of the world.

'I'm a terrible spendthrift,' she admitted. 'But I regard money as pieces of paper which I hand over in exchange for something else. I buy on impulse; I make the most of my payments by credit card – and that's extremely dangerous. It's terrible to find your bank account's in the red – and it happens to me so often.'

In March, Mario Oliver told *Elle* magazine that he and Stephanie would soon be mailing our wedding invitations once they had agreed on a date for the ceremony. A week later an angry Rainier summoned his daughter to a family summit at the St James Club in Antigua. During a stormy showdown, during which Stephanie kept provocatively referring to Mario as 'my husband', Rainier threatened to take away her title. He also reminded her that, under Monaco law, no member of the ruling family could marry without the permission of the sovereign. Eventually Stephanie stormed out in a huff, catching the first plane back to Los Angeles.

'We had some hard and grave talks about all this – and especially as to Mario, and his behaviour,' Rainier wrote to Rupert Allan on his return to Monaco.

'It was painful but indispensable. She is warned, and of course is mad at me. In the doghouse am I. But it will pass over, I am sure.'

That summer Stephanie and Mario settled down to a life of relative domesticity, mostly staying at home and entertaining their small circle of French friends. On the rare occasions on which they did venture out, it was to Hollywood's fashionable restaurants – Silvio's or Prego – or to hang out at Oliver's Vertigo Club with regulars like Mickey Rourke, Rod Stewart and Eddie Murphy. The Princess – who had been rumoured to have a drinking problem – had stopped drinking vodka and now sipped only Coca-Cola.

During the day she was hard at work on her voice-training classes and acting lessons at the Nina Foch studio. Her classmates included Victoria Sellers, daughter of Peter Sellers and Britt Ekland, and Hugh Hefner's girlfriend, Carrie Leigh.

In those days the Monaco Princess was a common sight racing around town in her black VW Rabbit convertible, on her way to the health club or shopping in Beverly Hills. She favoured size four zippered minis and oversize sweaters; and she spent about $1,000 a month on Italian shirts and sweaters for Mario.

In August, Princess Stephanie returned alone to Monaco for the Red Cross Ball; Rainier had refused to allow Oliver to be her official escort. Asked by reporters whether her father disapproved of her live-in lover, Stephanie replied that Mario hadn't met Rainier yet 'because the opportunity has not presented itself'.

Realising that Rainier might never allow Oliver to set foot in Monaco, Stephanie bought a million-dollar house in nearby St Tropez as a defiant gesture to prove her independence. And Mario too launched a pre-emptive strike against the Monaco ruling family, giving an interview to the Spanish magazine *Hola!* in which he threatened to present Prince Rainier with an illegitimate grandchild.

'Stephanie believes having a baby would be a bond,' declared Oliver, adding that he was fed up with being labelled a 'gangster' and a 'pariah'.

'Security is what [Stephanie] needs most, and that's what I want to offer her.'

Oliver pointed the finger at Princess Caroline as the major stumbling-block to their marriage, claiming that she had turned Rainier against him.

'She is entirely opposed to me entering the family,' he said. 'She does everything to convince her father not to accept me. I would hate [to cause] a worldwide scandal similar to Edward VIII when he abdicated for Wallis Simpson.'

CHAPTER SIXTEEN

STRANGER
THAN
DYNASTY

IF PRINCESS GRACE could have returned to Monaco on the fifth anniversary of her death, she would have been appalled at what had happened to her family. As Prince Rainier and his children gathered for a private memorial mass in the Palace, Grace's presence was pervasive – but her influence was sadly lacking. Five years on, without their matriarch, the Grimaldis had fragmented into scandal and disgrace.

Almost every week there was an embarrassing new plot twist in the ongoing soap opera that Monaco had become. Would Princess Stephanie make good her promise to marry convicted sex-offender Mario Oliver? How stable was Caroline's marriage to Stefano Casiraghi, and were the stories about his Mafia connections true? When would Prince Albert find a suitable girlfriend, marry and take over the throne? Or would his ambitious elder sister Caroline win the battle and take control of the principality?

'Grace would have been terribly upset,' says Gwen Robyns, who was ostracised by the family after Grace's death for accepting a magazine assignment reporting her death. 'She tried to prevent scandal at any cost. It just all fell apart without her.'

As Prince Rainier approached his sixty-fifth birthday he finally acknowledged that he would never remarry. Many Monégasques now expected him to abdicate in favour of Albert, but there was a growing suspicion that the Prince did not have the necessary qualities to rule Monaco and that he should step aside in favour of his more statesman-like sister, Caroline.

As he neared thirty, Albert was quite happy to postpone the responsibilities of rule for as long as possible.

'[The delay is] giving him a little more time to be independent,' his cousin Christine de Massy tactfully explained. 'Once he takes over, any semblance of freedom comes to an end.'

Although his hairline had noticeably receded, Prince Albert was still considered to be one of the world's most eligible bachelors. He always carried a French button badge with a slogan which translated as: 'Being a Bachelor is Fun'. In the last few years his name had been linked to dozens of women. Prince Rainier took a fatherly pride in his son's amorous activities, delighted that virile Grimaldi blood was coursing through his veins.

'He's a very wonderful young man and a super ambassador for the principality,' Rainier wrote to Rupert Allan; 'as he covers, may I say, all fields of activities, including the feminine one.'

Albert's friend Cassiana Elwes said to be seen having fun was a vital part of the Prince's job.

'I don't think it hurts in any way for Albert to project a glamorous existence,' said Elwes.

But all that changed when the Prince was hit by the first of several paternity suits. An alleged one-night stand in Munich in 1986 with a West German topless model Bea Fieldler, who claimed 'he tore my panties off with his teeth', had resulted – or so she said – in a son: Daniel.

In a 1991 interview with veteran English journalist George Clare in her home town of Witten, Germany, Fieldler said she first met Prince Albert when he walked into her restaurant in Ibiza with his bodyguards and struck up a conversation.

'He told me I reminded him of his mother Princess Grace,' said Fieldler. 'It was the ultimate compliment.'

For the next two weeks the couple saw each other every day, taking long walks and kissing, but they never had the opportunity to go further as Albert did not want his friends to find out about the relationship. When Albert left the island he invited Fieldler to meet him a few weeks later in Germany.

Albert soon sent word that he would wait for Bea in Munich's exclusive P-One nightclub; Fieldler put on her sexiest dress and arrived early.

'He came down from the VIP bar to greet me and I knew at that moment we would be lovers,' she recalled.

After an hour of dancing they went back to Bea's hotel room where the Prince made his move. But just as they were about to undress Bea heard a noise outside her hotel door; when she went to investigate she discovered two of Albert's bodyguards listening at the keyhole.

'He looked really embarrassed but the guards seemed to find the whole thing amusing,' said Fieldler.

After the guards had left Bea says she let the Prince lead her back to bed.

'It was obvious I was not the first girl in his life,' said Bea. 'I wouldn't say Albert was a memorable lover, but he certainly had stamina.'

Nine months later she gave birth to a son and named Prince Albert as the father. The Prince denied the allegation but when she applied for child support he was ordered by a German court to take a blood test.

'Daniel has the same eyes, ears and colouring as Albert,' said Bea. 'He is the only one who *could* be the father.'

The matter was finally resolved in 1992 when Prince Albert agreed to take a blood test – which proved he was not the father of Bea Fieldler's child.

Perhaps even more damaging to the six-foot Prince were the persistent suggestions that he was gay; that the procession of beautiful women he was photographed with were merely a publicity smokescreen. Although the hurtful allegations had never been proven, Albert was upset and annoyed by them.

'I was hurt at first,' Prince Albert said candidly. 'It's not pleasant for anyone to question your maleness. But now I just laugh at it. I mean, the people that are important to me know that I have never even been close to that, so I have no problems. I mean, I do have problems with it, but I just don't pay attention.'

There was a general sigh of relief when the Prince turned up at the Red Cross Ball on the wholesome arm of the 1984 Olympic swimming gold medallist Mary Wayte. The blonde twenty-two-year-old from Mercer Island, Washington State, had met Albert at a Monaco swimming competition two years earlier and had become a regular companion. There was speculation that they might marry after a Seattle newspaper ran a picture of her and Albert captioned, 'Queen of the Water – and Princess of Monaco.'

When Mary's father, an executive at Boeing Aircraft, was asked about the rumours he added fuel to the fire:

'I can easily see her being the Princess of Monaco. I think it's great, as long as she's happy.'

The blue-eyed blonde spent a year with Albert before she ended the relationship, deciding she couldn't handle the pressure of dating such a public person.

'I think he was really in love with her,' a friend of the Prince's later told the *Washington Post*.

It was through his relationship with Wayte that the Prince began his ongoing involvement with the Olympic movement and founded the Monaco Bobsled Team. When the Prince saw bobsled racing for the first time at the 1980 Winter Olympics in Lake Placid he was immediately smitten.

'I looked at the track and thought, "Maybe I have to try that,"' he recalled.

But it was another four years before he took his first ride down a course in St Moritz. After that, he was hooked. Returning to Monaco he set up a bobsled team and began holding tryouts, whittling down the male applicants, athletes between the ages of twenty and forty, to about 200. Of those, only twenty had the potential to reach Olympic standard. Prince Albert's final selection for his six-man national team included a hotel management student, a casino dealer and a commerce department official.

In 1985 Albert was elected to the International Olympics Committee as its youngest member and only active Olympian. Following in the footsteps of his grandfather Jack Kelly, who won three gold medals for the US in the single sculls, Albert and his team managed to qualify for the 1988 Winter Olympics in Calgary.

His delighted father wrote to Rupert Allan, adding a cautionary note: 'Albert's really getting into the affairs and he's travelling quite a lot for the International Olympic Committee etc. He has, thank God, slowed down with girl-chasing . . . which is good.'

It was one of the proudest moments of the Prince's life when he led his team at the opening ceremonies at the Calgary Winter Olympics. Albert insisted on being treated like any other athlete and stayed in the Olympic Village with his team-mates.

'We call him Big Al,' said Mike Aljoe, a brakesman for the US Bobsled Team. 'We hit on him and stuff. We throw him around. He's a good guy.'

In his sky-blue Monaco track suit he blended in with his team-mates, carrying his own gear bag – and roll of toilet paper.

'You never know what you're going to find in some of these

places,' he said of the toilet paper. 'But I want the full Olympic experience, so I have to live in the village.'

Although the Prince's team managed to finish a respectable twenty-fifth in a field of forty-one, he was disappointed, immediately pledging to train harder and return for the next Olympics.

'I'm always hard on myself,' said Albert as he came off his fourth and final run. 'I like to do better and better.'

As Albert spent more and more time abroad on Olympic business, the power struggle between him and his sister intensified, particularly when a self-styled group of Caroline followers, the 'Monarchist Circle of Monaco' petitioned Prince Rainier to amend the constitution in her favour.

Many Monégasques were concerned that when Prince Rainier turned sixty-five in a few months' time he might retire and hand over power to his sports-mad son. The principality was thriving under Rainier, who had become known as 'The Boss' and was seen as having the Midas touch: affluent Monégasques wanted to make sure it stayed that way.

'If earthly paradise exists it's here in Monaco,' influential Monégasque restaurateur Francis Muschietto told *McCall's* magazine.

'We are aware that we owe this to our monarch, Prince Rainier – but some say he is tired and considering abdication, which would be in favour of his son, Albert, according to our constitution. And they fear that Albert might not be up to the task. Prince Rainier has spoiled us. In forty years he has never made an error, either in his private or public life. Some of my fellow citizens worry that Prince Albert is seen a little too often with girls who change all the time and who are not always – how can I say? princess-like.

'They also think that he spends too much time on sports. I personally see nothing to object to in his eternal student life, but it has made the majority of us accustomed to thinking of him as the country's child rather than the country's father – as we all think of Prince Rainier.'

His views represented a growing feeling among Monégasques that the naturally regal and self-confident Caroline would make a more appropriate ruler than the immature Albert.

'Some fellow citizens are wondering whether it wouldn't be wise to change our constitution to allow her to ascend to the throne,' said Muschietto.

In early 1989 Rainier moved quickly and decisively to quell Albert's detractors by making his official position perfectly clear. His minister of state, Jean Ausseil, issued an official statement saying that there was no possibility of changing the constitution and that Albert was the unequivocal heir.

'When I have the impression that he's well prepared to succeed me, I'll tell him,' Rainier told the French newspaper, *Figaro*. 'But I don't want to give any date for this event, because then life speeds up and becomes full of risks.'

Prince Rainier also denied that there was any 'feud' between Caroline and Albert: 'Recently it was written that Princess Caroline hoped to supplant her brother as the head of the [principality]. This is ridiculous and completely without foundation.'

And Albert, too, felt compelled to tell *Newsday*'s columnist James Revson during a visit to New York: 'I'm much more comfortable with responsibility. I don't like to party as much as I used to.'

However, there was no question that Princess Caroline and Stefano Casiraghi were now actively promoting themselves as the *responsible* members of the Grimaldi family. Caroline came out of the shadows to start granting interviews to the press in order to enhance her position – but she was always careful to lay down ground rules banning any questions about her wayward sister Stephanie, her application for marriage annulment and the death of her mother.

She also co-operated with her close friend, fashion designer Karl Lagerfeld, on an intimate photo essay showing her both at home informally with her family and carrying out her official duties. The pictures went around the world and were a triumph of public relations.

'Princess Caroline is in Control,' said another profile of the Princess in *European Travel & Life*. 'Protector of Monaco's mystique, passionate patron of the arts, devoted wife and mother – she's nothing if not a woman of her times,' it declared.

In a rare interview the immaculately-groomed and ambitious Casiraghi even suggested the following scenario for Caroline's succession to the throne:

'If Prince Albert failed to succeed Prince Rainier for some reason, then my wife would rule the principality and I would become Prince Stefano of Monaco.'

For a brief period in the late 1980s, Caroline and Stefano symbolised a new age in Monaco. There was a massive economic boom with the arrival of rich Italian businessmen from the industrial heartland of Turin and Milan; there was also an unprecedented building bonanza that seemed to be making just about everyone in Monaco rich. Prince Rainier's life-long dream to take Monaco's dependence away 'from the bad luck of gamblers' was nearing fulfilment. And, for a brief period, anything seemed possible.

Casiraghi and his Italian partners in the firm Engenco-Pastor played a key role in Monaco's intensive building programme. In 1988 the company – of which Casiraghi was the main shareholder – had a huge annual turnover.

Casiraghi had absolutely no qualms about using his position as Caroline's husband to his advantage. 'The final result is the only thing that really matters,' he would declare in 1989.

But many questioned where Casiraghi's money came from as he lavished millions of dollars on his passion for powerboat racing. In 1989 he became world champion. Some Monégasques wondered about the real identity of his 'dubious' Italian business partners; there were even rumours of Mafia involvement.

'There was certainly an unpleasant odour coming off some of his business associations,' said *Daily Express* diarist Ross Benson. 'They were property and things – the kind of area that, if you had a lot of money and you were trying to wash it clean, you'd resort to.'

In April 1988 the *National Enquirer* reported that four of Stefano's closest associates had been arrested. Antonio Barca, Princess Caroline and Stefano's long-time chauffeur and friend, was charged by Italian police with being a member of an international drug-smuggling operation. Daniel Gasparri – the second in command at Casiraghi's Monaco real estate company – was under house arrest in Italy, charged with falsely declaring bankruptcy and cheating investors in one of his companies.

Another former partner in two of Stefano's Italian companies, Giancarlo Miorin, was about to stand trial for failing to pay $15 million in customs duties to the Italian government. A number of Stephano's friends and business associates were also arrested around this time in connection with several alleged illegal activities.

In September Rainier was forced to take tough action after the government-owned SBM was tainted by scandal; it was revealed that it had made investments through a near-bankrupt Paris brokerage and had lost some $2.5 million. The Prince was furious at what he called the 'laxness and incompetence' of the SBM and he ordered the firing of two top SBM officers and a complete overhaul of the principality's oldest and biggest company.

'All right, this coast will always attract some shady people – a sunny place for shady people,' conceded the Prince, paraphrasing the often-quoted Somerset Maugham phrase. 'What has come out of this affair is that there is a complete disorganisation of the whole structure of the SBM. It grew too much and had this silly conception of having to run everything.'

By the following June, as Prince Rainier celebrated forty years at the helm of Monaco, the SBM had already become a leaner, meaner and more effective organisation. And by princely decree SBM casino income could no longer exceed four per cent of the state budget.

The 'building prince' had irreversibly transformed Monaco during his time in office; it was now a million miles away from the tin-pot principality he had inherited. And although it didn't exert any meaningful power on the world stage, it was no longer an entirely obscure principality such as Liechtenstein or San Marino.

'When I was young, I was always annoyed by the fact that we were not taken seriously,' Rainier told Prince Michael of Greece in an interview for *You* magazine to mark the fortieth anniversary of his reign. 'My country was called the Monaco of Offenbach, of operetta, a fiscal paradise of casinos. It was said that the principality lived off those poor people who were ruined and committed suicide by throwing themselves under a train or jumping off a rock.

'Bit by bit, I wanted to re-establish the prestige of the principality and to change its reputation from one of Sodom and Gomorra. I wanted to prove that Monaco was a country in which one could certainly have fun, but where people also worked.'

His Serene Highness also condemned the constant barrage of publicity about his children, saying that it deflected attention from Monaco's more serious achievements. Although Princess Stephanie no longer lived in Monaco, Rainier pointed out that she remained responsible for her eponymous Youth Centre and the International Festivals of Circus and Magic. He also felt the press coverage of Albert and Caroline and their supposed feud was frivolous and irrelevant.

'They say he's chasing such and such a girl,' complained the Prince. 'They'd rather go into a four-page spread of Caroline changing her bathing suite on a motorboat taken with a long-range lens. To my mind it's not very interesting.'

Recently the ruling family have gone on the offensive to counter bad press and intrusive paparazzi; Rainier and Caroline have both successfully sued European magazines and it's not unusual to see half the front page of a French magazine blacked out by a court order.

'When you read certain articles that are derogatory or insulting and downright untrue you can't let these sort of things go by,' said Prince Albert. 'So that's why we've been more and more active in the last few years in legal procedures toward the press.'

But many businessmen in Monaco quietly applauded the Grimaldi children's romantic escapades in the 1980s, considering the headlines they generated good for business. The bottom line was that the children were highly effective marketing agents, maintaining Monaco's high profile. Besides, it was felt, scandals helped to bring in the tourists — which filled everyone's pockets.

Although the tourists might flock to the more glamorous Belle Époque Casino or Jimmy'z, those in the know considered the real hub of Monaco to be a shabby Tex-Mex saloon called Le Texan. Tucked away in a back street in the old port district next to Monte-Carlo's Ferrari dealership, Le Texan had started life as an Italian pizzeria. It was bought in the mid-1980s by Princess Grace's recently widowed friend Jeanne Kelly van Remoortel ('Kelly'), who had always dreamed of starting a restaurant in Monaco. But with no catering experience she soon ran into difficulties and sent for her children, Michael and Kate Powers, who were now living in Texas, running a chain of family-owned steak houses.

They immediately returned to Monaco, where they had grown up, and gave the shabby pizzeria a facelift, transforming it into a Tex-Mex bar and restaurant. Prince Rainier himself added the final touch by suggesting the name: Le Texan.

As soon as Le Texan opened its doors, in Grand Prix week 1988, it was a hit. It soon became the favoured hangout of the Grimaldis, who could relax there, away from prying eyes. On one particular night Prince Albert even hand-carved his Texan nickname – 'Al-Bob' – into the giant wooden sculpture of the Battle of the Alamo hanging behind the bar.

'Albert often comes down in his cowboy boots and jeans and has a few margaritas with me while we close the place,' says Michael Powers. 'It's not a fancy place by any stretch of the imagination. I call it shabby chic; it's shabby but there's chic people in it. It's almost become an institution in Monaco.'

Le Texan quickly revived Princess Grace's American-style barbecues, softball games and Fourth of July parties, all of which had been discontinued after her death. Prince Rainier, Albert and Caroline eagerly attended the first celebrity barbecue and gave it their official seal of approval.

'It was Grace's idea to have a Tex-Mex restaurant originally,' remembers Kelly.

'Grace always loved food and was very interested in it. She discovered Tex-Mex from her days living in California.'

American writer Robert Eringer arrived in Monaco in Summer 1988 for a year-long sabbatical and found himself drawn to Le Texan. Later he would immortalise the bar in his book *Monaco Cool*.

'You step inside, greeted by the piquant aroma of ham hock stewing in a crock of beans, and this Tex-Mex saloon is immediately as comfortable as your favourite pair of old jeans. For a couple of bucks you can linger over a bottle of Heineken, corn chips and salsa at the long Alamo Bar and watch the diverse cliques of Monaco mix it up: young international professionals here to transform the principality from an upper-crust community to *the* financial centre of Europe; the Monégasque establishment; royalty; the neighbourhood eccentrics. You see them all.

'I saw an elegant madam dump her twenty-grand mink coat on a stand near the door and disappear to a table round the back. And then, as a corpulent, fruity American expounded about Monaco's absence of crime, the [coat] stand, laden with Italian leather and furs, toppled over and mugged him.'

Most nights, when he was in town, Prince Albert could be found at Le Texan's Alamo Bar accompanied by his uncle, Louis de Polignac, the head of the SBM.

'Prince Albert, decked out in a cowboy shirt and blue jeans, was throwing back slammers with the boys while his eighty-year-old uncle, Prince Louis de Polignac, held court with strolling *mariachis*.

'Albert hangs out at Le Texan. His bodyguards, unequipped with dark glasses and wires sticking out their ears, hang there too: a couple of ordinary Pierres in sports dress. And then there's Shorty – always Shorty – rounding up girls too young for Roman Polanski.'

The man Eringer had nicknamed 'Shorty' had once been an Arizona public relations consultant; he had moved to Monaco while in the grip of a mid-life crisis, together with his wife and three stepdaughters. The wife had decided Monaco was a bad influence and had left with the children, but Shorty had stayed on.

The diminutive mustachioed man who nervously peered through wire-rimmed glasses had attempted to ingratiate himself with the Prince by trying to procure dates for him. Albert, always goodnatured, had played along, allowing him to become his sidekick. Suddenly Shorty was basking in the Prince's glory, rubbing shoulders with beautiful models, film stars, and professional athletes.

He also took it upon himself to become the Prince's personal pimp, casually dropping Albert's name to procure dates with the many young and beautiful female tourists who would never turn down the opportunity of meeting a real live prince.

'It was certainly not a case of Prince Albert appointing anybody to go out and find women for him,' explained Eringer. 'He was perfectly capable of drawing women himself. It was more that [Shorty] took it upon himself to ingratiate himself with the Prince by saying, "Guess what? I've lined us up two dates for tonight", or, "Look at those blondes over there, I'll go and sort it out."'

On one occasion Jeanne Kelly had to step in and ask Shorty to be more discreet when he was with Prince Albert.

'I'm a good influence on him,' Shorty had replied. 'I'm trying to get rid of the riff-raff around him. I take care of Albert.'

When it came to meeting women Prince Albert was anything but shy. Naturally chatty and gregarious, he would often strike up a conversation with a young blue-eyed blonde during his frequent visits to America. Then, after a couple of nights on the town, the Prince would politely suggest that, if ever she was in Monaco, she should look him up.

Robert Eringer witnessed what he describes as 'The Royal Destiny Phenomenon' at first hand.

'The girl quits her job,' he explains in *Monaco Cool*, 'blows her savings on a new wardrobe and arrives in the principality, expecting a romantic week with Prince Charming. Each one uniformly believes it is her *destiny* to tie the knot with a prince, become a princess and live happily-ever-after inside a fairytale. This is what she tells her friends; often the *National Enquirer* gets wind of her song and dance and proclaims an engagement, a 'world exclusive'. Sometimes it evolves into erotomania. The result is a letdown of royal proportions: she gets a few hours with the Prince, maybe a ride in his beamer, with all its fancy hi-tech doo-dahs, and a *few days* with Shorty.'

Over the years scores of women dreamed of becoming the next Princess Grace and settling down with Prince Albert in the pink Palace. But Albert himself is well aware of the unique qualities any prospective bride will need to be his Princess of Monaco. He is realistic; he does not want to make a disastrous mistake, like Prince Charles and Diana.

'I would love to have a wife and have kids,' the Prince said in 1997. 'But it will be a tremendous problem for her. The inevitable comparison to my mother will be there and she'd have to be a very strong woman to withstand these comparisons and these pressures, mainly put on by the press. It is going to be very, very difficult.'

His aunt Lizanne LeVine said Albert certainly had enough young women throwing themselves at him:

'He placed his mother on such a pedestal,' she said; 'he was mad for her. I said, "You're going to have trouble finding a girl like your mom." And he has. He has a little problem.'

Lizanne says that Albert was once deeply in love with a girl but the pressures of his position broke up the relationship.

'I once asked my son Chris, who is very close to Albert, if he had ever been involved with any lady who was special,' recalled Lizanne. 'Chris said, "There was a girl." But he refused to tell me a thing: he wouldn't gossip at all. Anyway, there was one that was very close.'

If the course of true love was not running smoothly for Prince Albert things were even rougher for his sister Stephanie. As part of her twenty-second birthday present Mario Oliver hired a plane and trailed a huge banner across the skies of Los Angeles saying: STEPH – WILL YOU MARRY ME? LOVE MARIO. Confident of success, Oliver had taken Stephanie to the beach to surprise her with the proposal; instead she had been embarrassed and humiliated.

In May, when the Princess flew into New York City for a Princess Grace Foundation USA benefit, Mario was nowhere to be seen. While she was in New York Stephanie went into the studio with songwriters Billy Steinberg and Tom Kelly – who had penned Madonna's breakthrough song 'Like a Virgin' – to record a dance track. Perhaps aware of her tinny voice and narrow range, the Princess was visibly nervous as she laid down her vocals.

'She's humbled by the music industry,' said Tom Kelly tactfully. 'She acts more like a nervous teenager than an arrogant princess.'

By June Stephanie had broken up with Mario Oliver, after the Frenchman demanded that she choose between him and her career.

'I decided on my career,' explained Stephanie at the time. 'My dad wasn't exactly thrilled about him – but then nobody was. And I can understand why. But I look at it this way: I did what I had to do and eventually realised it wasn't what I wanted, so I got out of it. I don't regret anything.'

But within a month the Princess was telling *Paris-Match* that she didn't know whether she could 'live without a man'. And then she moved in with Los Angeles-based record producer Ron Bloom, who had been hired by Sony Music to produce her first American album.

Jerry Greenberg, a producer at Sony, had signed Princess Stephanie to her first American record contract for a reported $1.5 million.

'The president of Sony at the time played me a demo tape of Stephanie and asked if I would consider putting her on this new label,' said Greenberg. 'So we entered into an agreement.'

With his shoulder-length hair, pot-belly and black leather jackets, thirty-seven-year-old Ron Bloom was a real departure for the fashionable Princess. She swapped her designer-label clothes for jeans and leather as she went into the studio with Bloom and started writing new songs for her album.

'Ron Bloom was very good-looking, very outgoing and very warm,' says Los Angeles columnist Belissa Cohen.

'He enjoyed immensely being around Stephanie. Being invited everywhere. Being the centre of attention.'

Stephanie and Bloom moved into a hotel room together as they started looking for a place of their own. The impetuous Princess had wanted to get a place immediately, but for once she found a man who was mature and sensible enough to take things slowly.

Bloom told her he wanted them to have "a real relationship," and didn't want them to rush things until she was ready. No one had ever treated her with such respect, she admitted later.

In September Stephanie and Bloom went suburban, buying a small wooden house for $200,000 in Toluca Canyon and settling down to shared domesticity. A charming market area in the San Fernando Valley, Toluca Canyon was very family-oriented and as far away from Hollywood glitz as you could possibly get. Stephanie and

Ron hired a couple to come in twice a week to do the housework and gardening, but the Princess was determined to do her own shopping and cooking. Princess Stephanie had reinvented herself once again; but this time, surprisingly, as the all-American housewife.

'There are certain parts of town where you'd think Stephanie would go settle,' said Judy Balaban Quine. 'She didn't go there at all. [Toluca Canyon] does not have any of the panache of the Hollywood highlife.'

Most nights Stephanie and Bloom would drive into town and do the rounds of the Los Angeles clubs, returning home in the early hours of the morning.

Stephanie had always had trouble getting up in the morning, beginning her day at midday and watching her favourite soap opera, *Days Of Our Lives*.

Most days the Princess would take vocal and acting classes, or go and audition for parts in movies. At that time there were so many offers pouring in from directors who wanted to add Grace Kelly's daughter to their project that she had to hire an agent to sift through them.

'My agent is tough,' explained Stephanie. 'She won't send me for anything if she isn't 100 per cent sure it's absolutely right for me.'

Over the following year the aspiring actress read for numerous parts; but somehow she never made the grade and was constantly turned down by casting agents. Acting, as her hard-working and ambitious mother would have been the first to tell her, was one profession you could not walk straight into at the top.

In November, Prince Rainier and his errant daughter had an emotional reconciliation when he visited Los Angeles for a Princess Grace Foundation gala dedicated to the memory of the late Cary Grant. One morning Rainier turned up at the Toluca Canyon house unannounced and armed with gifts, to be warmly greeted by a tearful Stephanie and her new boyfriend. A paparazzo waiting outside caught the moment of deep emotion when Stephanie hugged her father before they went into the house.

The Prince was quickly won over by the pony-tailed Bloom's charm and much impressed with his apparent sense of character. At last his beloved daughter had found a man he could relate to! The doting father walked around their new home, making a list of kitchen equipment – including a microwave – that he felt the couple needed. Then he dispatched an assistant to buy them from a nearby mall.

The next day Ron Bloom was summoned to a meeting with Prince Rainier and the Consul of Monaco to discuss his relationship with Princess Stephanie. And Bloom gave such a good account of himself and his intentions that the Prince gave him his blessing.

Rainier genuinely liked Bloom and appreciated his sense of family values. After her rift with her father, who had strongly disapproved of Oliver, it was Bloom who counselled her to repair the rift with Rainier. He told her that family was very important and steered her back into the Grimaldi fold.

Prince Rainier was so delighted by Stephanie's wholesome new lifestyle that he extended his US trip by five days so the two could get to know each other again. Each morning at 10.30 sharp a beaming Rainier would arrive from his hotel laden down with presents for his daughter. Then they would spend the day together reliving old times before meeting up with Ron Bloom for dinner. All too soon, however, the week came to an end; Ron Bloom drove the Prince to the airport while Stephanie waved her goodbyes.

Over the next few months Princess Stephanie became a common local sight as she shopped for clothes and groceries in the mall at Toluca Lake. As a rule she could go out in a pair of dark glasses with her bodyguard and remain unrecognised – which would have been impossible in Europe. The Princess – who had always been singled out as someone special – delighted in her new anonymity.

One afternoon British photographer Alec Burn's wife Kim was standing at the check-out in her local supermarket when she spotted

Princess Stephanie in front of her with an EPT (Early Pregnancy Test) kit in her basket. She immediately telephoned her husband, who said he'd be right over to try and get a photograph.

The Princess was still in the supermarket when Burn arrived. He quickly set up outside with a long lens focused on the supermarket exit.

'Sure enough, out comes Stephanie, all alone with a bag on her shoulder,' says Burn. 'She jumps into her Cherokee jeep and drives off.'

As he set off in pursuit, Burn ran her numberplates through a police contact and found the jeep had been leased to her record company. But within five minutes she'd spotted Burn and tried to lose him by back-doubling around the block. The photographer stayed with her, planning his strategy in order to get a saleable photograph out of the encounter.

'I figure there's no chance of getting any kind of candid, unusual pictures,' he explained. 'So sure enough at the next stop sign I see her door open. I think. "Oh, okay, it could be interesting". She might want to get out and do a confrontation or something. But the next thing is I see a hand come out and she just slips me the finger.'

Burn's shots of the irate Princess sold well and appeared in tabloid magazines all over Europe and America.

Although, to the Princess's relief, she hadn't been pregnant with Ron Bloom's baby, by the end of the year there were reports that the couple were planning a summer wedding in Monte-Carlo. It was said that Prince Rainier would like the Jewish-born Bloom to convert to Catholicism, although all he would in fact need to enable the marriage to go ahead was a letter of dispensation from the Archbishop of Monaco and a declaration from Stephanie that her children would be brought up as Catholics.

The rumours of marriage seemed substantiated in February

1989, when Ron Bloom flew to Monaco with the Princess and sat with the Grimaldis at the annual Monte-Carlo Circus Festival. Since their meeting in Los Angeles three months earlier, Bloom and Rainier had often spoken on the telephone. At one point, when Stephanie had become sick, refusing to slow down and take it easy, Bloom had asked her father to talk some sense into his daughter; and he had.

During the trip to Monaco, Bloom was feted like a future member of the family. He was a regular guest at the Palace.

In June, Ron Bloom was back in Monaco for the celebrations to mark Prince Rainier's forty-year reign. But during his visit the London tabloid *Sunday Mirror* printed a series of explicit shots of Princess Stephanie and Bloom together in their backyard. The photographs, taken a year earlier by Los Angeles paparazzi, caused a sensation when they were published.

Prince Rainier was livid: once again his daughter had managed to embarrass him and mar the pomp and ceremony of his forty years in power. But the person he blamed most was Ron Bloom, whom he had treated as a future son-in-law. The Prince's displeasure made itself felt; Bloom was noticeably absent at the Monte-Carlo Sporting Club's black-tie gala honouring Rainier.

Within six months, depressed about her failure to make it either as a singer or as an actress, Princess Stephanie walked out on Bloom and returned to Europe. She had grown tired of Los Angeles; the city was no longer in awe of the spoilt Monaco Princess who lacked her mother's class and talent.

The final humiliation for the fashion-designing Princess – who now had her own perfume named 'Stephanie' – came when she topped Mr Blackwell's annual worst-dressed list.

'Her royal unisex wardrobe entitles her to use either bathroom,' said a scathing Mr Blackwell, the Hollywood arbiter of bad taste.

'Well, I'm not surprised that Stephanie was on Mr Blackwell's worst-dressed list,' said Belissa Cohen; 'because although she was a beautiful girl and she had all the money in the world, she did not have any style. She wore expensive clothes with no personality.'

CHAPTER SEVENTEEN

CURSE OF THE GRIMALDIS

JEAN-YVES LEFUR had a silver tongue. With his dark piercing eyes and easy manner, the twenty-six-year-old Frenchman had an air of mystery that had stolen the heart of many a young girl. And when Princess Stephanie first met him in September 1989, while staying at a friend's country home outside Paris, she was bowled over.

'It was love at first sight,' the twenty-five-year-old Princess declared to *Paris-Match*. 'My heart is now in Paris.'

Lefur's past seemed too good to be true. He claimed to be the son of a fabulously wealthy architect; Jean-Yves, by the age of eighteen, had apparently become a successful tennis professional before quitting the game to start his own Paris modelling agency. He span a fabulous tale of how he had moved from the world of modelling to real estate when he was only twenty-four and claimed ownership of several prime buildings in the centre of Paris.

But the truth was far more mundane. After dropping out of school Lefur trained as a tennis teacher but gave it up for lack of talent. For a while he drifted around different apartments in Paris, living on the generosity of friends.

In his early twenties his good looks and immaculate grooming helped him become a fixture around the clubs of Paris. Through his connections he became a chauffeur for a top modelling agency, escorting beautiful women around the clubs.

He soon acquired a new set of wealthy playboy friends who accepted him into their circle in exchange for an introduction to his model acquaintances. Lefur was soon living the life of a wealthy playboy himself, financed by his new friends; he enjoyed hanging around with leading members of the jet set such as Thierry Roussel, the millionaire ex-husband of Christina Onassis.

After weaving his magic on Paris society, he set his sights on Princess Stephanie. Lefur, who was almost broke, began courting her in earnest.

'I succumbed to her charm,' he said at the time, adding that he was attracted to Stephanie's 'femininity, her sensitivity, her need for affection.'

The gullible Princess spent Christmas with Lefur in the Caribbean. In February she took him on the annual Grimaldi family skiing holiday to St Moritz.

Prince Rainier too was impressed by the young Frenchman's character and by April Lefur was publicly given the public seal of approval when he appeared between Prince Rainier and Prince Albert in the Royal Box at the Monte Carlo Festival of Music.

On April 21 the happy couple announced their engagement to eighty friends and relatives at Le Telegraph restaurant in Paris. Toasting each other with champagne and caviar, Stephanie and Lefur declared their undying love for each other.

'I've never been engaged before,' the Princess gushed to *Hello* magazine as she spoke of her plans to be a June bride in Monaco. 'This has been the first time – the real one, the best.'

But within weeks their relationship was in tatters. Soon after Stephanie showed her commitment to Lefur by removing a tattoo bearing ex-lover Mario Oliver's name from her bottom, her fiancé's past came back to haunt him.

First there was the damaging story in a French magazine that he had served five weeks in jail in 1985 for theft and fraud. Then it was alleged that, instead of being a fabulously-rich architect, Lefur's father was actually a butcher's-equipment salesman whose business had collapsed.

By July, Lefur had left Monaco in disgrace. But it didn't take the irrepressible Princess Stephanie long to find a new love in the shape of German ice-hockey star Roger Kluh.

'She is very anxious when it comes to new relationships,' Kluh told an English journalist. 'I want to show Stephanie that there are other things in life than discos and false friends, but she is scared of new disappointments.'

In September 1990, Princess Caroline flew to Philadelphia with Stefano Casiraghi and their three children to visit the Kelly family. It would be the Kelly's first opportunity to see Caroline's new baby, Pierre.

The years had been cruel to the Kellys of Henry Avenue, who had once had the world by the tail. Ma Kelly had suffered a debilitating stroke in 1975, but had survived until January 1990; because of the effects of the stroke she never knew of the deaths of her daughter Grace and son Kell, who suffered a heart attack in March 1985 while out jogging. Peggy, the eldest of the Kelly children, was an alcoholic; she had just a year left to live.

'Unfortunately Grace was the first of many that went,' said Lizanne Kelly LeVine, now the last surviving member of her generation. 'It's been very hard for me.'

After the family reunion in Philadelphia the Casiraghis travelled to New York to meet up with Prince Rainier, Albert and Stephanie for the fifth Annual Princess Grace Foundation, USA fundraiser. The cream of New York society attended the event, held on the *Crown Princess* moored on the Hudson River. And it provided a rare opportunity to see Caroline and Casiraghi carry out an official engagement together, greeting the 650 guests, and looking very much like the First Couple of Monaco.

A week later Stefano was back in Monaco to defend his world powerboat title along with his close friend and co-pilot, Patrice Innocenti. A year earlier Caroline and her Aunt Lizanne had watched the intrepid Italian win his first world championship in Atlantic City, New Jersey.

'I watched that and there was a man killed in one of those boats,' recalled Lizanne. 'And I said, "Oh, goodness Caroline, can't you tell him not to do that?" And she said, "Yeah, I think he's going to stop."'

That summer Stefano and Caroline celebrated his thirtieth birthday by flying fifty of their friends to Marrakech. Stefano had finally agreed to give up racing, promising Caroline he would retire after defending his world championship for the last time. Stefano had recently bought a $100,000 helicopter as a next new toy and was in the process of learning to fly.

'He was no hothead, but he loved to take risks,' said close friend Franco Bartolino.

It was a dull, overcast Wednesday morning as Stefano Casiraghi brought his three children to the dock and kissed them goodbye. Caroline had left the night before for Paris, having watched her husband compete in the first day of trials for the World Offshore Championship.

When Stefano and his pilot Patrice Innocenti boarded their forty-foot red, white and orange catamaran, *Pinot di Pinot*, they were firm favourites to retain the championship. Prince Rainier and Stefano's parents Giancarlo and Fernanda Casiraghi, who were watching from another boat, saw Stefano and Innocenti race off at 11 AM at the start of the ninety-seven-mile race. The conditions were windy – but far calmer than they had been a couple of days earlier at the race trials.

'We were heading out to sea,' Innocenti would later recall.

'I remember looking at the speed – we were travelling at about 100 mph. I asked Stefano to test the radio and he said it was fine. We were quite relaxed – everything was going well and there were no signs of anything likely to go wrong.

'Then, in a fraction of a second, I felt the boat rising up and flipping over. The wind blew on the port side and the waves therefore followed in that direction, so if we had been the victims of a wave, the boat would have been lifted to the right. There's no doubt about that. I was seated on the right and Stefano on the left. The boat was raised up two or three metres, flipped over and then hit the sea on Stefano's side. I felt the thud – it was tremendous. Poor Stefano.'

Casiraghi, who was wearing a seatbelt, took the full impact of the crash. He was killed instantly.

The race was immediately halted as emergency crews convened on the crash site to save Innocenti. As the accident had happened so far away from shore Prince Rainier didn't see it and he only knew something was wrong when rescue helicopters flew overhead. The Prince, who returned to the Palace, was initially informed that his son–in–law was unhurt. But an hour later a race official telephoned with the tragic news. On hearing that his son–in–law was dead at thirty the Prince began screaming – and then broke down in tears.

Princess Caroline was having her hair cut at Carita's salon in Paris when her world collapsed for the second time in eight years. A distressed Rainier had called his French industrialist friend Jean-Paul Scarpita, who managed to reach the Princess's car phone and give the sad news to her chauffeur Tony. He was so shocked that he was almost speechless when he burst into the hair salon.

'Madame must return to Monaco,' he stammered. Caroline knew immediately that something dreadful had happened. She rushed out of the salon and telephoned Scarpita, who broke the news of her husband's death. The distraught Princess left immediately for Monaco, where she went straight to the funeral home to view her husband's body, still clad in his red and white racing suit. Prince Rainier himself broke the news of Stefano's death to Caroline's three young children and Casiraghi's father, Giancarlo.

'When I saw Prince Rainier, who was visibly troubled, I guessed the truth,' recalled Giancarlo.

'"Stefano is dead," the Prince told me, his voice choked with tears. "I wanted to give you the terrible news myself, because I looked on Stefano as a son, and only I could understand your pain." We looked at each other, and at that moment we were two fathers suffering together.'

As thousands of Monégasques filed past Casiraghi's body where it lay in the mortuary, Stefano's older brother, Marco Casiraghi, called for a murder investigation. Only a few weeks earlier, Stefano had told friends that he had received death threats; he had recently taken the precaution of having his Mercedes bulletproofed.

'Stefano had many enemies,' said Patrice Innocenti, who was hospitalised with injuries received in the crash.

'Some of them drank to his death with champagne that day in Monte-Carlo.'

At the time of his death Casiraghi had built up a massive fortune from successful business ventures and his construction companies. He had a half-share in a real estate company that owned 3,000 apartments in Monaco and he was in the process of building a $160 million housing complex in the principality.

Many people in Monaco believed Stefano had been assassinated by the Mafia for attempting to sever his relationship with them. Initially, it was said, he had been happy to use their money to finance his businesses; but as he had become more successful he had assumed a new air of respectability, and turned his back on them.

Three days after his death Stefano Casiraghi was buried at Monaco's St Nicholas' Cathedral. For the second time in almost exactly eight years the Grimaldi family knelt in mourning on the front row of the

Cathedral for a funeral mass. At Princess Grace's funeral it had been Caroline who had supported her faltering father; now it was the other way around.

Clutching a white handkerchief against her plain black widow's dress, the Princess was numb with shock as Rainier helped her climb the fifteen cathedral steps. She looked pale and gaunt, her swollen eyes hidden behind dark glasses and a black mantilla. She seemed oblivious of the 1,600 mourners made up of the rich and famous of European society, including ambassadors and politicians, as she stared at her dead husband's mahogany coffin; slowly shaking her head as if in stunned disbelief. Then she placed a small bouquet of flowers on the casket and joined the rest of her family in the front row.

'The brutality of his death adds to our pain,' said Monaco's Archbishop Joseph Sardou, who had baptised each of the couple's three children. Turning toward Caroline, he told the weeping Princess that her children would have 'a double need for you now'.

After Archbishop Sardou delivered the Requiem Mass, Stefano's coffin was carried by a solemn guard of honour to a private chapel, where he was buried in the red and white racing suit he was so proud of.

Soon afterwards the Mafia left the Grimaldis in no doubt that they had been responsible for Casiraghi's death when they issued a macabre warning.

'There was a disturbing incident,' said *Nice-Matin's* Roger Louis Bainchini. 'During the night unknown individuals – who have never been arrested – entered the chapel where Casiraghi was buried. They lifted the tombstone and stood the coffin upright.

'According to Mafia experts, the coffin was deliberately left in this upright position as a warning from the Mafia to the Grimaldis that they wanted back the anonymous shares they had given to Casiraghi.'

★ ★ ★

Six weeks later, Prince Rainier cancelled all celebrations for Monaco's National Day on November 19, with the exception of a Holy Mass at the Cathedral. Making her first public appearance since the funeral, Princess Caroline was the picture of devastation. Since her husband's death, the Princess had been inconsolable, trying desperately to come to terms with this latest tragedy.

During the fifty-minute mass, the Princess repeatedly broke down in uncontrollable tears. She had to be helped out of the Cathedral and into a waiting Mercedes by Prince Albert.

Two weeks earlier Caroline had made the sad journey to Stefano's Italian home town of Fino Mornasco. She joined Stefano's friends and family at the unveiling of a memorial plaque at Sanctus Stephanus Church. It read: 'To Stefano. Ill-Fated Champion in Sport and Life.'

'It's unfathomable what Caroline's gone through,' said Judy Balaban Quine. 'How can anyone cope? And all of it again, on the great public stage.'

Each day, shrouded in her black widow's weeds, Caroline would leave her Clos Saint-Pierre home for the short walk across the Rock to the Cathedral where she would visit her dead husband's tomb and pray. When things become too overwhelming, Caroline would take her children to Roc Agel for some peace and solitude.

'They gave me strength because they relied on me,' the Princess would recall later of this dark time.

'Strength comes when you are in a very narrow alley and have no way of turning back, I think. It's circumstances.'

The tragedy reunited the Grimaldis. For the first time since Grace's death the family seemed to find comfort in being with each other. Even Princess Stephanie rallied round to the sister to whom she had never been particularly close. Rising to the occasion, Stephanie moved into Caroline's house to help her take care of the children. She walked six-year-old Andrea to and from school. She also put her singing career on hold and tried to take the strain off Caroline by fulfilling many of her official engagements in Monaco.

'My sister needed me,' recalled Stephanie. 'She was devastated. When you have three young children you have to keep going for their sake and she has been marvellous.'

There were reports that Caroline was on around-the-clock medication, and chain-smoking six packs of Winstons a day. As the Princess retreated from public life the principality erected a fortress of silence to shield her from the world.

That Christmas Monaco's official card featured a simple photograph of a decorated tree in the palace courtyard instead of the traditional Grimaldi family portrait. It was a mark of respect that spoke volumes.

'Tragedy, tragedy, tragedy,' said the Countess of Lombardy, who received the card. 'A lot of people in Monaco believe the Grimaldi family is cursed – but oh, how we pity them!'

On Christmas Day, as the rest of the world anxiously watched the Gulf War develop in Iraq, Caroline and the entire Grimaldi family flew to Jamaica to stay at the luxury Half Moon resort outside Montego Bay. Once there, they were joined by the Princess's former boyfriend Robertino Rossellini, who had so sensitively helped her cope with the death of her mother.

When the official mourning period ended in early January 1991, Princess Caroline showed no signs of returning to normal. After a brief skiing trip to the Austrian resort of St Anton with two girlfriends, Caroline went back to Monaco to continue the grieving process.

She remained in seclusion, failing to appear at official functions; her grief cast a dark shadow over Monaco. When she finally made two brief public appearances, at the Sainte Dévote Festival and her son Andrea's first violin recital, Caroline still wore deepest black. She had cut her long hair into a severe bob and had lost so much weight she looked gaunt.

To make matters even worse she had to deal with the enormous debts that Casiraghi's Monaco companies owed investors who were now demanding their money. In early March she had to choose between selling the companies – which employed 520 Monégasques – at a loss, or trying to make a success of them.

On the advice of Robertino Rossellini, Caroline pledged some of the jewellery and art her mother had left her against her debts.

By April Caroline's misery had so affected the principality that Monégasques wondered if their beloved Princess would ever smile again. Therefore, it came as something of a shock when the grieving widow left Monaco in May and moved with her children to Provence, prior to installing a new man in her life.

Princess Caroline first met rugged French actor Vincent Lindon the previous summer, only four months before her husband's accident, at a literary luncheon in Paris. Caroline and Lindon, who found themselves sitting next to each other, had struck up a conversation.

The unconventionally handsome actor was totally different from anyone Caroline had ever encountered. He had a pronounced nervous tic; he seemed to be in a constant state of agitation and hardly ever smiled. Although, at twenty-nine, he was five years younger than the Princess, he looked far older than his age.

After that lunch they agreed to meet the following day to see Lindon's latest film. After spending an enjoyable few hours together, they agreed to keep in touch after Caroline returned to Monaco.

Ironically, it would be Casiraghi's death that would actually bring them together again. In the spring of 1991 Caroline had to go to Paris and telephoned Lindon on the spur of the moment; the recovering widow found the actor sympathetic and easy to talk to and they became friends. The Princess felt it was therapeutic for her to have someone outside her family and close circle of friends in whom she could confide.

While Caroline and Lindon were on a short trip to visit Inès de la Fressange – the former Chanel model who was the Princess's closest friend – they spotted a delightful seventeenth-century farmhouse in the tiny village of St Remy de Provence. The Princess began renting it as a sanctuary for herself and her children but before long she signed a ten-year lease and decided to move her family away from Monaco for good. She hoped the move would help them escape the public pressures of being Grimaldis.

'My children really hate the press,' said the Princess. 'They see them as the bad guys.'

Returning to Monaco temporarily, Caroline sold off most of Casiraghi's possessions, believing it would help her progress to the next stage in her life. Amidst reports that his Monaco businesses were in deep financial trouble, with investors demanding the return of millions of pounds of loans, the Princess sold Stefano's £500,000 Ferrari F40 sports car, his Rolls-Royce and his prized collection of Harley Davidsons.

It was as if the Princess were deliberately eradicating all traces of Stefano's high-speed, flashy, daredevil world in favour of the far slower, more intellectual one represented by Vincent Lindon, whose family were 'old money'.

'Caroline seemed to have dealt with a lot of that by basically removing herself,' says Judy Balaban Quine; 'which was probably a very good move for her and the kids.'

Although publicly she still wore black, Princess Caroline was getting her life back on track. Most days, in between sorting out her affairs in Monaco, she would make the forty-minute drive out to the Cercle Hippique Saint-Gérogers stables to ride her Irish hunter Wintertown, a present from her late husband. But all her mental energies were concentrated on the move to Provence, where she wouldn't be constantly reminded of Stefano.

With Lindon's help, she selected rustic furniture for the wooded farmhouse, buying up the entire stock of a local antique store. Her children – Andrea, six, Charlotte, four, and Pierre, three, all loved being in the country where they could play in the woods and have lots of pets.

'I felt it was healthier for them,' explained Caroline. 'It started off as a weekend place, a summer place, and then they said, "Why don't we stay here? Because we don't like living in the city." So we live where we can have animals; the children can ride – and they bicycle every day.'

Lindon, who lived alone in a cramped one-bedroom Paris apartment, was a frequent visitor to St Remy that summer. The children became fond of him as he read to them and took them on long country walks. Slowly the sparkle returned to Caroline's eyes and she emerged from mourning.

For weeks the couple managed to keep their new relationship a secret, realising discretion was essential while Caroline was still officially in mourning. But eventually the French paparazzi found out; Caroline and Lindon were even chased through the Paris Metro by photographers.

When news of their relationship became public, eyebrows were raised in Monaco. The Monégasques wondered if Caroline shouldn't have waited a little longer, out of respect to Casiraghi. But the biggest shock was that Caroline appeared to have abdicated her role as First Lady for good by moving 200 kilometres away to Provence.

When reporters finally tracked her down to her new home, she was forced to place armed guards around it, with instructions to confiscate the intrusive paparazzis' films and equipment.

'We do have light security,' said Caroline, minimising her precautions, 'but my big battle with the press was not to mention where [the children] go to school. Then a French magazine published the name of the school. You can sue – but it's out.'

When Caroline first moved to St Remy the local storekeepers and neighbours were only too happy to talk to journalists about the royal stranger in their midst. But when articles started appearing about Caroline's new life she made it abundantly clear that she did not appreciate being the subject of gossip. Now the residents of St Remy are as closed and discreet as the Monégasques; and reporters are repeatedly stonewalled if they dare to inquire about the Provençal Princess.

CHAPTER EIGHTEEN

———— ⚜ ————

ROCK 'N' MONACO

P RINCESS STEPHANIE WAS not the only member of the Grimaldi family who was interested in pop music. Prince Albert too was an avid music lover; on occasion he could even be persuaded to perform his favourite Elvis Presley song, 'I Can't Help Falling in Love'.

With his eye for a pretty girl and his love of music, it was only natural that the Prince should introduce himself to Melissa Corken when she moved to Monaco in the late 1980s. After a successful career as a teenage pop singer in Italy, pretty blonde, blue-eyed Melissa had married and gone into public relations, producing celebrity events.

When she arrived in Monaco the Irish-born businesswoman saw that the principality desperately needed a more modern image. And her influence on Prince Albert would have a profound effect.

'I went to see the tennis all on my own and I just bumped into the prince,' said Melissa. 'He turned around and said, "Who are you?" I said, "I'm Melissa – who are you?" And he smiled and said, "Welcome to Monaco."'

Melissa soon became good friends with Prince Albert, joining his inner circle of friends, along with Michael and Kate Powers, and becoming a regular at Jimmy'z. One night the Prince told Melissa that he would like to see a music-related event aimed at young people in Monaco. It didn't take Melissa long to come up with an idea. Inspiration struck while she was watching the 1988 Grammy Awards on TV.

'It was the year Michael Jackson was nominated, together with U2,' recalls Melissa. 'And U2 had sold about nine million records, but Michael had sold over twenty million. And when Michael didn't win the award Quincy [Jones] had tears in his eyes. I just thought it was real cruelty to have this poor guy suffering torture and then having to go on and perform without winning an award. So I thought, why not do an awards show where the artists know that they've won beforehand so they don't have to suffer?'

Corken's plan was to stage an annual international awards show in Monaco, honouring artists for their total record sales. First she secured the co-operation of the London-based International Federation of the Phonographic Industry; then she presented the idea to Prince Albert. The Prince liked the idea, but told Corken that she would have to have the backing of the Monaco government before he could officially provide royal patronage.

'He's not going to do it on his own,' explains Melissa. 'Actually, thanks to him we got the whole thing off the ground. Without him it never would have happened.'

With the Prince's blessing Corken presented her concept – now called the World Music Awards – to the head of the Monaco press office and the SBM – who approved it. The first World Music Awards were held in the Monte-Carlo Sporting Club in 1989, with Prince Albert on hand to present awards to Julio Iglesias, Barry White and the Gipsy Kings.

'The first year was a tough cookie,' remembers Melissa, who worked closely with Albert on the project. 'He's so analytical and wants to get to the bottom of every problem. Albert's into the nitty-gritty and analyses everything, including the budgets. I think he's quite a money guy. Yes, I do.'

Over the years the World Music Awards would become a showcase event for Monaco, drawing superstars such as Michael Jackson, Prince and Jon Bon Jovi. Albert and Stephanie have both hosted the ceremony.

'It was difficult at first to convince people that it wasn't to be a poor man's Grammy Awards,' explained Prince Albert. 'There are so many ceremonies, but I hope we can establish ourselves within a few years as a recognised awards ceremony.'

The World Music Awards are carefully packaged and have few surprises. But in 1992, when the raunchily camp English trio Right Said Fred came down into the audience and started dancing suggestively during a performance of their hit 'I'm Too Sexy', Prince Albert walked out in disgust.

'Perhaps he found it too much to his liking,' quipped group leader Fred Fairbrass.

Since its inception the World Music Awards has become almost as popular as the Grammys. In 1997 it was broadcast to 120 countries all over the world.

'We're certainly putting Monaco on the map,' boasts Corken.

Unfortunately the sales of Princess Stephanie's second album did not qualify her for an award at the third World Music Awards in 1991. Following the death of Stefano Casirgahi, the record's release had been postponed yet again; it was finally set to come out in America and Europe that summer.

A massive publicity blitz for the Princess began in June, amidst reports that she had sued former finance Jean-Yves Lefur for £75,000, covering the cost of their engagement party, rent on their shared home and gifts she had showered on him during their short relationship.

'That was a big boo-boo,' admitted the Marlboro-smoking Princess, as she told interviewers of her new-found sense of responsibility. 'We got engaged and then suddenly we were spending a lot of time together and we simply didn't get on.'

As she announced plans for a concert tour, promising not to mime on stage like other performers, Stephanie cited her musical influences as Peter Gabriel, Rod Stewart and Elton John. As proof of her new-found maturity Stephanie revealed that she had exchanged partying for golf – although she had more proficiency at the former than the latter, as evidenced by her twenty-four handicap.

'I was considered a rebel when I was eighteen,' she told an English interviewer. 'But an eighteen-year-old wants to have fun. I'm now twenty-six, I've changed. I've grown up. When I was eighteen I used to get into fights and shout the place down if something went wrong. But that's no good – people don't hear you when you're screaming. Now I choose my words more carefully.'

Stephanie's frank soul-baring seemed almost cathartic. But cynics questioned if Stephanie – who, with Ron Bloom, had written a song about her mother's death called 'Words Upon the Wind', was exploiting her tragic past to justify her million-pound record deal.

'The song was very hard to [write], but the feelings had been in there since 1982 when my mother died and they wanted to come out,' she explained. 'I kept breaking down and saying "I can't sing it." Eventually, when I sang it, I felt this incredibly strong presence of my mother next to me. I could almost see her.

'Everybody has knocks in their lives, but everybody talks about mine more. Every day there are families that have tragedies around them and nobody talks about them because they're just not public people.

'So I don't want pity. Things happen and you have to make the best of it and not close yourself in, because then you won't live. I no longer think life has been unfair to me. I believe the day you are born, everything is already written down. What happens is meant to happen. You just have to make the best of it. I do feel that one day I'll see my mother again – I hope so.'

When asked whether she owed her new career to being a Princess of Monaco, Stephanie claimed it was a hindrance rather than a help.

'In fact lots of doors have closed to me because people don't think

I'm a serious person and don't trust me. I had to work hard to convince the record company to invest their money in me. They didn't want to spend it on a fluke.'

But the Princess's lack of musical knowledge was amply illustrated in an interview with the American magazine *Details* when she was asked about her octave range.

'It depends,' answered Stephanie – not realising that even a top opera singer would only have an octave range between two and three. 'I think – about six or seven.'

When Stephanie's record was finally released it was universally panned by critics, who advised her to quit singing and concentrate on being a Princess.

'Her self-titled new album is a slumber-party soundtrack for princess wannabes,' wrote *USA-Today*'s respected music critic, Edna Gundersen, awarding the album one out of a maximum of four stars.

Calling Stephanie a 'royal pain in the ear', Gundersen decried the album for being full of 'pea-brained pop tunes' and 'bubble-gum laments'.

'Only the awkward geography and weather metaphors offer comic relief from a stream of insipid romantic cliches,' wrote Gundersen. 'Wake me up when this is over.'

When the *Stephanie* album was released in the US it sank without trace, despite heavy airplay and a video seen on MTV.

'Radio's very finicky sometimes,' explained her record boss Jerry Greenberg. 'And, ahhh . . . they've got this princess making a record. So it was a bit tough promoting it because there was always a negative backlash.'

After the record's dismal performance in France and America Sony/CBS decided to cut their losses. They didn't even bother releasing it in England.

'I'm not surprised this album hasn't sold,' said Pierre-Louis Berlatier of Sony Music in France. 'Quality does count.'

During the interviews to promote her record, Princess Stephanie may have displayed a new maturity – but in the privacy of her hotel she had reverted to her old behaviour. The impulsive Princess had fallen madly in love with her massive French bodyguard Daniel Ducruet, a former Monaco policeman sent by Rainier to protect his youngest daughter. And Ducruet and Stephanie would eventually sow the seeds of the biggest scandal yet to hit the Grimaldis.

CHAPTER NINETEEN

PRINCE CHARMING

IN THE HISTORY of Monaco Prince Albert will undoubtedly go down as 'The Sporting Prince'. With his passionate love of games the Prince has transformed the tiny principality into an all-year-round international sporting Mecca.

Michael Powers – who, with his sister Kate, opened Monaco's first American-style sports bar, Stars & Bars, in the early 1990s – believes that sports will play a key role in the principality's future.

Prince Albert's Monaco 'will be an international sports centre,' Powers told the *Washington Post*. 'He's bringing in events, and he's very much behind his country's athletics, from the little local kids playing soccer to the professional team. He's going to bring a lot of youth and energy and vigour into Monaco with his drive and interest in athletics.'

Indeed Stars & Bars most treasured item of sporting memorabilia is one of Prince Albert's old shiny red bobsleds which hangs from the ceiling, inhabited by a plastic replica of the Prince himself. Other trophies on show in the bar include a basketball donated by Chicago

Bulls' star Michael Jordan and motor-racing suits belonging to Jacques Villeneuve and Michael Schumacher.

With its generous tax advantages and easy-going lifestyle, Monaco is now home to some of the world's richest sportsmen and women. Current Monaco residents include tennis stars Boris Becker, Bjorn Borg, Richard Krajicek and Thomas Muster; Formula One motor-racing drivers Jacques Villeneuve and Gerhard Berger; and athletes such as Russian pole-vaulter Sergei Bubka.

As well as the sports stars there are supermodels Claudia Schiffer, Helena Christensen and Karen Mulder; fashion designer Karl Lagerfeld; photographer Helmut Newton; former Beatle Ringo Starr; and Julian Lennon. They all reap huge financial advantages from residing in the tiny principality.

In the late 1980s and early 1990s a number of financial specialists moved into Monaco, offering expertise on the best ways of establishing and maintaining legal residency in Monaco.

'To come to me is not enough,' says Swedish financial advisor Gunnar Everhed, himself now based in Monaco. 'A client must also listen to me. And a client must do as I say. They must play the game.'

In order to become a player in the Monaco game and live tax-free, an applicant has to show proof of a bank balance of at least $100,000. After successfully clearing that hurdle, it is possible to get a residency card that must be renewed each year. In order to maintain resident status an athlete must either spend at least six months of the year in Monaco or prove that the principality is a primary domicile between sporting events. Many millionaire sports stars keep up the pretence that they live in Monaco by maintaining tiny studio apartments which are little more than crash pads with a mattress and mountains of dirty laundry.

'Resident status is so prized that, once granted, athletes will do almost anything to retain it,' says Alexander Woolf of *Sports Illustrated*. 'There are slapstick tales of their rushing into Monaco, turning on the taps and flicking on the lights, trying to run up meter readings so their documentation will look more impressive when their permits come through.'

But it's not only athletes that flock to the financial oasis of Monaco. Headquartered in Monte-Carlo are many international sports governing bodies, including the International Amateur Athletic Federation, The General Association of International Sports Federations, the European ATP Tennis Tour and the International Association Against Violence in Sport.

Monaco is also the venue for three world-class sporting events: The Monte-Carlo Tennis Open, the Monaco Grand Prix and the Monte-Carlo Grand Prix track meet. Monaco's national soccer team is one of the top teams in Europe, consistently finishing near the top of the European Championships. Even the World Monopoly Championships have been held in Monaco.

Prince Albert has a huge appetite for sports. There is no doubt that, whatever his other achievements in Monaco, his sporting ones are formidable. He's president of Monaco's Yacht Club and of the principality's bobsled, swimming and track federations. As a member of the International Olympics Committee he was instrumental in having the Special Olympics held in Monaco, as well as bringing in the US Basketball Dream Team, who held their pre-Barcelona Olympics training camp there.

One of the Prince's favourite events is the World Push Championships. Held every September, the two-and-four-man teams push a wheeled bobsled along special rails lining the old port. When they've built up enough speed they jump into the bobsled and coast to the finish.

'It does look kind of funny,' admits the Prince, who uses the activity to train his Olympic bobsledding team.

In February 1992, Prince Albert and his six-man Monaco Bobsled team flew to Albertville, Canada, to compete in his second Winter

Olympics. After finishing halfway through the field four years earlier in Calgary, Albert was hoping for a much better showing in Albertville.

When he arrived at the athletes' village with the name Al Grimaldi scrawled on his gear bag in magic marker, the Prince felt undertrained. Because of his official duties he had missed nearly all of last year's bobsled competitions and had only been training full-time since October. He was also upset by Monégasque criticism about the wisdom of the heir to the throne being involved in such a dangerous sport.

'If I don't do well, people will say, "Why is he doing this?"' the Prince said in Albertville. '"What's he trying to prove?"'

'It's true that bobsledding is a notoriously dangerous sport. The helmeted competitors jam themselves tightly into a capsule to hurtle at speeds reaching seventy miles an hour down the side of a mountain. When the bobsled hits the 270-degree Kriesel turn, a competitor's body has to endure a crippling four Gs of pressure, driving the head into the shoulder-blades. Only the fearless would want to finish the course.

'I do this for the speed and thrill,' explains the Prince, who is as devoted to bobsledding as his grandfather Jack Kelly was to sculling. 'It's a little like a roller-coaster – only faster.'

To achieve the necessary concentration required for competition, Albert, who is the driver of his two-man team, executes a series of Kabuki-like motions at the start of a race. This, he explains, will allow him to visualise the route he will steer his red bobsled – emblazoned with the Grimaldi coat of arms – down the twisting, icy race course.

Although he had hoped to finish in the top fifteen in Albertville, the Prince's team finished a miserable forty-third out of forty-six, well behind the Jamaican team and only managing to beat teams from the Virgin Islands and Puerto Rico.

Prince Albert's Olympic bobsledding performance may have been disappointing – but he was having no trouble with his love life. In spring 1992 Prince Albert was introduced to six-foot German super-model Claudia Schiffer at the World Music Awards: the ravishing blonde, who many thought bore a stroking resemblance to Grace Kelly, had just moved to Monaco to escape German taxes.

That summer Schiffer accompanied the Prince to most of the Monaco season's high-profile events, fuelling press speculation of a romance, with the inevitable forecasts that the supermodel was soon to follow in Grace Kelly's footsteps. The couple were constantly being photographed in public – but in private the Prince still displayed a keen eye for other women.

In July, Stevie Parker and her niece Nicole were passing through Monaco on their way to the Barcelona Olympics. The beautiful blonde in her mid-thirties had been given Michael Powers' telephone number by a mutual friend; when she called him up he invited her to Jimmy'z to meet his friend Prince Albert.

'The prince was standing with Claudia Schiffer and some friends when I walked in,' recalled Stevie, who was raised in San Antonio, Texas, before moving to New York to work in public relations.

'I just remember him leaving his date with Claudia and bounding up and climbing over people and chairs to say hello. I was wearing a white suit and he commented on how nice I looked. When he asked my name I said it was Stephanie but I told him he could call me Stevie as he already had a Stephanie in his life. He thought that was very funny and the name stuck.'

Although Stevie didn't see Prince Albert again while she was in Monaco, fate soon brought them together. A week later she and Nicole took a train from Paris to Barcelona for the Olympics. During the journey they struck up a conversation with a fellow passenger, who was a doctor from San Francisco. They admitted they didn't have anywhere to stay in Barcelona and the doctor immediately offered to introduce them to a very influential friend of his who was helping to run the Olympics.

'I didn't even ask who this person was,' said Stevie. 'We were just enjoying this guy's company.'

When they arrived in Barcelona in the early hours of the morning their new friend took them to a hotel to meet his contact – who turned out to be Prince Albert.

'He recognised me right away after our meeting at Jimmy'z,' explained Stevie. 'So Albert invited Nicole and I to sit down for breakfast and asked where we were staying. And I said I didn't know, so he recommended a couple of places. Then, out of nowhere, he looked me straight in the eyes and said, "I'd love to be your alarm clock." I was so surprised I didn't respond to him. Actually I thought it was rather sweet and he was so very flirtatious about it that I didn't turn him down.'

The Prince had to leave as he was busy with Olympic business, but he arranged to meet up with Stevie and Nicole for dinner that evening. Later he sent a message to their hotel, telling them that he was running late and they should meet him in a disco at midnight.

'We had a great time dancing together,' remembered Stevie. 'And at the end of the evening the Prince asked Nicole and I if we wanted to go back to his hotel room. So we did.'

When they got into his hotel suite the Prince opened a bottle of champagne. They talked about Texas and he told them how much he loved the States. Before long Nicole had fallen asleep on the sofa and Albert suggested Stevie join him in the bedroom. 'Albert was one of the nicest, most considerate men I've ever met,' said Stevie.

After only a couple of hours' sleep they had just resumed their love-making when the telephone began ringing and the Prince dutifully answered it. Without missing a romantic beat Albert began discussing affairs of state.

'We'd already started making love so we continued while he was on the phone,' she recalled. 'He was speaking in Spanish and conducting his business while we were making love. It was very funny, as the calls were coming in one after another.'

Their affair continued throughout the Olympics; Stevie sneaked up to Prince Albert's suite late every night. Although Claudia Schiffer had flown in especially to be the Prince's date at an official dinner which he had to attend as the president of the Monaco Olympic Committee, it was always Stevie with whom he finished off the evening.

At the end of the Olympics Prince Albert told Stevie how much he'd enjoyed their time together, giving her his private mailbox number in Monaco so they could keep in touch. During the next few months they exchanged intimate gifts and love letters which they signed with their pet names: Al Bob and Stevie.

'I would send him things like silk boxer shorts, personal photographs and suggestive cards,' she said. 'I always felt that he would be the only one to open them.'

In November, Prince Albert arrived in New York with his father and Princess Caroline for the tenth anniversary of the Princess Grace Foundation. There, he resumed his affair with Stephanie Parker. The Prince was conveniently staying in room 2121 of the Regency Hotel on Manhattan's East Side – just a couple of blocks from where Stevie was living.

'I sent red roses up to his room and had them placed on his pillow,' said Stephanie, who'd been inspired to become a member of the Princess Grace Foundation USA by Albert. 'It became a custom and I did it every time he came to New York during the four years we were together.'

The Prince arranged for his bodyguard Captain Bruno Philipponat to let Stevie into his room before he arrived after a hectic day of business meetings. But on that first US trip she found herself having to console the Prince, who was very distressed by another paternity suit which had just been served against him.

The previous July a young Californian girl called Tamara Rotolo had saved up all her money and gone to Monaco with a friend for a dream holiday. Soon after her arrival the attractive brunette had gone to a tennis tournament and caught Prince Albert's eye.

'He approached me and we struck up a conversation,' recalls Tamara. 'He asked me to stay and watch him play in the tournament and join him at a dinner party later that evening.'

The Prince was charmed by the 31-year-old and after dinner invited her back to his yacht where they embarked on a two-week love affair. He took her to his favourite spots in Monaco like Stars & Bars, introducing her to friends like Michael Powers. They went sailing and the happy couple were even photographed embracing on his yacht. For once Albert found himself letting down his guard with Tamara and was very upset when the time came for her to return to California.

'The day I was to leave he repeatedly asked me to stay behind,' says Tamara, who had to return to her job.

Back in California Tamara kept in close touch with Albert by telephone and letter. But a few weeks later she realised she was pregnant with his baby and broke the news to the Prince in October when he telephoned from Canada.

'He was scared and surprised,' said Rotolo. '[He was] worried that I would tell his father before he had a chance to.'

The Prince had every reason to be concerned. For any child of his would automatically be in line to the Monaco throne. According to Tamara he readily accepted his responsibility, even devising a plan to keep the baby a secret from Prince Rainier until it was born.

During her pregnancy Albert kept in regular contact and even discussed possible names when doctors told Tamara she was carrying a baby girl. He told Tamara he was delighted at the thought of having a daughter and suggested calling her Grace in honour of his mother. And he assured Tamara that although he didn't quite know how to address the issue, he realised it was not the baby's fault.

'Albert said he would not allow her to grow up as his grandmother did,' said Tamara. 'He promised he would sort things out before she got old enough to understand.'

But everything changed when Jazmin Grace Grimaldi was born 6 weeks prematurely on March 4, 1992. Albert was out of Monaco on business and out of contact for days. When he finally heard the news he sheepishly told Rainier who was furious, ordering his son to sever all ties with Tamara and deny any responsibility.

'The moment the child was born they just slammed the door and stopped returning her calls,' said a friend of Tamara's, columnist Bruce McCormack, who would later champion her case in his Wyoming newspaper. 'I think it was Rainier's doing as Albert was constantly phoning before.'

Finally, after failing to get any response from the Palace, Rotolo retained top Beverly Hills lawyer Robert Kaufman, suing for child support and asking the Prince take a blood test.

Tamara says that originally the Prince's lawyers agreed to a blood test and she and Jazmin Grace both provided blood for analysis. But when it came to Prince Albert's turn he balked, fearing the monumental consequences of his mistake. 'He knew he was her father,' says Tamara. 'We both know it. However by taking the test he would be forced to acknowledge that she is his first born and heir to the throne. Despite my assurances I wanted nothing other than him to be a father to our daughter, his family feared an outsider would ultimately control the family.'

Six months later a process-server arrived at the Regency Hotel in New York to serve a paternity suit on Prince Albert.

'He spent his whole time trying to avoid the summons server,' recalled Stephanie. 'Finally, when the man tried to serve it [in the Regency lobby] Albert fell over and broke his right arm. It was in a cast for the whole trip.'

Friends of the embarrassed Prince put out the word that he had been knocked off his bicycle by an over-zealous paparazzo in the Riviera; Prince Albert himself laughingly told guests at the Princess Grace Foundation event that he'd 'punched out a jealous husband'.

'I do not believe that Albert is going to be able to hide behind palace walls forever,' said Kaufman, as a California judge set an early-1993 court date to hear the case.

Rotolo's paternity suit sent shivers through Prince Rainier and the Grimaldi family lawyers. For they realised that, if it were legally ruled that Jazmin Grace was Albert's daughter, the six-month-old girl would take precedence over Princess Caroline's children in the ladder of succession. It would be an identical situation to that which took place a century earlier, when the illegitimate birth of Prince Rainier's mother irrevocably diverted the path of the Grimaldi dynasty.

Whatever pressure he might be under from his father, Albert would always return to his non-smoking Regency suite late each night to find the condoms which his handlers had started placing in the ashtrays in readiness for his rendezvous with Stevie Parker. On their nights alone in the suite they'd drink champagne, talk and make love. But the Prince would always be up early to leave for his appointments, giving Stevie the run of his suite.

During her time with Prince Albert, Stevie learned to be discreet, never asking any questions about his family or his other girlfriends. She was happy just to see him a couple of times a year in New York or Monaco; she realised there were probably numerous other girls scattered across the world who enjoyed relationships with Albert.

'I think that's one of the things that kept me interesting,' she said. 'I didn't demand a lot of answers. I was in love with him but he never told me he loved me. I think he reserves that. He isn't very free with *that* word. He can be a little distant with that level of intimacy. He tries to play it very safe and I don't blame him at all.'

If Albert tended to be reserved with lovers, his younger sister Stephanie was just the opposite. In May 1992, Stephanie – to the abject horror of her father – announced she was having her ex-bodyguard Daniel Ducruet's baby. And she was having it out of wedlock. It was a humiliating blow for the Grimaldis.

The heavily-tattooed Daniel Ducruet, who favoured a uniform of gold chains and cowboy boots, was an unlikely choice to sire a possible heir to the Monaco throne. His parents, Henri and Maguy Ducruet, were a struggling working-class couple from Marseilles who lived in a two-bedroomed council flat in Beausoleil, just outside the borders of

Monaco. Soon after Daniel's birth in 1965, Henri walked out on the family and Daniel was raised by his mother.

Daniel was not a gifted student at the local state school in Beausoleil; he excelled only in sports. At the age of eighteen he took up body-building and also began his first serious love affair, with a young bank-clerk called Sandra Naccache, whom he married a couple of years later. To support his new wife he worked as a pet-shop salesman during the week and helped out at a friend's fish stall at weekends for extra money.

Ducruet's big break came in 1986 when he enlisted in the Monaco police force as a trainee officer. The handsome, muscular six-footer was good at his job and within two years he had been singled out to become a palace bodyguard.

Prince Rainier himself was highly impressed by the level of dedication Ducruet showed on his first assignment guarding the heir, Prince Albert. But the casual Prince felt uneasy around the over-enthusiastic Ducruet, complaining that he stuck too close.

Ironically it was Prince Rainier — much to his later regret — who suggested that Ducruet accompany Princess Stephanie on her ill-fated tour to promote her record album. By the time it was over the impressionable Princess had fallen for the newly-divorced Ducruet, who immediately cleared the way for an affair by deserting his new girl-friend, Martine Malbouvier, who was then five months pregnant with his baby.

'That woman stole my baby's father,' Malbouvier fumed to the local press when she heard Ducruet had left her for Stephanie.

Just two days after the Palace angrily denied reports of the pregnancy, Stephanie and Ducruet proudly made the announcement themselves. Showing off their new matching tattoos, the couple gave an exclusive paid interview to *Hello* magazine, posing for pictures in their eighteenth-floor Monte-Carlo apartment.

'My mother came from Catholic Irish stock — but I've changed,' declared the twenty-seven-year-old Princess.

As she nestled in her lover's arms, Stephanie said that after their baby boy was born they would probably sneak away and have a small wedding without any Grimaldis present.

'I think [my father] will let me choose how I want to get married,' she said. 'If I get married in church I'm sure he'll be thrilled. But if I decide otherwise it's not that important.'

Once again the Princess declared her undying love for Ducruet. This time, she assured *Hello*, she had definitely found Mr Right.

'My life has been one enormous doubt,' she explained. 'But now it's full of certainty, and of that I'm proud. He loves me for myself. He has shown me that it is I who count, not what I represent.'

And the burly ex-policeman/high-class fishmonger declared that he planned to name his son Jonathan. He boasted about his parenting skills, saying he paid child support for the five-month-old son by his former girlfriend; he also announced that he and Stephanie would produce a TV series called *Welcome To Monte Carlo* once the baby was born.

Although, publicly, Prince Rainier kept a discreet silence about his wayward daughter, privately he was furious; he and his daughter were hardly on speaking terms. The ageing Prince, who had turned sixty-nine in June, was totally opposed to Stephanie's relationship with this Frenchman of humble birth; and particularly tormented by the fact that his newest grandchild would be born out of wedlock. But Princess Stephanie resolutely refused to give up Ducruet and bristled at any criticism against him.

'She was willing to support him at any cost,' says her cousin Megan van Arkel. 'And I think it hurt her that she really lost her father for a little while. She really didn't have any chance to have him for dinner and have that father/daughter relationship for some time during this courtship with Daniel. And that really bothered her. She was more upset by that than anything.'

Stephanie's Aunt Lizanne believes that Stephanie would never have rebelled against her family if her mother had been alive.

'My sister would have been very upset,' said Lizanne. 'I don't know if [Stephanie] would have quite done all that.'

When she was five months pregnant the Princess donned a daring bikini thong at the Monaco Beach Club and proudly showed off her fuller figure as she embraced Ducruet, prompting the London *Sun* headline PRINCESS CHEEKY.

Enraged and humiliated by Stephanie's outrageous behaviour, Rainier ordered his lawyers to change his will. He placed all family monies and property into trust on his death to ensure that his children's spouses would never be able to inherit the Grimaldi fortune.

But Stephanie's pregnancy was temporarily forgotten when the Vatican finally annulled Princess Caroline's 1978 wedding to Phillipe Junot. Her marriage to Stefano Casiraghi – and their three children – were finally legitimised in the eyes of the Church after twelve years of campaigning and two papal commissions. It was rumoured that the deciding factor in the annulment had been Prince Rainier's refusal to pay Monaco's multi-million pound tithe to the Church until it was granted.

The annulment also meant that Caroline could once again take holy communion and remarry within the Catholic Church. Soon after the annulment Vincent Lindon started escorting Caroline in public, leading to speculation that they would soon marry. That November they travelled to New York together for the Princess Grace Foundation awards. The Jewish-born Lindon was said to have agreed to become Catholic so he could marry Caroline in a traditional ceremony, in church.

CHAPTER TWENTY

FRACTURED
FAIRYTALE

WHEN MONACO CELEBRATED its National
Day on November 19, 1992, it was plain for all to see that there was
trouble in paradise. The annual festivities of parades and fireworks
were overshadowed by the imminent arrival of Princess Stephanie's
illegitimate child. And as Prince Rainier appeared on the Palace balcony with Caroline and his three grandchildren there was general
relief that Stephanie had not humiliated the family further by giving
birth on National Day.

Earlier in the day, when the Prince led the official parade through
the winding narrow streets of the Rock, he had looked a sad and broken man. Even his self-designed military uniform overflowing with
medals and gold badges couldn't hide the fact that he was hugely overweight and he looked ill.

'The sixty-nine-year-old ruler looked morose and distracted as a "*Te
Deum*" was sung in his honour at the Cathedral,' wrote William Droz-
diak of the *Washington Post* in an article headlined, ARE THESE THE LAST
DAYS OF THE GRIMALDI DYNASTY?

'In the Palace courtyard he somberly doled out decorations to members of his staff and security forces, then he retreated to the privacy of his chambers. At a climactic gala at Monte-Carlo's opera house he turned and briskly fled his *loge* without acknowledging the applause from his subjects. Rainier seems to be struggling, in his forty-third year on the throne, as he tries to cope with a prolonged family crisis that could affect the future of one of Europe's oldest reigning dynasties.'

Only a week earlier Rome's *La Republica* had reported that Italian drug baron Larbi 'Bibi' Daghmane – who had links with the notorious Medellín Colombian drug cartel – had admitted supplying cocaine to Princess Stephanie in Paris during her modelling days. It was also claimed that Stephanie had been interviewed by Interpol as part of an ongoing investigation, and that she was being guarded around the clock. Daniel Ducruet had also run foul of the law; he'd been arrested on assault and battery charges after beating up a doctor in a driving altercation. Ducruet was later given a fifteen-day suspended jail sentence and fined £750.

These events certainly did not fit the wholesome image of Monaco that Prince Rainier and Princess Grace had worked so hard to create.

'In Monaco, the royal (sic) family means everything,' declared the recently-retired palace spokesperson Nadia Lacoste. 'This place takes its identity from them, and we all adapt as they evolve.'

Summing up the present situation in Monaco, the *Washington Post*'s Drozdiak questioned whether the principality was suffering from a 'detachment from reality'.

Wrote Drozdiak: 'With Rainier showing the fatigue and sorrow of his years, and his offspring looking so untested and uninspired as custodians of the Rock's future, some observers are predicting the dynasty might succumb to a future round of political turmoil in Europe and reach the end of the line when Rainier leaves the scene.'

Rainier's second cousin Lionel Noghes said it had been very hard for the Prince to control Princess Stephanie.

'It's been a drama,' said Noghes. 'There's a lot written about [her] and without the mother it's been very difficult for the father to be strict. To tell the truth Monégasques are just like one big family and they never criticise. I don't mean that they enjoy everything but they never criticise.'

Exactly one week after National Day Princess Stephanie gave birth to a seven-pound baby boy by Caesarean section at the Princess Grace Hospital. At the last moment, as a conciliatory gesture to the family, the baby had been named Louis after Rainier's grandfather.

But the only official response from the Palace was a terse public statement: 'Princess Stephanie and the child are doing well.'

Princess Stephanie's current estrangement from her family now became obvious to all when neither Prince Rainier, Albert nor Caroline visited the hospital to see the newest addition to the family. And the day after the birth, as Stephanie lay in hospital recovering from her operation, the Grimaldis left Monaco en masse. Albert went to Paris, while Caroline joined her father to hunt at his Chateau Marchais country estate.

In the aftermath of the birth Stephanie and Daniel Ducruet defiantly negotiated a reported £360,000 deal with *Hello* magazine for the first pictures of their new baby.

'Our love is deeper now,' said the Princess. 'Yes, I think our love is stronger now. It has a reason to be different.'

And the proud new father, who appeared visibly moved by the birth of his second son, waxed philosophical:

'There's a sense of continuation and progression in our love and we now have the goal of building a future and a family.'

Six weeks later it appeared that family stress was taking its toll when Prince Rainier was rushed to the Princess Grace Hospital after collapsing at dinner with chest pains. The overweight Prince – who loved rich food and was a heavy smoker – feared he was having a heart attack, but tests showed that he merely had an ulcer and would have to go on a special diet.

He was soon let out of hospital to recuperate, but it was obvious that the Prince was not in good health and the question of succession was again hotly debated in Monaco. Any hopes that Prince Albert would marry Claudia Schiffer and bring some much-needed glamour back to the principality were dashed when, in early 1993, she announced her engagement to a French businessman.

'I live in Monte-Carlo in Monaco and I know [Albert] very well,' she said. 'And that's it.'

It was widely believed that the whole relationship had been a set-up all along, a subterfuge arranged by Schiffer's boss and head of Chanel, Karl Lagerfeld, and his close friend Prince Rainier. A resulting marriage would have netted Chanel invaluable publicity and provided Monaco with a new Grace Kelly icon.

But the whole Schiffer affair struck fear into Prince Albert's heart.

'I was never romantically involved with her,' the Prince told the *Washington Post* in 1993. 'I think the visibility of it all scared me. There was too much hoop-la around it and I didn't want to deal with it.'

The publicity-wary Prince breathed a sigh of relief in March when a judge dismissed Tamara Rotolo's paternity case, ruling that a Californian court could have no jurisdiction as the alleged affair had happened 7,000 miles away in Monaco. Tamara Rotolo decided to keep a low profile in Newport Beach as she waited to make her next move. She was still determined to have her fair-haired one-year-old daughter recognised by the Grimaldi family. Indeed, *New York Post* columnist Cindy Adams even reported (falsely) that Albert had already accepted responsibility for the baby and had agreed to pay off Tamara if the matter was settled out of court.

In April Pope John Paul II fuelled the question of the Monaco succession when he legitimised Princess Caroline's three children, making the boys eligible to succeed to the throne. As Monégasques debated the pros and cons of Caroline's eldest son Andrea – now eight – taking over with his mother as Regent, the future of the principality seemed precariously uncertain.

★ ★ ★

On May 31, 1993, Prince Rainier turned seventy. The small family birthday celebration was not attended by his youngest daughter Stephanie. Nevertheless, it was a groundbreaking occasion for the silver-haired monarch, who used it to launch a public relations offensive in an attempt to offset some of the recent bad publicity. He and Prince Albert gave an exclusive interview to the *European*, which was owned by his friends and Monaco residents, the notoriously reclusive multi-millionaire Barclay Brothers.

In a wide-ranging 'state of the principality' interview entitled 'Steering His Country into Pole Position', the Prince told *European* editor Charles Garside he was still preparing his son for power.

'In the end you are alone in this position,' said Rainier. 'I think my son is learning this too. He says he can count his friends on the fingers of one hand, which I think is the right proportion. You have very few friends in this position, if friends are people who don't ask for anything.'

Without mentioning Princess Stephanie by name the Prince attacked the press for 'hurting' and 'paralysing' some younger members of royal families:

'The press can destroy someone very quickly,' he said. 'I don't think this can be justified when the person they choose as their victim can't fight back.'

Asked what he had left to accomplish in Monaco, Rainier said he wanted to see through to completion a number of projects he'd initiated. 'The Builder Prince' said he looked forward to the new underground railway station – which would free more land for development – and the new jetty outside the harbour to service cruise ships. Acknowledging that his modern Monaco was, financially at least, democratic and no longer purely for the rich, Rainier now planned to turn Monaco into a departure point for Mediterranean cruises.

'The sort of people who go on these cruises are precisely the sort of people we want in Monaco,' he explained.

The Prince also applauded Delta Airlines' newly-introduced New

York to Nice route; he saw this as directly benefiting Monaco in the current European recession.

'We are suffering like everyone else in the recession,' he admitted. 'Fewer people are travelling and they have less money to spend.'

And Prince Albert, who was photographed in his official uniform of state next to his father, declared that he was now ready to lead Monaco into the next century. Defining his job as a mixture of diplomat, charity president, sports administrator and businessman, the Prince said there was never a dull moment.

'I think I'm capable of taking on the role,' he said. 'I hope to have enough strength, courage and will-power to be able to face up to it.'

But when asked about his primary responsibility of getting married and siring a future heir, Albert sounded decidedly less statesmanlike.

'I am enjoying the bachelor life,' said the Prince. 'Perhaps I view marriage too highly and see it as too important. I feel that I am just not ready for it.'

Albert's uncle Prince Louis de Polignac, viewed his nephew's lack of marital commitment as a dereliction of official duty and urged him to marry for the sake of Monaco.

'He said that Albert must get married soon,' recalled de Polignac's friend, Sylvia Kahane. 'We need Albert to get married. And Louis complained [that] Albert's always saying that he wants to marry a woman like his mother . . . and I keep saying to him, "Albert, you will never find a woman as perfect as your mother. Find someone else. Just please marry somebody."'.

The Prince certainly didn't seem ready to settle down into domesticity as he mixed with the world's most beautiful and famous stars at that year's World Music Awards. That spring the Prince had personally invited the self-declared King of Pop, Michael Jackson, to Monaco to receive three awards; the eccentric superstar helicoptered into the principality for 'a family holiday' accompanied by his manager and two young children. The party stayed at the Winston Churchill Suite of the Hotel de Paris, which afforded an excellent view of the pink Palace.

The highlight of Jackson's trip was a personal Palace tour by Prince Albert, who then hosted a special dinner in his honour. The following day Prince Rainier accompanied the singer to a recital by Italian opera star, Luciano Pavarotti.

'Michael has a lot of respect for Prince Albert,' said a spokesman for Jackson. 'And he loves Grace Kelly movies.'

The 1993 World Music Awards, which starred Michael Jackson, Rod Stewart and Tina Turner, also marked Princess Stephanie's first public appearance under the same roof as the other Grimaldis since the birth of her son. And it was the first sign of the thawing of her frosty relationship with the family.

A week after Prince Rainier's birthday Princess Caroline accidentally ran into her sister at the Monaco Beach Club. Deliberately, to make a point, she made a fuss of her new nephew, Louis: she willingly posed for photographs as she played with the baby, poking out her tongue and making funny faces, to the delight of Andrea and Charlotte.

For the last few months Princess Stephanie had kept an unusually low profile. Recently Daniel Ducruet's mother Maguy Ducruet had moved into the couple's modest apartment overlooking the Mediterranean to help look after Louis. Most days Stephanie could be seen pushing the pram on her daily stroll in the park accompanied by a bodyguard. She seemed to delight in being photographed changing Louis' nappies and she seemed happier than she had ever been to be an ordinary mother. She even began putting on a little weight as she socialised with her husband's policeman friends and stayed at home to cook and watch television.

But while Stephanie took care of their baby, Daniel Ducruet spent his days pursuing expensive hobbies: racing cars and powerboats, paragliding, helping to deplete Stephanie's allowance. Stephanie resolved to mend fences with her father and staged a series of secret, highly emotional meetings; Rainier, who loved Stephanie deeply, was only too willing to have her back in the fold. But it would take far longer for him to accept Ducruet, the former bodyguard he still believed had betrayed his trust.

'As Uncle Rainier came around [he] came to accept Daniel and to accept Stephanie's love for him,' said Megan van Arkle.

The Prince was certainly all smiles when he publicly heeled the rift with his daughter by turning up at the Princess Stephanie Youth Centre and joyfully posing for photographs with Stephanie. It was the first time in over a year that father and daughter had been photographed together – it gave a clear sign to Monégasques that the Grimaldis had reunited.

'I really have to give Rainier enormous credit for the way he has not shut doors on his kids forever,' says Judy Balaban Quine, who stayed in close contact with Rainier during this period; 'So that, even though he himself may be angry, distraught or sad at what the world may consider scandalous, they are still his family. And his involvement with his grand-children and in the lives of his children is always very strong. The doors are always open, and they are always his kids.'

CHAPTER TWENTY-ONE

———— ❧ ————

COWBOYS AND INDIANS

O N MAY 28, 1993, Monaco was accepted into the United Nations as a full voting member. As befitted its new place in international diplomacy, the principality rented a new townhouse on Manhattan's swank East Side for the principality's delegates; Prince Albert was tipped to head Monaco's UN delegation.

Stevie Parker was excited by the prospect of seeing Albert in New York once again. Since he had last been in the city the previous November, she had been active in the Princess Grace Foundation as well as doing public relations for the National Museum of Catholic Art and History. She had also kept in touch with the Prince through his personal mailbox.

In August Stevie and the Catholic Museum's executive director Christina Cox were invited to Monaco by two museum patrons to attend the Red Cross Ball. Delighted at the unexpected opportunity to meet Prince Albert, Stevie wrote to give him news of her forthcoming visit; he replied saying that his friend Michael Powers would come and see her at the Hermitage Hotel during their stay in Monte-Carlo.

When the two women arrived, on the night before the Ball, Michael Powers came straight over to the Hermitage and immediately made them a proposition:

'He wanted to know if we would fly to Texas with him and the Prince straight after the Ball and spend a long weekend as their guests on a ranch,' recalled Stevie.

'We were so surprised that we said we'd have to think about it. But it didn't take us long to decide to go.'

As president of the Red Cross Prince Albert was busy throughout the weekend hosting various events. But he did manage to seek out Stevie and Christina during the glittering ball at Monaco's Sporting Club, and even posed for photographs with them.

The only members of the family who attended the Ball that year were Prince Albert, Princess Caroline and their aunt Princess Antoinette. Prince Rainier was in Brussels for the state funeral of King Baudouin of Belgium and Princess Stephanie was holidaying in Madeira with Daniel Ducruet and their son.

'It was a really glamorous occasion, with Whitney Houston performing,' recalls Stevie.

The next evening Stevie went to the newly-opened Stars & Bars, where they met Prince Albert and the girl who had attended the Ball with him the night before.

On Monday morning Stevie and Christina flew back to New York, unpacked and caught the first plane to San Antonio, Texas. There they were met by Michael Powers, who drove them to the ranch, two hours outside the city. On their arrival they found a party atmosphere with a relaxed Prince Albert enjoying his annual vacation.

'We've made it a tradition for the last eight years to come to Texas once a year and go to a friend's ranch,' explained Michael Powers, who organises the trip. 'We work cattle and ride horses and act like a bunch of drugstore cowboys. It's a great time together. It's great bonding and we meet a couple of friends and have a great time.'

The Prince loves coming to the Texas ranch, where he dons cowboy clothes and lets his hair down without fear of the paparazzi. The owner, a rich industrialist and an old family friend of the Grimaldis, used to hunt big game in Africa and originally built the 10,000 acre ranch, complete with its own landing strip, as a place to house his trophies. Stuffed lions' heads, elephants tusks and antlers line the walls of the main house and there is a private game reserve where giraffes, horses and zebras run wild.

Prince Albert first fell in love with the American Wild West when he saw his mother's film *High Noon* in the Palace screening room as a very young boy.

'Well, mother was hardly noticed,' Princess Grace told an interviewer when Albert was just eight-years-old, 'because Albert is very cowboy-minded and he was watching the cowboys most of the time.'

As children Albert and Michael Powers had played Cowboys and Indians in the Palace Gardens; now, as adults, they were doing it for real.

'When I was very young I wanted to be a cowboy,' explained Prince Albert. 'I just love the whole atmosphere and the whole close-ness-to-nature aspect of it all'. 'It's just a love of the beauty of mountains and of prairies. Maybe it's also a fascination with the American West and what it means to be a pioneer; what it means to be a Native American.

'When we go to pay a visit to our friends down there on the ranch it's usually very, very private. You know, we do a lot of outdoor activities.'

Stevie Parker and Christina Cox had their own rooms while Prince Albert stayed in the guest house by the pool. But it wasn't long before the beautiful American had rekindled her affair with the Prince.

'I slept out by the pool one night on the chaise longue, right outside the prince's door,' she recalled. 'It was such a beautiful night. The next morning I knew he was up so I went into his bedroom and spent some time with him. It was like we had never been apart.'

During the visit Michael Powers organised trail rides and cook-outs with ballad-singing around the campfire for the Prince's amusement.

'He loves doing these fun trail rides with country and western singers and guys singing ballads,' said Powers. 'And we take chuck wagons and cross very exciting historical countryside and national forests. It's something that I think Albert truly enjoys. He feels right at home.'

Back at the ranch Stevie and Christina spent most of their time walking and sunbathing by the pool. But they soon learned that, although almost everything else was allowed, cameras were strictly off-limits.

'Everybody takes off their clothes poolside and goes skinny-dipping,' said Stevie. 'On one occasion someone had a disposable camera and tried to take a picture of Prince Albert while he was undressed. Mike Powers just grabbed it away.'

As a devout Catholic, Christina Cox was uncomfortable around all the nudity and informal behaviour on the ranch. She began locking her door at night.

'She was acting very shy and prudish,' laughs Stevie. 'She wanted to try and keep everything proper, which I thought was funny. I mean, here we are for this weekend with the Prince and Michael . . . I was going, "Christina, what are you *worried* about?"'

Every afternoon Prince Albert would work out, doing aerobics and stretching exercises before going off for a run before dinner. Most evenings old college friends of the Prince's would arrive and they'd drink and tell stories long into the night.

During this trip Stevie really began to fall in love with Prince Albert. But she had to face reality: they could not possibly have a future together.

'We were deeply attracted to each other,' she says, looking back. 'It just seemed like the normal thing to do. He never told me that he loved me but I've always presumed that there were very high, strict standards as far as who he could marry. On the other hand he didn't seem bothered. I always felt like it was a regular guy I was with. He never had any sort of attitude toward me.'

It was an emotional farewell for Stevie when she and Christina left the ranch after five days with Prince Albert to fly back to New York. Michael Powers took a photograph to commemorate their time on the ranch as Albert eagerly hugged the two women by the pool. And when Albert next met up with Stevie in New York he gave her the signed photograph: 'To Stevie, with fond memories of South Texas. Love, Albert.'

In September 1913, Albert's great-great-grandfather Prince Albert I made history by becoming the first European reigning monarch to visit America. At the beginning of the century the 'Navigator Prince' had attended the famous Buffalo Bill's Wild West Show during a European tour; and after the show, he met the legendary cowboy, Buffalo Bill, whose real name was William Frederick, got his nickname after slaughtering 5,000 buffalo in just eight months to feed workers who were building the Kansas Pacific Railway.

'Buffalo Bill must have heard that Prince Albert I was keen on hunting so he invited him to come out and hunt deer and elk in Wyoming,' said his enthusiastic descendant Prince Albert. 'So he took him up on that and he went in the summer of 1913 and stayed for ten days hunting with him up in the mountains by Yellowstone National Park, where they killed a deer and a bear. And there is even early movie footage of the Prince meeting Crow Chief Plenty Coups at a camp they established, which was called Camp Monaco in his honour.

'Apparently there's a tree that still exists which is engraved with "Camp Monaco,"' said Prince Albert.

As a young boy Prince Albert loved hearing the stories of his ancestor's meeting with Buffalo Bill and Chief Plenty Coups. So together with Michael Powers he decided to commemorate the eightieth anniversary of the meeting by making a sentimental pilgrimage to Cody, Wyoming.

Back in California Tamara Rotolo had read that Prince Albert would be in Cody and decided to take Jazmin Grace there to meet him. She had become increasingly frustrated with Albert's refusal to acknowledge Jazmin Grace and believed that if he saw his daughter face to face he would have to accept her. Tamara was convinced that Albert had tested Jazmin Grace's blood samples and now knew beyond doubt he was her father.

'I know Albert,' says Tamara. 'This is eating at him every breathing moment. You can rest assured, and he had to be more than curious, that if Albert took our blood and had his own testing done, and it confirmed he is *not* her father, he would have announced it to the world.'

Tamara and Jazmin Grace flew into Wyoming and checked into a Holiday Inn. Then Rotolo paid $50 to join the Buffalo Bill Historical Center's patron's association to gain admittance to the events and began preparing her 18-month-old daughter to meet her father.

Prince Albert and Michael Powers made a far grander entrance in a 1910 Yellowstone coach drawn by four horses driven by Buffalo Bill's great-grandson Bill Garlow. And as the coach drew up outside the Buffalo Bill Historical Museum, there was a crowd of eager parents and children waiting for a glimpse of His Serene Highness.

The Prince seemed delighted by his reception and began shaking hands with the children who had brought him flowers and making casual small talk. Then suddenly to his horror Tamara lunged forward out of the crowd and thrust baby Jazmin Grace to within inches of the Prince, declaring: 'Albert, say hello to your daughter.'

'It was a remarkable moment,' recalls *Cody Enterprise* editor and publisher Bruce McCormack who was standing by the Prince. 'I'm telling you Albert's jaw just dropped. He looked stricken.'

As Michael Powers, who had met Tamara at Stars & Bars in Monaco, firmly escorted her out of the crowd, Prince Albert regained enough composure to smile weakly to the stunned crowd as he disappeared into the museum.

Later that evening Tamara turned up at an official outdoor reception for Prince Albert planning another confrontation if he refused to meet her. Recognizing Tamara from earlier, McCormack struck up a conversation, persuading her not to approach Albert and make another scene.

'Everyone was treating her like a leper,' recalls McCormack. 'The word had gone out from the museum that she was a kook. I felt sorry for her.'

The *Cody Enterprise* publisher managed to keep Tamara well in the background as a nervous Albert, who had noticed her, danced the Western two-step to the music of Bucky Beaver and the Ground Grippers and joined the local ladies for a 'boot-scootin' line dance. It was a tough evening for the Prince who made an early exit.

The following morning McCormack ran a story about Tamara's outburst, prompting her to telephone his office and complain. McCormack agreed to go over to the Holiday Inn to hear her side of the story.

'This is not about money,' said Tamara, as she cuddled little Jazmin Grace by the pool. 'This is not about publicity. This is about acknowledging a child. I just wanted Jazmin to see her father. My whole goal in coming to Cody was for him to see this beautiful child. I want him to think about that when he closes his eyes at night.'

Although the palace has always denied Tamara's claim and Albert has always refused a blood test, McCormack is convinced that Jazmin Grace is a real Grimaldi. He has spent many hours talking to Tamara and has kept in touch since she went into seclusion with her daughter in 1993.

Tamara now lives as a single mother in California, struggling to bring up her child on a meager wage. She says she doesn't want a penny from the Grimaldis and only hopes that one day Prince Albert and the Grimaldis will recognize Jazmin as one of their own.

'She's his own flesh and blood,' says Tamara. 'If he chooses to fail to love and nurture her throughout her childhood – it's his loss. He's the one who must wonder every day about her. How can he not?'

Now a very independent six-year-old, Jazmin Grace bears a striking resemblance to Grace Kelly with the same fair hair and perfect features. Her mother prays that in time Albert will stand up to his father and get to know his daughter, who has inherited her grandmother's love of the theatre, ballet and music.

'Jazmin's fully aware of who her father is and has adjusted quite well,' said Rotolo in December 1997. 'To her he's "Albert, my biological father who's busy and lives far away." Albert himself has never privately or publicly denied he's her father. There's not a published or broadcast report anywhere on earth where he denies Jazmin – and that's all I ask – all I expect. Jazmin is recognized by me, her family and those who love her.'

Each Christmas Tamara sends Bruce McCormack a card with a new picture of Jazmin Grace, whom she dresses like a little Princess.

'I sent Albert updated photos of *our* precious daughter,' Tamara wrote McCormack at Christmas 1996. 'What a loss for him and a beautiful gain for me.'

In October 1993 Prince Albert gave a speech to the United Nations representing the Monaco delegation. Later he lunched with his fellow delegates, setting forth the principality's position on world affairs. And when he arrived back at his suite at the Regency he found a red rose from Stevie Parker on his pillow.

Although Stevie would spend nights with the Prince at the Regency, aided and abetted by Captain Philipponat, they had to keep their affair secret. On one occasion Albert and Stevie both attended the annual Princess Grace Foundation gala in New York; but they had to bring along separate dates. They sat opposite each other at dinner.

'Albert kept flirting with me during the speeches,' recalls Parker. 'It was very funny. He kept giving me the eye and winking when my date wasn't looking.'

Afterwards Stevie's companion dropped her off outside her apartment. As he drove off she ran straight over to the nearby Regency, still wearing her long evening dress.

Prince Albert was in his suite partying with his inner circle of friends, including Michael Powers and an ophthalmologist from St Louis who had known the Prince for years. Stevie had also arranged for a couple of her girlfriends to come along.

'They were like little kids,' she recalls. 'They were telling jokes and being very funny. We stayed up late drinking champagne and talking. Then I stayed over.'

On his trips to New York, Prince Albert would often take Stevie to art galleries and on to dinner before going back to the Regency for a romantic night together. Stevie Parker's relationship with Prince Albert was well known among his friends, but they always maintained the utmost discretion.

'The real girlfriends he has had over the years are the ones you are least likely to have heard about,' Michael Powers told the *Tatler* in early 1995. 'He has had a nice relationship with the same person for the last year or so but he certainly won't discuss it with any outsiders.'

Explained the Prince: 'It's not *that* serious, so there's no chance of marriage for some time yet.'

Princess Caroline had disliked being on show for family photo opportunities as she was growing up but her own children certainly did not shy away from the camera. Andrea, Charlotte and Pierre were becoming seasoned veterans; they were pictured giving out Christmas presents to Monégasque children, appearing with their grandfather on the Palace balcony, or applauding enthusiastically from the Royal Box at the Circus Festival.

Although they spent most of the time in St Remy, on their frequent visits to Monaco they loved to visit Stars & Bars and play the video machines.

'Princess Caroline's children love to come in and play the games,' said Kate Powers, who had now moved from Le Texan to Stars & Bars. 'They love the video games centre and especially the ski machine.'

Lizanne Kelly LeVine says that the next generation of Grimaldis are growing up in a more normal atmosphere than their parents; hopefully, they won't face the same pitfalls.

'Grace would have loved to have seen her grandchildren,' said Lizanne. 'Whenever I see them I think, "Oh God, Gracie would love them!" It's such a tragedy.'

But how Grace would have reacted to the sorry state of her own children was another matter. Now in their late thirties Caroline had two marriages behind her; Albert was still single. In early 1994 Princess Stephanie announced that she was pregnant again and would soon be presenting Daniel Ducruet with a second illegitimate child, this time a daughter.

In a somewhat bizarre move the Princess also announced that she would be donating the neck brace, which she wore after the car accident that killed her mother, to a charity auction. Although Rainier condemned the gift as being in poor taste, the Princess insisted it was her own property to do with as she wished.

In February, Prince Albert gamely competed in his third Winter Olympics in Lillehammer, Norway. But again his team finished near the bottom.

'We have a small country, we do the best we can,' he said sadly after a disappointing run.

Prince Albert seemed far happier at the 1994 World Music Awards where he joined the rock star Prince at a post-awards party at Stars & Bars. There, Prince thrilled the partygoers when he played an impromptu ninety-minute set.

'I want to thank Prince Albert – the funkiest man in showbusiness,' the American star told the crowd after Albert jumped on stage at 3 AM, calling for an encore.

Princess Stephanie gave birth to a daughter, Pauline Grace, on May 5. Daniel Ducruet was still refusing to sign the pre-nuptial agreement drawn up by Rainier's lawyers to ensure he could never inherit the Grimaldi fortune. An ailing Prince Rainier was insisting that Ducruet would get no more than £300,000 if the couple split after five years:

£650,000 if the marriage lasted more than ten years. Although this time round all the Grimaldis came to the Princess Grace Hospital to congratulate Stephanie on the birth, she and Ducruet were still unofficially banned from all the official functions in Monaco.

But Rainier had finally resigned himself to Ducruet's presence. He awarded the former bodyguard's new security company, Monaco Watch Investigations and Protection, valuable contracts for several of the principality's sporting events, including the Monaco Grand Prix.

That summer the Grimaldis' public image had sunk to an all-time low. After Prince Albert felt compelled to publicly deny that he was gay to a French newspaper, the influential fashion magazine *W* branded the Grimaldis 'Europe's tackiest royal [sic] family.'

'With the antics of the Grimaldi cast these days, events that once had the glamorous glow of a Hollywood fairytale seem more like a sordid script for a daytime soap,' wrote *W*'s Paris correspondent, William Middleton.

'But the fact is that Monaco was always slightly embarrassing, that the ruling family is just drifting back toward their former reputation and that the only really unusual thing has been the illusion of elegance that swirled up around the wedding of Grace and Rainier.'

In September, Prince Rainier was devastated when British author Robert Lacey published a well-researched biography of Princess Grace. In *Grace* he claimed that Rainier's indifference during the marriage had driven Princess Grace first to drink and then to extra-marital affairs with young men during her final years.

'This book severely violates the memory of Princess Grace as well as the personal rights of HSH Prince Rainier III of Monaco,' thundered the Prince's lawyer as he took out a French court injunction. But, without giving a reason, the Prince withdrew it several days later after Lacey's publishers vowed to fight it.

When the seventy-one-year-old Prince appeared on the Palace balcony for the 1994 National Day celebrations he seemed to be carrying a heavy burden. Beset by rumours that he was soon to abdicate in favour of Prince Albert, Rainier seemed vacant and lethargic as he reviewed the troops and awarded decorations, while Caroline and her children looked on.

A week later, during a routine check-up, cardiologist Dr Jean Joseph Pastor discovered that the Prince's left coronary artery was blocked. He would need an emergency double heart by-pass if he was to survive. The stricken Rainier was operated on at Monaco's Centre Cardio-Thoracique by a team of five doctors led by Professor Vincent Dor, who successfully inserted two replacement internal arteries.

The medical emergency threw Monaco in a panic. As Prince Albert, now thirty-six, rushed home from a bobsled competition in Canada, the future of the principality looked precarious. However, with regular visits from Princesses Caroline and Stephanie the Prince's condition soon improved and he was released after ten days of convalescence.

Monégasques had good reason to be concerned about the effect that Rainier's poor health could have on Monaco's future. Rumours about Rainier's abdication were bolstered by a report in *Paris-Match*, not only confirming the abdication but also claiming that Monaco's police had been given a 'superior and secret order' cancelling all vacations in February and March. It also claimed the Palace had ordered new buttons for official uniforms, with Albert's initial 'AG' replacing the present 'RG'.

As Prince Rainier appeared publicly for the first time since leaving hospital at the annual Monaco Children's Christmas Party, together with Princess Stephanie – significant in itself, as it was their first official appearance together since Daniel Ducruet had arrived on the scene – the Palace issued a strong statement to Reuters' press agency denying an abdication.

'The sovereign Prince expresses the most formal denial of this fantasy that lacks all foundation. You can imagine that, if such an important decision had been made, there would have been a press release.'

CHAPTER *T*WENTY-TWO

❧

SEND IN THE CLOWNS

JUST TWO MONTHS after his open-heart surgery Prince Rainier seemed in excellent spirits as he presided over the Monte-Carlo International Circus Festival. As a boy the Prince had been captivated by the circus; he especially loved clowns. All through his unhappy days of being bullied as 'Fat Little Monaco' at Stowe School, he had dreamed of running away and joining the circus. Now, as his country's ruler, he had the power to bring the circus to him.

In 1974 the Prince had been the driving force in the creation of the Monte-Carlo International Circus Festival, in which young circus performers from all over the world compete against each other. During the eight-day festival, Prince Rainier and the other judges watched assorted acrobats, trapeze artists, clowns, jugglers and trained animals compete to be the best in their categories.

Although there is no evidence that the Prince is related to the great Italian clown Grimaldi, Monaco's ruler often uses a crudely-drawn smiling face of a clown to sign letters to friends. In anticipation of his eventual retirement, Rainier has a custom-made camper-bus sitting in his garage; which one day he plans to drive off in it and follow the circus, just as he had wanted to do when a boy. Yet some might wonder if the spectacle that has become Monaco is enough – or, indeed, too much – of a circus for the Prince already.

The nineteenth annual Circus Festival in January 1995 gave Rainier a perfect opportunity to recuperate and forget his family problems. He sneaked out of the Palace to watch rehearsals; he attended every single performance and voted in his capacity as president of the jury.

The ageing Prince appeared to have found a new lease of life as he cheered and applauded like a schoolboy. After Princess Caroline, wearing a sophisticated full-length black gown with a plunging neckline, had presented the awards, the Prince invited the winners back to the Palace for a private dinner where they could tell jokes and trade circus stories. It was one of the rare occasions on which Rainier could throw off his state responsibilities and truly enjoy himself.

In the wake of his heart surgery the Prince had been forced to recognise his own mortality. Finally, he saw that his days were numbered. He had become much closer to his youngest daughter; to please her he had softened his attitude toward Daniel Ducruet, whom he still referred to privately as 'that servant'. At Christmas Ducruet had been invited to the Palace to join the Grimaldi festivities for the first time since he'd left the police force. Since Louis' birth, Princess Stephanie had not accepted any family invitations because they never included Ducruet, so this was the first time Rainier and his three children had been together in more than two years.

Although Rainier still distrusted Ducruet's long-term motives, he tried his best to be polite to the father of his two newest grandchildren and forced himself to make small talk. The Prince had to admit that his former 'wild child' had finally calmed down; since meeting Ducruet she was at least behaving herself.

Since moving back to Monaco, Princess Stephanie had deliberately kept a low profile, leading a quiet life with her young family first in a comparatively modest apartment and then following Pauline Grace's birth, in a large tangerine-coloured villa, Clos Saint-Martin.

Shunning the limelight, the Princess seemed content to be a housewife, staying at home, watching television and caring for her babies. The girl who had always not wanted to be a Princess had finally found an inner peace and happiness with her new, very ordinary family. Princess Stephanie took her children to the supermarket and for walks in the park – as her bodyguard discreetly followed behind. She became a common sight on the streets of Monaco.

In March, Prince Rainier gave Stephanie and Daniel Ducruet permission to marry. The Princess favoured a big Cathedral wedding but her father was determined to keep the ceremony quiet and discreet to avoid the public spectacle of Stephanie's two illegitimate children tugging at her wedding dress.

To pave the way for the wedding, Louis and Pauline were baptised on Easter Monday at Princess Grace's beloved St Dévote's Church. A smiling Prince Rainier drove himself to the chapel and formally shook hands with Ducruet and his mother Maguy at the afternoon service. Caroline and Albert were named as godparents to Pauline and Louis.

It was a moving ceremony; Stephanie and Ducruet broke into spontaneous embraces and kisses. Everybody felt the unseen, watchful presence of Princess Grace.

'That's really the time when I missed her the most,' recalled Princess Stephanie; 'because I would have wanted her to see my children and know them.'

After living in sin for four years, Princess Stephanie's marriage to Daniel Ducruet was a pale shadow of her parents' wedding almost forty years earlier. The pink-ribboned invitation card was plain, without the Grimaldi coat of arms – and to the point.

'On the occasion of their marriage, Stephanie and Daniel invite you to join them at 20.30 on Saturday July 1, on the terrace of Loews Hotel, Monte-Carlo.'

The once-sophisticated and mythical Grimaldis had gone suburban, selecting the principality's Atlantic City-style concrete tourist hotel instead of the Victorian splendour of the Hotel de Paris or the Hermitage. It was not even the wedding of the day; the Grimaldis had deliberately chosen the same day Crown Prince Pavlos of Greece was marrying in London, to try and deflect press attention away from Monaco.

But although the choice of venue may have been second-rate, the couple's gift list certainly was not; items by Lalique, Daum, Baccarat and Christofle bought the total value of items requested up to £400,000.

On the morning of her wedding Stephanie visited her mother's tomb in the Cathedral and left a bouquet of flowers before crossing the Rock to the civic ceremony. Nearly 400 well-wishers gathered in the hot sun outside the Palace to get a glimpse of the bride. Shortly before the couple arrived police moved in to clear the crowd who started booing as they realised they were being shut out of the wedding.

Doing her best to be invisible, Stephanie, wearing a white mini-dress, slipped in through a back door carrying her thirteen-month-old daughter, Pauline.

The twenty-five minute civic ceremony in the town hall was closed to all press and photographers. It was attended by just forty people who saw Monaco's Mayor Anne-Marie Campora perform the simple cere-mony. The official wedding photograph taken afterwards shows a relaxed Princess Stephanie standing between her grim-looking father and a visibly nervous bridegroom.

After the ceremony Rainier and Caroline toasted the newly-married couple at a champagne reception at their Clos Saint-Martin villa. But Prince Albert was the only close family member to attend the celebra-tory lobster dinner at Loews' rooftop terrace restaurant.

'The Princess was effusive and happy all night,' said Loews' manager Jacques Provence. 'And nobody did anything outrageous – thank God.'

Now that Princess Stephanie was married all eyes turned to Caroline. After nearly five years her relationship with Vincent Lindon did not seem after all to be heading for the altar. The relationship had stalled somewhat after Prince Rainier presented the Jewish actor with a demanding pre-nuptial list of requirements, including an insistence that he become a Catholic and give up all rights over any children of the marriage in the event of divorce.

In May – as Stephanie and Albert presided over the World Music Awards – Caroline was in London supporting the British debut of the Monte-Carlo Ballet at Sadler's Wells. Keeping his usual distance, Vincent Lindon, a recent winner of a French César award, joined Caroline for the meal and then left separately.

Recently there had been subtle signs that the reticent and shy Lindon might at long last be accepted as a future member of the Grimaldi family. He had appeared in the Royal Box at the Monte-Carlo Tennis Open and the Monaco Grand Prix. But the always introspective Princess Caroline was wavering about whether or not she wanted to commit herself to a third marriage.

She spent hours alone at her home in St Remy reading and writing poetry; even her closest friends and relations found her distant and hard to know. Although she still performed the duties of Acting First Lady, the Princess had become an enigma.

'I don't see her as often as I used to,' said Prince Albert. 'And sometimes she forgets to tell us or to inform us about different things that concern her or the kids. We always have to kind of pull information out of her.'

Now approaching forty, Caroline lived an elegant country life, with Lindon coming down to visit at weekends. She socialised with her best friend Inès de la Fresange – who lived nearby – and the late Jackie Onassis's sister Lee Radziwill, who moved into St Remy with her husband, film director Herbert Ross.

The Princess delighted in moving in liberal intellectual circles, meeting friends who were involved in the worlds of fashion and the arts.

'She has found her own equilibrium,' says family friend and Dior designer Marc Bohan. 'She has evolved. She is very conscious that she has an appearance to maintain in public and in her private life.'

'Caroline would have been a good left-wing intellectual,' says her friend Egon von Furstenberg. 'She would be happy in the West Village reading Freud or Kafka – but she was born a Princess. The role isn't her, but then she plays it as little as possible now.'

In October Caroline joined her father and brother in New York for a Princess Grace Foundation benefit at the circus-themed restaurant, Pomp, Duck and Circumstance. During the official trip Prince Albert – who'd recently been linked with English model Naomi Campbell.

The previous summer the Prince had invited Stevie back to the Texas ranch for her second visit. This time she brought along her twenty-four-year-old blond niece Nicole who, perhaps predictably, seemed to turn the Prince's head. But although Albert was still sleeping with Stevie, her woman's intuition told her their three-year affair was coming to an end.

'At one point we were all swimming,' recalls Stevie, 'and Albert paddled over to Nicole and asked her if she wanted to go away on a trip with him. She just looked at him and said "no."'

In March 1995, Albert saw Stevie again when he arrived in New York as special guest at a Cartier jewel auction to raise money for the Princess Grace Foundation. As had been the case during previous visits, she was a constant visitor to suite 2121 at the Regency where she came and went at her leisure.

In August she visited Monaco with her actress friend Tina Louise, who had starred in television's *Gilligan's Island*; the Prince had arranged a personal tour of the pink Palace for them both.

But two months later, when Prince Albert once more arrived in New York, he brought a new girlfriend called Camilla Olsson with him. He didn't even call Stevie, who had arranged to leave her usual red rose on his pillow.

'I wish he had said something before,' she said. 'The word was out that this girl was staying in the same hotel as him, so I didn't contact him as I might have gotten in the way. Well, I just tried to be sensible about the whole thing. That part of our relationship was over but we are still friends. In fact, he calls me his "fax buddy".'

But Stevie Parker did manage to greet Albert when they met at the black tie Pomp, Duck and Circumstance event, which she was attending as a member of the Princess Grace Foundation USA fundraising committee.

'He just said hello – and that was about it,' recalls Stephanie.

Prince Albert was at the clown-themed club, which encourages audience participation, with his father and Caroline. During the entertainment waiter Tim Ward, who was playing a wise-cracking clown, walked past Albert and began to roast him – to the embarrassment of the guests.

'You're Prince Albert now, but if there were elections, would you be plumber Albert?' joked Ward.

When the waiter suggested the balding Prince Albert join the Hair Club for Men, Prince Rainier could not contain his anger. Beckoning Ward over to the table, the Prince slapped him hard in the face.

'He was being very insulting to Albert,' says Stevie. 'Prince Rainier was just protecting his son.'

Prince Albert must have taken the clown's comments to heart. Three months later he completely shaved his head as a dare during a bobsledding trip to Norway.

The Prince, who had been given the task of organising the 700th anniversary of the Grimaldi rule of Monaco, was planning to retire from bobsledding after the February 1996 world championships in Calgary, Canada.

'I've juggled my schedule around enough in the last few years to know what it means to try and find different niches for training,' explained the Prince, who lays claim to making 300 official appearances a year.

'I count everything. I count meetings that I chair. You know – going to the opening of such-and-such a congress. Prizegivings.'

And Prince Albert, who had met with a London public relations firm to discuss a possible new image for himself a year earlier, admitted he had a credibility problem with Monégasques, who didn't seem to appreciate his hard work on their behalf.

'Maybe I should communicate it better,' he said.

'I know a lot of people who just think I go out and party, or just do sports. But you know, it was largely vehicled by the press, because they only seem to show me in extreme circumstances or in situations that could cause a scandal because it sells their magazines and papers. So of course they are going to look for me walking out of a restaurant, or talking to a girl, or dancing with a girl at a charity ball. I mean, they're not going to say it's a charity ball, or maybe they will, but it's in such small print that no one will really know where it was. They see me with a girl either laughing or having a good time . . . so I don't know.'

CHAPTER TWENTY-THREE

APOCALYPSE MONACO

As PRINCESS CAROLINE was growing up her mother had pored through the social registers searching for a suitable husband. The two men Princess Grace had earmarked as appropriate marriage material were Prince Charles – and Prince Ernst Von Hanover, who is Queen Elizabeth's godson.

Highly individual and independent in her late teens, Caroline detested the idea of having what she considered to be an arranged marriage. Although she never got to meet the Prince of Wales, Prince Ernst was invited to the pink Palace by Princess Grace after they'd met in St Moritz. But Caroline, to her mother's disappointment, seemed totally uninterested in Ernst and went on to marry Philippe Junot.

If Salic law – which banned females from succeeding to the throne – had prevailed in England, Ernst, as head of the German House of Hanover, would now be King. But Queen Victoria had succeeded to the English throne in the last century and diverted power away from the Hanovers.

Born in 1954 in Germany, into a privileged world of titles and wealth, Prince Ernst served in the army before attending university and going to England to study at Cirencester Agricultural College.

In his early twenties he moved to London to work in film production, living the life of a self-indulgent playboy.

'Ernst would never open a bottle of champagne – he'd open a magnum,' a close friend told the *Tatler*. 'Likewise you'd never see a tin of caviar on the table – it would always be a bucket.'

Through his influence and contacts in the media the Prince always managed to keep a low profile. He was never mentioned in the British gossip columns. In 1981, Prince Ernst seemed to cast off his playboy image, marrying Swiss heiress Chantal Hochuli and moving to Fulham in London. Ernst and Chantal, who were known respectively as 'Piggy' and 'Piglet', were very much in love. Their friends in Chelsea believed they had the perfect marriage. And in 1983 they had a son, Prince Christian, followed by a second child, Prince "Ernestie", two years later.

Chantal and Ernst moved in the same rarefied royal circles as Princess Caroline and the three became close friends in the early 1990s. Caroline, who was then dating Vincent Lindon, was a regular guest at their Hurlingham home whenever she was in London. Indeed Chantal considered the Monaco Princess to be one of her closest friends and confidantes.

In January 1996, Princess Caroline had a very public row with Vincent Lindon at a gala dinner after a performance to celebrate the tenth anniversary of the Monte-Carlo Ballet. The occasion had also marked a new official acceptance of Lindon: for the first time in their five-year relationship he had escorted Caroline to both the performance and the dinner afterwards, although for reasons of protocol he was seated well away from the Princess at another table.

But during the dinner at the Hotel de Paris the French actor had become increasingly annoyed that Caroline was ignoring him as he sat by himself, smoking a cigarette. Then, in front of the other guests, Caroline and Lindon started a heated argument. The usually reticent actor finally stormed out of the dinner – and out of the Princess's life.

Princess Caroline was particularly vulnerable as she realised that her relationship with Vincent Lindon was over. Over the next few weeks she would increasingly turn to Prince Ernst for support and help. And suddenly Princess Grace's long-cherished dream finally came to fruition, as Ernst and Caroline fell madly in love.

'Ernst was saying that their friendship had progressed a step or two beyond what would normally be regarded as friendship,' said the London newspaper diarist, Ross Benson, who is a friend of Prince Ernst.

'They move in the same kind of world. It's a world of the Riviera, it's a world of skiing the Swiss Alps, it's a jet-set lifestyle, so they were inevitably moving in each other's company on occasion. Their friendship appears to have overstepped the boundaries of propriety.'

In February, Caroline and Ernst threw caution to the wind, flying off to Thailand together for a ten-day holiday and staying in a $5,000-a-night penthouse suite. Back in Fulham, Chantal had no idea her husband was with her best friend until she saw pictures of the couple shopping in the Istanbul Bazaar in *Hello* magazine which, failing to recognise Prince Ernst, referred to him only as 'a Jack Nicholson looka-like'. But after Caroline issued a statement describing the trip as 'cultural' Chantal accepted Ernst's explanation and they kissed and made up.

Over the next few months Princess Caroline seemed happier than she had ever been since the death of Stefano Casiraghi. Friends noticed she had a new zest for life; her affair with Ernst was now an open secret. In June the usually sombre-looking Princess was pictured giggling uncontrollably at the Paris Opera House and was all smiles again soon afterwards at the Monte-Carlo Jumping International.

That summer Princess Caroline spent time in Monaco sorting through her mother's belongings for a forthcoming auction, which would raise money for the Princess Grace Foundation. In April a sale of Jackie Onassis's personal belongings had exceeded all expectations by raising £22.5 million in New York; now, fourteen years after

Princess Grace's death, the Grimaldis were looking into the possibility of setting a new record with Princess Grace's Hollywood momentos.

Among the treasures gathering dust in the pink Palace were £1.5 million of personal jewellery Grace had owned before her marriage; it had been locked away in a strongbox for more than forty years. There was her MGM wedding gown; and Hollywood memorabilia, including her personal Hollywood photograph album, signed by friends such as Frank Sinatra, David Niven, James Stewart, Liz Taylor and Bing Crosby. Experts predicted the collection could fetch more than £30 million at Sotheby's.

Prince Rainier, who had always been jealous of Grace's Hollywood past, was only too happy to get rid of it. But he insisted that all her official gowns and possessions from after their marriage be retained for a future Princess Grace Museum to be built in Monaco.

Now seventy-three, Prince Rainier cut a tragic, lonely figure during public appearances. Increasingly he seemed to live in the past, lacking the razor-sharp attention to detail which had outwitted so many business adversaries in the past.

'In conversation the Prince is there one moment – and then clouded over,' said American television interviewer Diane Sawyer, who spoke to him at length in the winter of 1996. 'Sentences trail off into his own thoughts . . . memories.'

Once, during a public appearance, the Prince actually fell asleep and began snoring loudly, to the amusement of the audience and delight of the paparazzi. It took an embarrassed Prince Albert to wake him up in time for the award presentation.

But although his health was declining, Europe's last surviving dictator still fully believed in his divine right to rule. He had not relaxed his iron grip on Monaco one bit. Rainier had never tolerated criticism of any kind and this was clearly illustrated in June 1996 when he found himself at war with the English actress and animal-rights activist Virginia McKenna over conditions at his zoo.

Some years earlier the star of the film *Born Free* had been horrified when she'd seen a video showing the deplorable conditions in the zoo at the foot of the pink Palace, which Rainier had so proudly shown to Grace Kelly during their first meeting.

Said McKenna, the founder of the Born Free Foundation: 'I always thought for a place like Monaco, which has enormous wealth and riches and where humans lead the most amazing lifestyles, to have a slum zoo stuck in the cliff below the Palace is an obscenity.'

After Prince Rainier's refusal to acknowledge a barrage of letters of complaint from McKenna, she asked zoo expert John Gripper to visit the zoo. The English Department of the Environment Inspector was shocked by what he saw. The Prince's rhinoceroses and hippopotamuses were imprisoned in cramped cages barely the width of their own bodies. He reported back that 'tormented and distressed' animals were being housed in 'barren cages and cramped conditions'.

'One monkey had chewed its own tail out of boredom and had not been treated. This suggests to me that vets are not regularly monitoring the animals,' said Gripper. 'I have seen bad zoos in bad places around the world. But at least owners can claim that they have no money to improve things. The situation at Monaco is inexcusable.'

After years of failing to elicit any response from the Palace, McKenna and her fellow Foundation trustee Joanna Lumley decided to stage a 'spectacular' stunt at the 1996 World Music Awards in order to draw international attention to conditions at the zoo and embarrass the Prince into action.

The two actresses and their supporters arrived in Nice, planning to hire a plane to tow a large protest banner over Monaco demanding Rainier improve his zoo. But in the end they failed to find a pilot who would agree to fly over Monaco airspace and had to abandon the protest.

'I hope we can persuade Prince Rainier to make some real changes,' said Joanna Lumley. 'The animals simply can't be left in this condition.'

The editor of the *Riviera Reporter* Patrick Middleton, who covered the protest against the zoo, said Rainier's complete refusal to acknowledge even the smallest criticism hurt the principality.

'What's stupid is that they always take this line of ignoring things,' he explained. 'A fairly high-profile person like Virginia McKenna can send nineteen letters and not get a single response – how they thought she'd leave it there I don't know. But their basic policy is, never to answer. Just ignore it.'

A month later Prince Rainier quietly hired a professional zoo-keeper from Paris to clean up the zoo and improve the conditions.

'I know Prince Rainier would never concede that he's been prompted to do something because of the pressure by campaigners,' declared a victorious Virginia McKenna; 'but I think we can all feel a little proud about this.'

If anyone had reason to feel proud in Monaco that summer it was Princess Stephanie. Now married with two young children, the thirty-one-year-old Princess finally appeared to have emerged from her crazy days as a mature and responsible woman. Being a wife and a mother had changed her immeasurably; she delighted in the pleasures of her young family.

'To find true love and enjoy your kids – that's about the best thing that could happen,' said the Princess. 'Children change your whole way of seeing things.'

She was also embarking on yet another career, this time as a television personality. The Princess had signed a deal with the American network ABC to co-host an annual *Champions of Magic* special from Monte-Carlo. But ironically, during rehearsals for the show at the Monte-Carlo Opera House, Grace Kelly's daughter had some problems playing a Princess.

With four cameras rolling Stephanie ran through her lines in a little-girl voice. She kept breaking down into fits of giggles. During take after take she fluffed her lines; at one point the frustrated Princess snapped at the director, 'Don't tell me to smile!'

By the end of the session the Princess was having a tough time coping with the tedium of television.

'The other night, I had to keep running up and down the stairs, saying, "Welcome to Monaco!"' she told *TV Guide*'s Janice Kaplan.

'The director was insisting – "Say it like you really mean it!" And I thought, "I meant it the first fifteen times, but not now! Now I'm getting tired and I want to say, "Good night!"'

On July 1, Princess Stephanie and Ducruet celebrated their first wedding anniversary. The former bodyguard from the other side of the tracks had now been fully accepted into the Grimaldi family – he regularly appeared with the ruling family at high-profile events.

Stephanie seemed more in love with him than ever; even Rainier begrudgingly had to admit that perhaps he had misjudged his new son-in-law. Once a week the young couple would go to Le Texan for a hamburger with their children, but most nights Stephanie would stay at home and cook.

The couple were also going into business together, opening a Monaco branch of the Italian-based Replay Store complete with an adjoining cafe in Monte-Carlo's Rue Grimaldi. The Princess explained her venture: 'When you come you can outfit the family and feed them next door.'

But when she talked about her love for Ducruet, the Princess's eyes would mist over as she tried to express her deepest feelings.

'We were born in two different directions and life put us together,' she told an American interviewer. 'That was our destiny, that was meant to be. We found each other and fell madly in love and still are. He's very sensitive and a very deep person. And, besides, he's gorgeous.'

At the end of July, Stephanie and her children went to Belgium to watch Ducruet compete in a car race. Before the race, while he was on his own in the pits, Ducruet was introduced to a beautiful stripper called Fili Houteman, who had the dubious distinction of being the previous year's 'Miss Bare Breasts of Belgium'.

The voluptuous twenty-four-year-old showgirl began flirting with Ducruet; after a couple of minutes chatting they exchanged telephone numbers. As she said goodbye, Fili playfully brushed Ducruet's cheek with her hand and smiled seductively.

The 'chance' meeting was in fact a set-up by an old enemy of Ducruet's called Stehane de Lisiecki. De Lisesky saw an opportunity to destroy Daniel Ducruet's reputation and make a fortune for himself at the same time. Later, conspiracy theorists would speculate about possible Palace involvement in the plan.

The week after the race de Lisiecki rented a villa with a swimming pool in Villefranche, a mere nine miles from the Monaco border. It was then a simple matter of Fili making a telephone call to Ducruet and inviting him over to see her the following Monday afternoon.

'The trap was set,' said *Paris-Match* investigative reporter Jean Ker.

Before Ducruet arrived on August 5, de Lisesky made his final preparations for recording the planned seduction on film and video-tape. He set up a video on a tripod hidden in the bushes and two paparazzi photographers were carefully positioned with a perfect view of the pool. Fili had been thoroughly briefed to ensure she stayed within camera-range and in focus.

At 2 PM Ducruet drove up to the villa in his Mercedes together with his bodyguard and friend Alain Launois, nicknamed 'the gorilla'. Fili and a girlfriend, Theresa Belle, welcomed them and made them comfortable by the pool, serving them with rosé champagne. After a few glasses Fili and Ducruet began kissing on their beach lounger. And as they started getting more intimate Belle and Launois slipped into the villa, leaving them alone.

As the video rolled and the photographers started shooting, Fili carefully placed the recliner mattress by the edge of the pool. And she and Princess Stephanie's husband stripped naked and began making love.

'It really was pornographic,' says Ker.

The following Friday, a tuxedoed Daniel Ducruet escorted Princess Stephanie to the 1996 Red Cross Gala at the Sporting Club. Self-assured and relaxed, he sat at the head table with Prince Rainier, Albert,

Caroline, Stephanie and Princess Antoinette. After dining on caviar, lobster and *filet* of beef, the 800 guests were entertained by American singer Michael Bolton as they sipped the finest champagne. As he made effortless small talk with his Grimaldi in-laws, the working-class boy from the wrong side of the tracks looked untouchable.

But less than two weeks later Daniel Ducruet's world came crashing down around him when he discovered that sexually-explicit photographs of him and Houteman were about to be published in two Italian tabloid magazines. In desperation he telephoned the editors of *Gente* and *Eva Tremila*, pleading with them to stop publication, but they refused.

On August 27, the magazines published twenty-six pages of photographs of Ducruet and Fili, promising even better shots the following week.

In an attempt to take the initiative and exercise some damage control, Ducruet broke the news to his wife, claiming he'd been drugged by Fili. A shocked and tearful Princess Stephanie grabbed her children and fled to Roc Agel, to be met by Prince Rainier and Caroline. They told her that she must file for divorce immediately; that she must exorcise Ducruet from the Grimaldi family.

It was a moment of sheer humiliation for Stephanie, who had spent so long persuading Rainier to accept the man she loved. At first she defiantly tried to find excuses for her husband's betrayal, but soon she collapsed in tears, finding comfort in her father's soothing embrace.

'I think children should know that there's not a judge sitting there to wave a finger at them saying, "I told you so,"' Prince Rainier would later explain.

Two days after the photographs were published a swimsuited Stephanie met her husband outside the Monte-Carlo Beach Club. With paparazzi looking on the Princess gave Ducruet a cold stare before kissing him and going into the club.

Although Ducruet claimed he'd been drugged and forced to have sex with Fili against his will, the pictures that were published the following week were definitely X-rated, as was the ninety-minute video now being sold across the border in Italy. The Palace kept a frosty silence on what was being called 'l'affaire Ducruet'; although strictly banned in Monaco, truckloads of smuggled magazines were readily available for £35 under the counter in the principality's bars and cafés.

As if the Daniel Ducruet scandal wasn't bad enough, Monégasques woke up a week later to see pictures of an inexplicably-bald Princess Caroline illustrating their morning newspaper. Paparazzi had snapped the now-hairless Princess at her St Remy home on September 5 after a shopping trip with Prince Ernst.

With just four months to go before the family's much-anticipated 700th anniversary, what should be a triumph for the principality now threatened to be overshadowed by shame and scandal. APOCALYPSE MONACO trumpeted *Paris-Soir*, while the London *Sun* noted that one of the world's most beautiful women now looked like a 'concentration-camp victim'.

Even the Grimaldis' spiritual advisor, Monaco's highest-ranking churchman Archbishop Joseph Sardou, felt compelled to comment on the family's current misfortunes:

'The personal problems confronting the Grimaldis sometimes add a bizarre touch to Monaco,' he admitted.

The extraordinary photographs of Caroline immediately sparked rumours that the Princess was undergoing chemotherapy for cancer, or had a mysterious disease. When the pictures appeared Caroline called her aunt Lizanne in New Jersey to reassure her that it was only nervous alopecia. One morning she had discovered that some of her hair had fallen out – so she had completely shaved her head.

'She said, "Lizzie, my hair started falling out!"' recalls her Aunt Lizanne. 'I think it was because of the stress.'

Over the past few months Caroline's affair with Prince Ernst had escalated. Romantic trysts in London and New York City had been reported; there had also been a dramatic face-to-face showdown between Caroline and Ernst's wife Chantal, who had now accused her one-time friend of breaking up her marriage. Many people had sided with Chantal; some of Caroline's best friends were no longer speaking to her. The pressures on the stoic Princess, who seldom showed any outer emotion, had had a dramatic physical effect.

Prince Albert, too, tried to reassure the world that his sister was not dying of cancer as he completed preparations for the 700th anniversary celebrations.

'It's a skin problem – a dermatology thing,' he said. 'It's nothing serious, and her hair will grow back. Other than that she's fine.'

Furious at being photographed in her home by paparazzi with telephoto lenses, Princess Caroline now defiantly appeared in public flaunting her skinhead look. She even turned it into a stunning fashion statement by wearing the same jewelled turbans her mother had once worn.

On September 16, Princess Stephanie sat down at her desk and, conforming to princely protocol, wrote her father an official letter requesting a divorce from Daniel Ducruet. The letter, which publicly admitted her mistake in marrying Ducruet, was the ultimate humiliation.

Two days earlier Ducruet had returned from Morocco, where he had fled to escape the press. He had already met his wife several times to beg for a reconciliation. The Princess – who still loved her betrayer – had finally been persuaded by her father that continuing her marriage would irreparably harm Monaco and the Grimaldis. After much crying and hand-holding between father and daughter, the Princess had reluctantly agreed to a divorce.

'Rainier was very relieved that Steffie had decided to get a divorce and get rid of that man,' Lizanne Kelly LeVine says. 'He was very happy with that.'

As Princess Stephanie took Louis and Pauline to Disneyworld in Orlando, Florida, where they enjoyed a very happy vacation together, Daniel Ducruet attempted to explain his actions to *Hello* magazine.

Self-pitying and tearful, the disgraced Ducruet delivered a pathetic *mea culpa*.

'My mistake has destroyed me,' he sobbed. 'I have betrayed my wife, I have betrayed her love and I have betrayed my children. I have humiliated Stephanie in the eyes of the whole world.'

Explaining how he came to be captured on film making love to Fili Houteman, Ducruet theorised that his drinks had been spiked, and 'cursed' the day he had met the stripper.

'I got there and she threw herself at me crying and I comforted her,' said Ducruet. 'We had a drink and then another one. I lost my self-control at that point.'

On October 5 – the very day that their quickie divorce was finalised in the Monaco courts – Princess Stephanie bought Ducruet a $1.2 million apartment and offered him financial help for the sake of their children. Under the divorce terms Ducruet would see the children every other weekend and for half their holidays. When her angry father demanded she sever all ties with her ex-husband, Stephanie said that she wanted the children to be able to visit their father, and to be able to do so in a pleasant environment.

Just days after their divorce Stephanie and Ducruet were together again at the official opening of their Replay Store and Café. They seemed friendly and relaxed, as if nothing had happened, as they inspected their new business and spoke to the press about their venture.

'We wanted to put Monaco on the map again,' explained the hapless Ducruet.

That fall a turbaned Princess Caroline was in Manhattan to preside over the Princess Grace Foundation Awards gala, which included a performance by the Monte-Carlo Ballet. Amidst reports that Prince Ernst was to separate from Chantal – who was said to have expressed surprise that her husband would choose a 'bald woman' – the Princess retained her composure throughout.

The American fashion bible *Women's Wear Daily* applauded the Princess for 'looking terrific in a turban'. Caroline gleefully posed for photographs with her head wrapped in a black and white polka-dot scarf at a luncheon at Mortimer's, and in a deep wine-coloured silk scarf during a shopping trip around Manhattan. And she visited leading New York dermatologist Dr Joel Kassimir at his Upper East Side offices; he started her on a treatment programme.

On her return to Europe, Princess Caroline turned her tragedy into triumph when she posed for a series of stunningly beautiful photos to be published in a book called *Past and Present* by the French artist and writer, Francois-Marie Banier. Shot from below, with the Princess's bald head bathed in heavy shadow, the picture was a silent statement to the Grimaldis' tenacity and determination to survive despite all the odds. And that strength of will had seen the family through seven centuries of absolute dominance in Monaco.

EPILOGUE

※

AT CHRISTMAS IN 1996 the beleaguered Grimaldis flew out to Jamaica to prepare themselves for the coming 700th anniversary of their ancestor Francesco the Spiteful's storming of Monaco. 1996 had been the Grimaldis' *annus horribilis*, but Caroline and Stephanie seemed blithely unperturbed as they frolicked, unscathed, in the warm Caribbean water of Montego Bay, surrounded by their children. The Curse of the Grimaldis may have struck with a vengeance – but the family were still standing.

Two weeks later, when Prince Rainier led his children out on to the balcony of the Palace for the 700th anniversary on January 8, 1997, he himself was just two years short of celebrating his own half-century of rule. During that time he had transformed his country from a gambling Ruritania into one of the world's richest financial centres.

But there were lingering questions to be answered: had the ageing monarch, now seventy-four, clung to power too long? Was he out of touch? Rainier's business innovations – which worked well in the 1960s and 1970s – were out of step in the 1990s. Many felt that in order to survive into the twenty-first century, the principality would have to become less autocratic, less dependent on one man.

'I think over the last few years there's been something of a cloud gathering over the horizon,' explained the *Financial Times*'s Andrew Jack.

'And there's a real question about its financial security, its diversity and really the future of its political institutions.'

In 1996 Monaco had a budget deficit for the third year running and the SBM was haemorrhaging money. With no land left to build on the real estate market was stagnant; prices had plummeted, leaving many apartments empty. The principality's future was uncertain – and the ageing Prince, who had already endured one heart by-pass operation, stubbornly refused to relinquish power.

Judy Balaban Quine, who has known Rainier for more than forty years, is convinced that he will never willingly abdicate. In the late 1980s, while preparing her book *The Bridesmaids*, Quine discussed retirement with Rainier several times.

'Rainier was speaking like a person who was contemplating retirement,' said Quine. 'I looked at him and thought, "You are not going to retire. They're going to have to carry you out."'

The tragedy of Monaco is that Rainier's refusal to entrust his son with any meaningful power and responsibility has prevented Albert from growing up and realising his full potential. Even on the eve of the 700th anniversary Rainier was belittling Albert, telling reporters that his son must 'sharpen his skills' and 'gain from experience' before he was ready to take over.

'Monaco's fortune is based on the past brilliance of Prince Rainier and the [ruling] family in generating publicity and investment,' says Roger-Louis Bianchini of *Nice-Matin*. 'The uncertainty about the future of the [ruling] family goes hand in hand with the uncertainty about the future of the principality in general.'

Although Albert talks a good game – forever declaring his willingness to follow his father, who involves him in all major decisions – he has yet to be put to the test.

Now almost forty, the Prince still waits in the wings. Ten years ago he might well have risen to the task of government and grown with it. But now, as he approaches middle age, he is still at play, whether it's with girls or bobsleds.

Dubbed 'Dirty Bertie' by the British tabloids, the Prince good-naturedly jokes that his reputation for having slept with more than 150 women is a 'conservative estimate'. The truth is, Albert is quite happy to be a bachelor boy. He is in no hurry to give up his pleasures to rule.

'Rainier says he's a little reluctant,' says his Aunt Lizanne. 'He's having such a good time! He's travelling around and doing things. And [besides] Rainier likes to keep his hand in. He's very active and he's not ready to be put out to pasture.'

Although he worked hard throughout 1997 on the 700th-anniversary celebrations, Prince Albert still dreamed of coming out of retirement and competing in his fourth Olympics in Japan in the year 1998.

'Well, I thought about this a long time and I'm going to try to,' he said in June 1997. 'It's going to be extremely difficult – especially with the coming year we're having – but I've juggled my schedule around enough in the last few years to know what it means to try.'

To ensure the success of the anniversary celebrations, Rainier and Albert spent millions of pounds, hoping to present a positive, dynamic image of the principality. But instead of a glorious ten-month-long round of galas, parades and festivals, the celebrations became an elaborate, prolonged exercise in damage limitation.

The year began with the Café de Paris placed firmly at the centre of a kick-back scandal. The SBM suspended fourteen employees – including a croupier – for helping certain customers win big in return for payment. As the main SBM stockholder, Prince Rainier was forced, yet again, to reorganise the troubled company, bringing in a new Director General to root out corruption.

Indeed, as the 700th celebrations wound to a close there were startling, uncorroborated allegations from England's Channel 4 investigative programme *Secret Lives* that in the late 1970s Princess Grace had become the high priestess of a bizarre Christian sex cult, donating six million pounds to prove her dedication. The documentary wildly speculated the Order of the Solar Temple may have been involved in Grace's death after she became disillusioned and demanded her money back.

To counter this negative publicity Prince Albert gave a series of interviews to selected publications to mark the Grimaldis' 700th anniversary. He accused the media of being directly responsible for the principality's poor moral and ethical record.

'In certain newspapers, sensationalism has overshadowed the "serious" economic reality of the principality,' the Prince told *Le Figaro*. 'That damages us a lot. We are compared unfairly to showbiz stars, people think they have the right to invade our private lives. I take great care to protect my privacy. It's the only way to have any freedom of action.'

By March 1997 Princess Caroline had turned forty. As her hair had begun growing back she dropped her turban look. Prince Ernst, a regular visitor to her home in St Remy, had been accepted by her three children as the new man in their mother's life. After spending months denying her husband's relationship with Caroline, Chantal Hochuli had finally stepped out of the love triangle, telling friends her sixteen-year marriage was over.

'A woman can only take so much humiliation,' said Chantal's friend, gossip columnist Taki Theodoracopulos. 'Chantal is a saint.'

Three months after the divorce papers were filed in London, Prince Ernst and Caroline were photographed cuddling off the coast of Spain in the Princess's yacht, *Pacha III*. And by October they made their first public appearance together at a high society wedding at the Palace of Versailles, prompting speculation that the Princess would soon marry for the third time – a marriage which would elevate her from a Serene Highness to a Royal Highness. On hearing the news, Prince Rainier quipped, 'Well, at least he's one of us!'

But her younger sister Stephanie's future looked far less secure. Although the Princess had marked her divorce from Daniel Ducruet by adding several new tattoos to her growing collection, most days found her quietly working behind the counter of her Replay Store while a bodyguard stood guard outside. But her fragility was illustrated in March when she fled the 700th Anniversary Rose Ball in tears, as soon as the dancing began.

'I don't know how long the wound will take to heal,' Stephanie said three months after her divorce.

'But I sure see men in a very different way now. It's like, I think men are all the same.'

She bounced back by hosting the World Music Awards, the highlight of which was an impromptu performance by Prince Albert of the popular dance, the 'Macarena'. And although she was linked to a colourful set of new boyfriends – including movie star Jean Claude Van Damme, model Marcus Schenkenberg, ski instructor Boris Brun, and soccer star Patrick Blondeau – Stephanie seemed melancholy.

In June Daniel Ducruet crassly tried to exploit his betrayal by writing a book taking the form of a letter of apology to Princess Stephanie. During a live interview on German television to promote *Letter To Stephanie*, he was ambushed as Fili Houteman walked out unannounced to confront him for the first time since their fateful tryst. Millions of viewers watched the hapless Ducruet go on a violent rampage, destroying the set before kicking down a door on his way out.

All through his publicity-hungry antics Princess Stephanie maintained her dignity, bringing up her children and getting on with life. After finally severing her business ties with Ducruet in the summer, Stephanie opened a new branch of Replay in Barcelona and was rumoured to be romantically involved with her new business partner, Claudio Buziol.

'She's doing very well,' said her Aunt Lizanne. 'She has her business and she has her children. She has done a fantastic job. She seems to be quite content.'

The Monte-Carlo Replay store and restaurant became a life-line for Stephanie during her darkest days. But by October she seemed to be back to her old self again as she took yet another bodyguard, Jean Raymond, as a lover and moved him into her Le Clos Saint-Martin home.

Princess Stephanie's roller-coaster love life was off again – at full speed.

The Princess's constant companion throughout her troubled life has been her mother, Princess Grace. Stephanie believes she is always there in the background, guiding her. She freely admits that she talks to her dead mother every day – and very often it is an appeal for help.

Indeed, more than fifteen years after her death, the haunting presence of Princess Grace still permeates every corner of Monaco. The Monégasques revere her as a saint; her picture is in almost every shop window and hangs on most restaurant walls. The beautiful young American Princess, who came to their country and changed it forever with her own special magic, will never be forgotten.

Without Princess Grace, the Monaco fairytale quickly became a nightmare. Since her passing, her husband and children have faltered badly; one can only speculate on what might have been if she had not taken that tragic last ride from Roc Agel.

'I think Grace and Rainier would have had a very happy old age together,' says Gwen Robyns. 'The children would have been better behaved, certainly. Rainier would have retired and Grace would have calmed down and gone along with her flower-pressing and her ballet. It's all so cruel – and a huge tragedy.'

As a tribute to Grace, Prince Rainier erected a statue to Grace in Fontvielle. She will stand there for eternity, looking out over her principality. Surrounding her in the memorial garden are beds of roses named after Grimaldi family members – 'Rainier', 'Grace', 'Stephanie', 'Caroline', 'Albert'. Each spring the garden bursts forth into bloom; but by some mysterious force of nature one rose always flowers a month earlier than the others. Named the 'Cinderella', this rose stands out from the others, as classically beautiful and unique as Grace Kelly herself. The Monégasque gardeners who lovingly tend the roses have no explanation for this phenomenon. But they agree that the Cinderella rose provides a fitting memorial, to Grace and to Monaco.

NOTES

———— ❦ ————

Information on the preparations for the 700th anniversary celebrations, interview with Prince Albert, 19 June, 1997.

CHAPTER ONE – THE CRASH

Details of Princess Grace's medical history and treatment, interview with the Countess of Lombardy, 17 May, 1997.
'She wasn't feeling too well', *Rainier and Grace*, Jeffrey Robinson, p 268.
Information on Princess Grace's telephone call, her depression and headaches, interview with Gwen Robyns, 21 July, 1997.
Background on Princess Grace's problems with Stephanie, *Grace*, Robert Lacey, pp 357 and 358.
Rainier leaving all parenting to Grace, interview with Lizanne Kelly LeVine, 10 June, 1997.
Account of the morning of Grace's death, *Rainier and Grace*, Jeffrey Robinson, p 260.
'I thought the car was going to blow up', *Rainier and Grace*, Jeffrey Robinson, p 270.
Background on Princess Grace's hospital arrival, interview with the Countess of Lombardy, 17 May, 1997.
'It took a long time' *Rainier and Grace*, Jeffrey Robinson, p 271.
'Grace's head shaved', interview with Countess of Lombardy, 17 May, 1997.
Information on CAT scan at Dr Mourou's office, *Grace*, Robert Lacey, pp 369–70.
Princess Stephanie's reaction to hearing of Grace's death, interview with Countess of Lombardy, 17 May, 1997.
Peggy's reaction at seeing Grace's wig and make-up, interview with Gwen Robyns, 21 July, 1997.
Stephanie's grief while watching the funeral, *Rainier and Grace*, Jeffrey Robinson, p 266.
Details on the private reception after the funeral, interview with Judy Balaban Quine, 29 July, 1997.

CHAPTER TWO – ONCE UPON A TIME

Perspective about Jean-Louis Marson, *Monaco: Une Affaire Qui Tourne*, Roger-Louis Bianchini, p 184.
'I think he's having. . . .', *People*, 15 November, 1982.
Insight on the state of Grace and Rainier's marriage, interview with Gwen Robyns, 21 July, 1997.
Description of Grace's arrival in Monaco, *The Bridesmaids*, Judith Balaban Quine, p 168.
'He's charming . . .', *Grace: The Secret lives of a Princess*, James Spada, p 142.
Rainier's wooing of Grace, *Rainier and Grace*, Jeffrey Robinson, p 73.
'Sometimes I saw her . . .', *Grace: The Secret lives of a Princess*, James Spada, p 151.
Background on the Kelly's, *Grace: The Secret lives of a Princess*, James Spada; *Grace*, Robert Lacey; and *Princess Grace*, Gwen Robyns.
'It used to be said in the city of Philadelphia', *The Grimaldi Dynasty: Life With Grace*, Meridian TV.
Jack Kelly's unfaithfulness, *Grace*, Robert Lacey, p 23.
'She was a strong martinet . . .', interview with Gwen Robyns, 2 September, 1997.
'Grace was always sniffling . . .', *Grace*, Robert Lacey, p 20.
'I was not too fond . . .', *Grace: The Secret lives of a Princess*, James Spada, p 25.
Grace's loss of virginity, *Grace: The Secret lives of a Princess*, James Spada, p 27.
'She had gotten a . . .', *The Grimaldi Dynasty: Life with Grace*, Meridian TV.
Description of Cassini's unhappy weekend with the Kelly's, *Grace*, Robert Lacey, p 177.
'When my father . . .', *The Grimaldi Dynasty: Life with Grace*, Meridian TV.
'It's too delicate a matter . . .', interview with Oleg Cassini, 14 August, 1997.

CHAPTER THREE – THE WEDDING OF THE CENTURY

'I made up my mind . . .', *Grace: The Secret lives of a Princess*, James Spada, p 159.
Background on Rainier's first meeting with the Kellys, *Grace*, Robert Lacey, p 222.
'His intentions . . .', *Grace*, Robert Lacey, p 38.
'Young ones', *Princess Grace*, Gwen Robyns, p 130.
'I think he's very fascinating . . .', *Grace*, Robert Lacey, p 223.
Grace's announcement that she and Rainier were engaged, *Grace: The Secret lives of a Princess*, James Spada, p 161.
'I hope you won't run around . . .', *Rainier and Grace*, Jeffrey Robinson, p 76.
'We happened to meet . . .', *Grace*, Robert Lacey, p 226.
'She didn't have time . . .', *Grace: The Secret lives of a Princess*, James Spada, p 162.
'I don't really believe in love . . .', *Prime Time Live*, ABC, 8 January, 1997.

NOTES

Background on Giselle Pascall's medical check-up, *Grace: The Secret lives of a Princess*, James Spada, p 164.
Details of Grace's letters to Don Richardson, *Grace: The Secret lives of a Princess*, James Spada, p 165.
Details of MGM's contract to film wedding, *Grace: The Secret lives of a Princess*, James Spada, p 187.
'It was a media circus . . .', interview with Rita Gam, 4 August, 1997.
Monégasques cashing in on wedding, *Grace: The Secret lives of a Princess*, James Spada, p 201.
'Grace kept saying . . .', *Rainier and Grace*, Jeffrey Robinson, p 86.
'The British Royal Family did not consider Rainier an equal', interview with Gwen Robyns, 21 August, 1997.
'Grace looked like Snow White . . .', *The Grimaldi Dynasty: Life with Grace*, Meridian TV.
'Watching Grace come down the aisle . . .', *The Bridesmaids*, Judith Balaban Quine, p 227.

CHAPTER FOUR – LIFE IN MONACO

'Grace had no idea . . .', interview with Gwen Robyns, 21 August, 1997.
'There was some suspicion . . .', interview with Judy Balaban Quine, 19 July, 1997.
'Naturally I was a stranger . . .', *Today Show*, NBC, 3 August, 1996.
'Grace had great problems . . .', *Rainier and Grace*, Jeffrey Robinson, p 214.
'For God's sake . . .', *Grace*, Robert Lacey, p 273.
'A European husband . . .', *Today Show*, NBC, 3 August, 1966.
'He was Mr. Flowers . . .', *The Grimaldi Dynasty: Life with Grace*, Meridian TV.
'Grace told me . . .', interview with Gwen Robyns, 21 July, 1997.
'Oh shucks . . .', *Grace*, Robert Lacey, p 276.
Grace's reaction to Caroline's birth, *The Grimaldi Dynasty: Life with Grace*, Meridian TV.
'My beloved life . . .', *Grace: The Secret lives of a Princess*, James Spada, p 223.
'She attracted people . . .', *The Grimaldi Dynasty: Life with Grace*, Meridian TV.
Details on Rainier's early PR strategy, *Grace*, Robert Lacey, p 279.
Background on Grace's breast feeding, *Grace: The Secret lives of a Princess*, James Spada, p 225.
Caroline kidnapping hoax, *Grace*, Robert Lacey, p 281.
'It's a family that was made by publicity . . .', *Prime Time Live*, ABC, 8 January, 1997.
'Grace had notions . . .', interview with Judy Balaban Quine, 29 July, 1997.
'It's a sort of playground . . .', *Princess Grace*, Gwen Robyns, p 254.
Details of Grace's parenting philosophy, *Grace: The Secret lives of a Princess*, James Spada, p 227.
'I've always treated children . . .', *McCall's magazine*, December, 1974.
'I don't think they realized . . .', *Princess Grace*, Gwen Robyns, p 180.
'When you're that young . . .', interview with Kate Powers, 16 May, 1997.
'There were sort of visions . . .', *Prime Time Live*, ABC, 3 September, 1997.
Character background of Princess Caroline as a young child, interview with Judy Balaban Quine, 29 September, 1997.
'I'm afraid I'm very severe . . .', *Grace*, Robert Lacey, p 294.
'Grace and Rainier included their children . . .', interview with Judy Balaban Quine, 29 September, 1997.
Caroline's behaviour in Saks, *Grace*, Robert Lacey, p 295.

CHAPTER FIVE – GRIMALDI INC

'It's a heavy weight . . .', interview with Prince Albert, 19 June, 1997.
Background on principality, Monaco government information statistics.
Grimaldi domination over neighbours, *Biography* magazine, December, 1997.
Background on Princess Charlotte-Catherine Grimaldi, *The Grimaldis of Monaco*, Anne Edwards, pp 34–46.
The legitimizing of Louise-Juliette, *Grace*, Robert Lacey, p 266.
Prince Louis aiding the Nazis, *Biography* magazine, December, 1997.
'It was not an especially joyous moment . . .', *Rainier and Grace*, Jeffrey Robinson, p 29.
Rainier's friendship with Jean-Louis Marsan, *Monaco: Une Affaire Qui Tourne*, Roger-Louis Bianchini, p 184.
Prince Rainier's time in Paris during the Second World War, *Rainier and Grace*, Jeffrey Robinson, p 30.
Monaco laundering Nazi money, *Daily Telegraph*, 19 July, 1997.
Washington's treatment of Monaco after the war, *Grace*, Robert Lacey, p 268.
Rainier's daredevil antics, *Grace: The Secret lives of a Princess*, James Spada, p 181.
Early Monaco banking scandals, *Rainier and Grace*, Jeffrey Robinson, p 37.
'Hot-bed of gossip . . .', *Grace*, Robert Lacey, p 268.

CHAPTER SIX – GRACE IN MONACO

'Well she did create . . .', interview with Rita Gam, 4 August, 1997.
Background on the banning of the pigeon shoot, *Palace: My life in the Royal Family of Monaco*, Baron Christian de Massy, p 58.
'Grace brought a great deal of pizazz . . .', interview with Michael Powers, 15 May, 1997.
'The American Princess . . .', *Palace: My life in the Royal Family of Monaco*, Baron Christian de Massy, p 101.
'She brought us heart . . .', *Princess Grace*, Gwen Robyns, p 187.
'The Red Cross will be the end . . .', *Grace*, Robery Lacey, p 293.
'She was heavily criticized . . .', interview with Gwen Robyns, 21 August, 1997.
'Monaco was such a glamorous place . . .', interview with Jeanne Kelly van Remoortel, 17 May, 1997.
Grace's subscription to Celebrity Bulletin, *Grace: The Secret lives of a Princess*, James Spada, p 239.
'He was always jealous . . .', *Grace: The Secret lives of a Princess*, James Spada, p 242.
'The palace accommodations . . .', interview with Lizanne Kelly LeVine, 10 June, 1997.

Jack Kelly's dislike of palace protocol, *Grace: The Secret lives of a Princess*, James Spada, p 240.
Details of Grace's last hospital visit with Jack Kelly, *Grace: The Secret lives of a Princess*, James Spada, p 263.
Grace's despair over the death of her father, *Grace*, Robert Lacey, p 278.
'He wasn't a bit faithful . . .', interview with Gwen Robyns, 21 August, 1997.
Rainier's Sunday afternoon trysts, *New York Post*, 29 September, 1994.
'I think first . . .', *Prime Time Live*, ABC, 8 January, 1997.

CHAPTER SEVEN – THE WONDER YEARS

'Over the phone . . .', *The Bridesmaids*, Judy Balaban Quine, p 334.
'Grace adored Stephanie . . .', interview with Gwen Robyns, 21 August, 1997.
'She was a most demanding child . . .', *The Bridesmaids*, Judy Balaban Quine, p 337.
Stephanie's worship of Albert, interview with Gwen Robyns, 21 August, 1997.
'I played with Stephanie a lot . . .', *Rainier and Grace*, Jeffrey Robinson, p 219.
'Caroline was clearly . . .', interview with Judy Balaban Quine, 29 July, 1997.
'The kids are . . .', interview with Lizanne Kelly LeVine, 10 June, 1997.
'A year off.', *Grace*, Robert Lacey, p 307.
'I think that the thing . . .', *The Today Show*, NBC, 3 August, 1966.
'He has me cornered . . .', *Grace*, Robert Lacey, p 309.
'In a way the principality . . .', *Rainier and Grace*, Jeffrey Robinson, p 143.
'Rainier was very astute . . .', interview with Gwen Robyns, 21 August, 1997.
Background on Monaco Economic Development Corporation, *Grace*, Robert Lacey, p 284.
Background on Princess Grace's state visit to Paris, *The Bridesmaids*, Judy Balaban Quine, p 271.
President de Gaulle orders Emile Pelletier to tell Rainier to relax ban on trading Radio Monte-Carlo stocks, *Grace: The Secret lives of a Princess*, James Spada, p 256.
Rainier's firing of Pelletier, *Rainier and Grace*, Jeffrey Robinson, p 40.
'They may enclose Monaco . . .', *Grace*, Robert Lacey, p 286.
Background on Onassis' relationship with Prince Rainier, *Grace*, Robert Lacey, p 305.
'He wanted to keep the principality . . .', *The Grimaldi Dynasty: Life with Grace*, Meridian TV.
Rainier's letter to Rupert Allan, *The Grimaldi Dynasty: Life with Grace*, Meridian TV.
'Monte Greco', *Palace: My life in the Royal Family of Monaco*, Baron Christian de Massy, p 130.
Princess Grace's attack on Onassis, *Playboy*, January, 1966.
Grace's belief in astrology, *Palace: My life in the Royal Family of Monaco*, Baron Christian de Massy, p 60.
'Grace said she found it hard . . .', *The Bridesmaids*, Judy Balaban Quine, p 378.
'Grace's greatest treat in life . . .', interview with Gwen Robyns, 21 August, 1997.
Princess Grace's daily routine, *Palace: My life in the Royal Family of Monaco*, Baron Christian de Massy, p 105.
'There's always a crisis . . .', *Philadelphia Evening Bulletin*, 23 July, 1971.
Background on the 1974 Red Cross Ball, *Woman's Wear Daily*, 2 July, 1974.
'She was unbelievable . . .', *Rainier and Grace*, Jeffrey Robinson, p 185.

CHAPTER EIGHT – GROWING UP IN PUBLIC

Nothing is more important to me . . .', *Grace: The Secret lives of a Princess*, James Spada, p 284.
Background on Caroline's time at St. Mary's Convent, *The Bridesmaids*, Judy Balaban Quine, p 382.
'Caroline had Rainier's Latin temperament . . .', interview with Judy Balaban Quine, 29 July, 1997.
Details on Prince Albert's stammer, *Palace: My life in the Royal Family of Monaco*, Baron Christian de Massy, p 211.
'Albie was shyer . . .', interview with Judy Balaban Quine, 29 July, 1997.
Curtis Bill Pepper's account of his day with Grace and the children, *McCall's*, December, 1974.
'She was spoiled . . .', *Palace: My life in the Royal Family of Monaco*, Baron Christian de Massy, p 210.
'Caroline went a little crazy . . .', *Grace: The Secret lives of a Princess*, James Spada, p 285.
'Grace was mortally terrified . . .', *The Bridesmaids*, Judy Balaban Quine, p 379.
'I remember as a girl . . .', *McCalls*, December, 1974.
She wants to fly . . .', ibid.
'It was clear to Grace . . .', *The Bridesmaids*, Judy Balaban Quine, p 379.
'She is not a normal girl . . .', *McCalls*, December, 1974.
'Stephanie was terrified . . .', interview with Judy Balaban Quine, 29 July, 1997.
Princess Caroline's 18th birthday interview, *New York Times*, 19 January, 1975.
'It was the first time . . .', interview with Judy Balaban Quine, 29 July, 1997.
Caroline's reaction to Grace's affairs, *Grace: The Secret lives of a Princess*, James Spada, p 289.
'She was careless . . .', *Chicago Tribune*, 20 March, 1977.

CHAPTER NINE – THE PRINCESS BRIDE

Background on Gwn Robyns' first meeting with Princess Grace, interviews with Gwen Robyns, 21 July, 1997 and 21 August, 1997.
'He was very charming . . .', interview with Lizanne Kelly LeVine, 10 June, 1997.
'She cried most of the week . . .', *Newsweek*, 26 June, 1978.
'Philippe has given me . . .', *Ladies Home Journal*, January, 1981.
'Caroline was mesmerized . . .', interview with Gwen Robyns, 21 July, 1997.
Prince Rainier's anger at Caroline's topless photographs, *Grace: The Secret lives of a Princess*, James Spada, p 294.
Junot's proposal to Caroline, *Ladies Home Journal*, January, 1981.
'Uncle Rainier thought . . .', *Palace: My life in the Royal Family of Monaco*, Baron Christian de Massy, p 227.

'There were strong principles . . .', *Prime Time Live*, ABC, 8 January, 1997.
'It's different with each child . . .', *McCalls*, December, 1974.
'Albie was a piece of . . .', interview with Judy Balaban Quine, 29 July, 1997.
Background on Prince Albert's childhood, *Interview magazine*, January, 1986.
'He was quiet . . .', *Palace: My life in the Royal Family of Monaco*, Baron Christian de Massy, p 211.
'It was embarrassing . . .', *Grace*, Robert Lacey, p 309.
'He had a temper . . .', *Prime Time Live*, ABC, 8 January, 1997.
Albert's early dating, *The Bridesmaids*, Judy Balaban Quine, p 410.
'He took to American College Life . . .', *The Grimaldi Dynasty: Life with Grace*, Meridian TV.
'He is friendly . . .', *Sun*, 30 October, 1977.
'He would never use . . .', *W* magazine, November, 1997.
'I would be driving a car . . .', *The Grimaldi Dynasty: Life with Grace*, Meridian TV.
'Quite frankly . . .', interview with Prince Albert, 19 June, 1997.
'He's very accommodating . . .', *People*, 15 November, 1982.
Albert's loss of virginity . . .', ibid.
'He created a certain kind . . .', interview with Judy Balaban Quine, 29 July, 1997.
Background on the pre-wedding ball, *Grace: The Secret lives of a Princess*, James Spada, p 296.
'I bought her a wonderful dress . . .', *The Bridesmaids*, Judy Balaban Quine, p 451.
Confusion over Junot's profession, *Washington Post*, 29 June, 1978.
Princess Grace's view of the curse of the Grimaldis, interview with Gwen Robyns, 21 July, 1997.
'That's when it started . . .', *Rainier and Grace*, Jeffrey Robinson, p 228.
Junot's visit to Studio 54, *Ladies Home Journal*, January 1981.
'She really loved him . . .', *Grace: The Secret lives of a Princess*, James Spada, p 298.
'Poor Caroline's marriage . . .', *The Grimaldi Dynasty: Life with Grace*, Meridian TV.
Caroline's break-up with Junot, interview with Gwen Robyns, 21 August, 1997.
Grace's advice to Caroline to divorce, *Rainier and Grace*, Jeffrey Robinson, p 228.
'There were problems . . .', *Grace: The Secret lives of a Princess*, James Spada, p 300.

CHAPTER TEN – HONG KONG ON THE RIVIERA

'First of all he gave . . .', interview with Andrew Jack, 29 May, 1997.
Details on the 25% AVT in the building sector, *Monaco: Une Affaire Qui Tourne*, Roger-Louis Bianchini, p 107.
Background on the Monaco economy and construction in the 1970s and 1980s, *Financial Times*, 7 January, 1997.
'It was a sacrifice . . .', interview with Lionel Noghes, 22 May, 1997.
Background on Monaco as a tax haven, *Grace*, Robert Lacey, p 315.
'We expanded our borders . . .', *Rainier and Grace*, Jeffrey Robinson, p 150.
The problems with Fontvielle, *Monaco Cool*, Robert Eringer, p 10.
Financial background on the Tisch brothers, *New York Post*, 17 August, 1997.
Loews' investment in Monaco, *Grace*, Robert Lacey, p 316.
Bob Tisch's annual Monte-Carlo Grand Prix Party, interview with Stephanie Parker, 11 July, 1997.
Insight on Prince Rainier and Grimaldi family life at Roc Agel, interview with Gwen Robyns, 21 August, 1997.
'You know I have . . .', *Grace*, Robert Lacey, p 326.
Prince Rainier's temper, *The Bridesmaids*, Judy Balaban Quine, p 414.
'I don't wake up in the morning . . .', *The Today Show*, NBC, 31 March, 1982.
Grace's daily transformation into Princess Grace, interview with Gwen Robyns, 21 July, 1997.
'I like to think they would consider me . . .', *The Today Show*, NBC, 31 March, 1982.
'My mom and dad did more . . .', *Rainier and Grace*, Jeffrey Robinson, p 223.
'She said she might not . . .', interview with Gwen Robyns, 21 July, 1997.
Grace's alleged affairs in middle-age, *Grace*, Robert Lacey, pp 335–336.
'These were charming young men . . .', interview with Gwen Robyns, 21 August, 1997.
Background on Princess Grace's new lease on life, *The Bridesmaids*, Judy Balaban Quine, p 491.
'Her bosoms were spilling out . . .', interview with Gwen Robyns, 21 August, 1997.
'For the first time . . .', *The Bridesmaids*, Judy Balaban Quine, p 520.
'I remember meeting . . .', *Diana – My True Story*, Andrew Morton.
Background on Grace's problems with Stephanie, *Grace: The Secret lives of a Princess*, James Spada, p 322.
Grace putting Stephanie under 'house arrest', *Blick*, 10 August, 1981.
'Princess Stephanie was standing . . .', interview with R. Couri Hay, 15 September, 1997.
'Well of course it does . . .', *The Today Show*, NBC, 31 March, 1982.
Background on Stephanie's relationship with Paul Belmondo, *Grace: The Secret lives of a Princess*, James Spada, p 323.
Insight on Grace's problems with menopause, *The Bridesmaids*, Judy Balaban Quine, p 496.
'I started to speak . . .', *The Bridesmaids*, Judy Balaban Quine, p 502.

CHAPTER ELEVEN – AFTER THE FALL

'This was a time of great sorrow . . .', interview with Prince Albert, 19 June, 1997.
Background on Princess Caroline trying on her mother's gowns, interview with Janice Gregory, 15 July, 1997.
'In other words . . .', *Prime Time Live*, ABC, 8 January, 1997.
'No-psycho-analysis . . .', *The Grimaldi Dynasty: Life with Grace*, Meridian TV.
Background on the family grieving for Grace, interview with Lizanne Kelly LeVine, 10 June, 1997.
'I think it was very difficult . . .', ibid.
Princess Stephanie's threat to elope with Paul Belmondo, *Star*, 8 February, 1983.

'It's a hard passage . . .', *Life*, March, 1983.
'She changed after . . .', interview with the Countess of Lombardy, 17 May, 1997.
'She was of course . . .', *Life*, March, 1983.
Prince Rainier's attacks on Hy Simon and Vinnie Zuffante, *New York Post*, 23 and 24 February, 1983.
Prince of Fury, *New York Post*, 25 February, 1997.
'He goes to New York . . .', interview with Lizanne Kelly LeVine, 10 June, 1997.
'After Grace died . . .', interview with the Countess of Lombardy, 17 May, 1997.
Caroline relationship with Robertino Rossellini, *New York Post*, 12 April, 1983.
Stefano Casiraghi's first meeting with Caroline, *People*, 31 October, 1983.
'I felt right away . . .', *People*, 9 January, 1984.
'Fancazzista', *Washington Post*, 20 December, 1983.
Caroline's trip to Milan with Casiraghi, *People*, 31 October, 1983.
'He's fine for a flirt . . .', *People*, 9 January, 1984.
Background on Caroline lobbying for an annulment, *New York Times*, 30 December, 1983.
'The Pope has a respect . . .', *New York Post*, 20 December, 1983.
'I propose to make . . .', *Rainier and Grace*, Jeffrey Robinson, p 283.
Speculation on Caroline's pregnancy, *New York Times*, 30 December, 1983.
Le Monde's editorial on Caroline, *Le Monde*, 23 December, 1983.
Background on Caroline's wedding to Casiraghi, *New York Times*, 30 December, 1983.
'It was a great occasion . . .', interview with Noel Museux, 20 May, 1997.
Background on 'An Evening in Monaco', *People*, 31 October, 1983.
'The discipline that Grace . . .', interview with Oleg Cassini, 14 August, 1997.
'Everyone was asking . . .', *New York Post*, 20 February, 1984.
Caroline's secret visit to Rome, *People*, 25 June, 1984.
Prince Rainier's fundraising, *New York Times*, 17 February, 1984.
'I don't believe . . .', *Life*, March, 1983.
'I would like to be around . . .', *New York Times*, 17 February, 1984.
'That was actually . . .', *Interview*, January, 1986.
'You almost have to use . . .', interview with Prince Albert, 19 June, 1997.
'He has a lot of dates . . .', *Grace: The Secret lives of a Princess*, James Spada, p 340.
'At the opening . . .', *Interview*, January, 1986.

CHAPTER TWELVE – PRINCESS PUNK

'That's something that . . .', interview with the Countess of Lombardy, 17 May, 1997.
'Princess Grace was a . . .', *People*, 25 June, 1984.
Background on Casiraghi's Monaco business, *People*, 25 June, 1984.
Casiraghi's skiing trip, ibid.
'Stefano has read . . .', ibid.
'Steph had way too much . . .', *The Bridesmaids*, Judy Balaban Quine, p 529.
'I worry when I see her pictures . . .', *The Bridesmaids*, Judy Balaban Quine, p 531.
Background on Anthony Delon, *People*, 27 August, 1984.
Palace injunction against *Paris-Match*, *New York Times*, 28 August, 1984.
'Look, it is our Dallas . . .', ibid.
'The image is what principally . . .', *The Grimaldi Dynasty: Life with Grace*, Meridian TV.
'There are circumstances . . .', interview with Prince Albert, 19 June, 1997.
'Rainier saves Stephanie . . .', *National Enquirer*, 25 September, 1984.
Police crackdown on Jimmy'z, interview with Alec Marr, 18 May, 1997.
'Princess Grace always thought . . .', interview with R. Couri Hay, 15 September, 1997.
Stephanie frequenting Paris nightclubs, *People*, 19 November, 1984.
'Everything Stephanie has done . . .', *Redbook*, November, 1985.
'She dares to try . . .', *Palace: My life in the Royal Family of Monaco*, Baron Christian de Massy, p 294.
'A guy put a gun . . .', *Rainier and Grace*, Jeffrey Robinson, p 213.
'We're in the 20th century . . .', *People*, 15 April, 1985.
Background on Stephanie's modeling career, *Vanity Fair*, July, 1985.
'It was a rebellious act . . .', ibid.
Stephanie's reported drug overdose, *National Enquirer*, 23 April, 1985.
'Were she any other . . .', *Daily Express*, 26 May, 1985.
'She's very shy . . .', *Vanity Fair*, July, 1985.
Stephanie's skiing vacation in Courcheval, *Redbood*, November, 1985.
Background on Pool Position, *Boston Herald* magazine, 17 November, 1985.
Pool Position's launch, *People*, 30 September, 1985.
'A very good collection . . .', ibid.
Princess Stephanie's New York nightclub outburst, *New York Post*, 28 October, 1985.
'I still see . . .', *The Bridesmaids*, Judy Balaban Quine, p 534.

CHAPTER THIRTEEN – A NEW COAT OF PAINT

Economic background on Monaco, interview with Martin Ricketts.
Details on Rainier's negotiations with *Dynasty* and *Dallas*, *Boston Herald*, 21 January, 1985.
'He somehow lacks . . .', *Vanity Fair*, October, 1987.

Background on Rainier's plastic surgery, *Boston Herald*, 20 May, 1985.
Background on Princess Ira von Furstenberg, *People*, 30 September, 1985; and *Vanity Fair*, October, 1987.
Speculation about an engagement between Rainier and Ira, *Boston Herald*, 18 August, 1985.
Details on the Princess Grace Foundation, *USA Weekend*, *New York Post*, 5 November, 1987.
'He is very playful . . .', *E! True Hollywood Stories*, E! TV, 10 August, 1987.
His self-proclaimed strategy, *W* magazine, November, 1997.
'It's kind of funny for me . . .', interview with Prince Albert, 19 September, 1997.
Background on Albert's tryst with Terri Weigel, *Daily News*, 4 November, 1991; and *People*, 18 November, 1991.
'Now I'm back in Monaco . . .', *Los Angeles Times*, 4 November, 1985.
'It's like a dog biting its tail . . .', *Prime Time Live*, ABC, 8 January, 1997.
'Grace worked hard . . .', *Vanity Fair*, October, 1987.
'I want to point out . . .', letter from Judith Mann to *Riviera Reporter*, 23 June, 1992.
'Without Princess Caroline the arts . . .', interview with Andre Peyregne, 19 May, 1997.
'Puffing Princess . . .', interview with Neil Marr, 16 May, 1997.
'Some people need friends more than others . . .', *McCalls*, September, 1986.
Archbishop Sardou's secret report, *Monaco: Une Affaire Qui Tourne*, Roger-Louis Bianchini, p 267.
The Italian investigation into Casiraghi, *New York Post*, 7 August, 1997.
'Their marriage has always been . . .', *People*, 12 August, 1986.
Princess Caroline's car accident, *USA-Today*, 28 August, 1986.
Background on Stephanie's Pool Position American mall tour, *Washington Post*, 3 March, 1986.
'It was driving me crazy . . .', *Rainier and Grace*, Jeffrey Robinson, p 213.
Details on the West Coast leg of the Pool Position tour, *Los Angeles Times*, 11 April, 1986.
'I felt betrayed . . .', *Rainier and Grace*, Jeffrey Robinson, p 212.
Stephanie's meeting with Dodi Fayed, *Star*, 3 March, 1986.
'She's an idol . . .', *New York Post*, 27 January, 1988.
'You can't sell a record . . .', *Los Angeles Times*, 11 April, 1986.
Background on Stephanie's German TV appearance, *National Enquirer*, 30 September, 1986.
'I decided that I couldn't handle things . . .', *Rainier and Grace*, Jeffrey Robinson, p 213.
'There was so much magic . . .', ibid.

CHAPTER FOURTEEN – THE DISNEY DICTATORSHIP

'Yes, the police', interview with Jane France, 15 May, 1997.
Background on CEPAM, *Monaco: Une Affaire Qui Tourne*, Roger-Louis Bianchini, p 261.
Background on police surveillance in Monaco, *Financial Times*, 7 January, 1997.
Monaco security details, interview with Patrick Middleton, 21 May, 1997.
'Our system is preventative . . .', *Financial Times*, 7 January, 1997.
Details on the principality's plainclothes police, *Monaco: Une Affaire Qui Tourne*, Roger-Louis Bianchini, p 96.
'I was just sitting . . .', *The Grimaldi Dynasty: Life with Grace*, Meridian TV.
Prince Rainier's drugs crackdown, *Monaco Cool*, Robert Eringer, p 57.
'Monaco is just like Russia . . .', interview with Patrick Middleton, 21 May, 1997.
Background on the BIM scandal, *Monaco: Une Affaire Qui Tourne*, Roger-Louis Bianchini, pp 15–22.
Rainier's tightening of Monégasque banking regulations, *Monaco: Une Affaire Qui Tourne*, Roger-Louis Bianchine, p 32.
'Banking in Monaco has developed . . .', *Financial Times*, 7 January, 1997.
Background on SAMs, *Monaco: Une Affaire Qui Tourne*, Roger-Louis Bianchini, p 53.
'Because everything in Monaco is small . . .', *Financial Times*, 7 January, 1997.
Details of Mafia infiltration into Monaco, *Guardian*, 5 July, 1997.
'The Mafia's all over the place . . .', *Prime Time Live*, 8 January, 1997.
'Everyone leaves you alone . . .', interview with John Haley, 21 May, 1997.

CHAPTER FIFTEEN – HOLLYWOOD REVISITED

'I do not think I'm the ideal woman . . .', *McCalls*, September, 1986.
'She is the First Lady . . .', *Palace: My life in the Royal Family of Monaco*, Baron Christian de Massy, p 295.
Caroline upsetting Nancy Reagan, *Vanity Fair*, October, 1987.
'I don't know . . .', ibid.
Caroline's bid for power, *New York Post*, 11 June, 1987.
'Her character is stronger . . .', *Palace: My life in the Royal Family of Monaco*, Baron Christian de Massy, p 296.
'He and I used to fight . . .', *Rainier and Grace*, Jeffrey Robinson, p 225.
'She was bugging . . .', *Interview* magazine, January, 1986.
'Caroline had some . . .', interview with Judy Balaban Quine, 29 July, 1997.
Background on Stephanie's night out with Rob Lowe, *People*, 10 November, 1986.
Rainier's request to Rupert Allan for information on Rob Lowe, *The Grimaldi Dynasty: Life with Grace*, Meridian TV.
Stephanie telling friends of engagement, *Daily News*, 24 October, 1986.
'It is obvious . . .', *The Grimaldi Dynasty: Life with Grace*, Meridian TV.
'He's a good waiter . . .', *Daily Express*, 9 February, 1987.
'I am proud to show our happiness . . .', *People*, 23 March, 1987.
'I live with it all my life . . .', ibid.
'I pray to God . . .', *The Grimaldi Dynasty: Life with Grace*, Meridian TV.
'She was in love with this . . .', Interview with Judy Balaban Quine, 29 July, 1997.
'She was just going through . . .', *The Grimaldi Dynasty: Life with Grace*, Meridian TV.

'It was extraordinary . . .', ibid.
'There was a series of . . .', interview with *Alec Burn*, 22 July, 1997.
'Prince of Pop . . .', *Daily Star*, 18 December, 1986.
'I saw her occasionally . . .', interview with Judy Balaban Quine, 29 July, 1987.
Background on Stephanie's life with Mario Oliver, *People* 23 March, 1987; and 28 April, 1987.
'It's much less than those . . .', *Daily Express*, 11 February, 1987.
'I'm a terrible spendthrift . . .', ibid.
Background on Rainier's Antigua meeting with Stephanie, *Daily Mail*, 17 April, 1987.
'We had some hard . . .', *The Grimaldi Dynasty: Life with Grace*, Meridian TV.
Background on Stephanie's new house in St. Tropez, *Daily News*, 30 September, 1987.
'Stephanie believes having a baby . . .', *Daily News*, 13 November, 1987.

CHAPTER SIXTEEN – STRANGER THAN DYNASTY

'Grace would have been . . .', interview with Gwen Robyns, 21 July, 1997.
'It's giving him a little . . .', *People*, 29 September, 1987.
'Being a bachelor . . .', *Cosmopolitan*, February, 1990.
'He's a wonderful young man . . .', *The Grimaldi Dynasty: Life with Grace*, Meridian TV.
Background on Albert's affair with Bea Fieldler, *Sun*, 28 March, 1991.
'I was hurt . . .', interview with Prince Albert, 19 June, 1997.
'I can easily see her being . . .', *Daily News*, 11 April, 1987.
'I think he was really in love . . .', *Washington Post*, 1 December, 1993.
'Albert's really getting into . . .', *The Grimaldi Dynasty: Life with Grace*, Meridian TV.
'We call him . . .', *Newsday*, 23 February, 1988.
'You never know . . .', *Wall Street Journal*, 11 February, 1992.
Background on Albert's Olympic bobsledding, *New York Times*, 10 February, 1988.
Background on the Monarchist Circle of Monaco, *McCalls*, March, 1989.
'If earthly paradise exists . . .', ibid.
'When I have the impression . . .', ibid.
'I'm much more comfortable . . .', *Newsday*, October, 1989.
Background on Caroline's interview stipulations, *US* magazine, 30 May, 1988.
'Princess Caroline is in Control . . .', *European Travel & Life*, April, 1988.
'If Prince Albert failed . . .', *Hello*, 1 April, 1989.
Background on influx of Turin and Milan businessmen into Monaco, 5 July, 1997.
Background on Casiraghi's business affairs, *Hello*, 1 April, 1989.
'There was certainly an unpleasant odour . . .', *The Grimaldi Dynasty: Life with Grace*, Meridian TV.
Background on the SBM scandal, *New York Times*, 21 October, 1988.
'All right, this coast . . .', ibid.
'When I was young . . .', *You* magazine, 18 June, 1989.
'They say he's chasing . . .', *New York Times*, 21 October, 1988.
'When you read certain . . .', interview with Prince Albert, 1 June, 1997.
Tabloid headlines are good for Monaco business, *New York Times*, 21 October, 1988.
Background on Le Texan, interview with Robert Eringer, 1 July, 1997.
'It's not a fancy place . . .', interview with Michael Powers, 15 May, 1997.
'It was Grace's idea . . .', interview with Jeanne Kelly van Remoortel, 17 May, 1997.
Description of Le Texan, *Monaco Cool*, Robert Eringer, p 40.
'Albert hangs out at Le Texan . . .', *Monaco Cool*, Robert Eringer, p 64.
'It was certainly not the case . . .', interview with Robert Eringer, 14 August, 1997.
'I'm a good influence . . .', *Monaco Cool*, Robert Eringer, pp 148–49.
'The girl quits her job . . .', *Monaco Cool*, Robert Eringer, p 99.
'I would love to have a wife and kids . . .', interview with Prince Albert, 19 June, 1997.
'He placed his mother . . .', interview with Lizanne Kelly LeVine, 15 July, 1997.
Oliver's marriage proposal, *Boston Herald*, 29 February, 1988.
Background on Princess in the studio, *USA-Today*, 9 May, 1988.
'She's humbled by the music industry . . .', *USA-Today*, 21 September, 1988.
'I decided my career . . .', *Chicago Sun-Times*, 24 June, 1988.
Background on Stephanie's recording contract with Sony Music, *You* magazine, 15 September, 1991.
'The president of Sony . . .', *E! True Hollywood Story*, E! TV, 10 August, 1997.
'Ron Bloom was very good looking . . .', ibid.
'Ron kept saying . . .', *Rainier and Grace*, Jeffrey Robinson, p 218.
'There are certain parts of town . . .', interview with Judy Balaban Quine, 29 July, 1997.
'I can't get up in the morning . . .', *Rainier and Grace*, Jeffrey Robinson, p 216.
'My father likes him . . .', *Rainier and Grace*, Jeffrey Robinson, p 217.
Background on Rainier's visit to Los Angeles, *Hello*, 19 November, 1988.
'Sure enough out comes Stephanie . . .', interview with Alec Burn, 22 July, 1997.
Speculation that Stephanie and Bloom would marry, *Daily News*, 23 December, 1988.
Background on Bloom's visit to Monaco, *Hello*, 18 February, 1989.
The explicit photographs of Stephanie and Bloom, *Sunday Mirror*, 25 June, 1989.
'Her royal, unisex wardrobe . . .', *USA-Today*, 22 January, 1989.
'Well I'm not surprised . . .', *E! True Hollywood Story*, E! TV, 10 August, 1997.

NOTES

CHAPTER SEVENTEEN – CURSE OF THE GRIMALDIS

'It was love at first sight . . .', *People*, 19 March, 1990.
Background on Lefur, *Star*, 26 June, 1990.
'I succumbed to her charm . . .', *Hello*, March, 1990.
'I've never been engaged before . . .', *Hello*, 12 May, 1990.
'She's very anxious . . .', *USA-Today*, 24 August, 1990.
'Unfortunately Grace was the first . . .', interview with Lizanne Kelly LeVine, 10 June, 1997.
Background of Casiraghi's defense of his world powerboat title, *New York Post*, 5 October, 1990.
'I watched that . . .', *E! True Hollywood Story* E! TV, 10 August, 1997.
'He was no hothead . . .', *Washington Post*, 4 October, 1990.
'We were heading out to sea . . .', *Hello*, 12 October, 1990.
Background on Casiraghi's death, *Hello*, 10 November, 1990.
'Stefano had many enemies . . .', *Hello*, 12 October, 1990.
Rumours of Mafia involvement in Casiraghi's death, *National Enquirer*, 23 October, 1990.
Background on Casiraghi's funeral, *People*, 22 October, 1990.
'There was a disturbing incident . . .', *The Grimaldi Dynasty: Life with Grace*, Meridian TV.
Caroline's pilgrimage to Fino Mornasco, *People*, 3 December, 1990.
'It's unfathomable . . .', interview with Judy Balaban Quine, 29 July, 1997.
'And they gave me strength . . .', *Prime Time Live*, ABC, 8 January, 1997.
'My sister needed me . . .', *Today*, 20 May, 1991.
Background on the Grimaldi Christmas in Jamaica, *People*, 8 April, 1991.
Details on Caroline's grieving, *Hello*, 26 February, 1991.
Casiraghi's debts, *Hello*, 30 March, 1991.
Caroline's meeting with Vincent Lindon, *Daily Mail*, 31 May, 1991.
'My children really hate the press . . .', *Harper's Bazaar*, 1 October, 1996.
'Caroline seemed to have dealt . . .', interview with Judy Balaban Quine, 29 July, 1997.
'I felt it was healthier . . .', *Harper's Bazaar*, 1 October, 1996.
Details on St. Remy security, *New York Post*, 29 May, 1992.
'We do have light security . . .', *Harper's Bazaar*, 1 October, 1996.

CHAPTER EIGHTEEN – ROCK 'N' MONACO

Background on the World Music Awards, interview with Melissa Corken, 20 May, 1997.
'It was difficult at first . . .', *Hello*, 1 June, 1991.
'Perhaps he found it too much . . .', *Sun*, 16 May, 1992.
Details of Stephanie suing Lefur, *Hello*, 23 March, 1991.
'That was a big boo-boo . . .', *Today*, 20 May, 1991.
'I was considered a rebel . . .', ibid.
'The song was very hard . . .', *Daily Express*, 18 June, 1991.
'I kept breaking down . . .', *Today*, 20 May, 1991.
'Everybody has knocks . . .', *Daily Express*, 18 June, 1991.
'In fact a lot of doors have closed . . .', *You* magazine, 15 September, 1991.
'Her self-titled new album . . .', *USA-Today*, 30 July, 1991.
'Radio's very finicky . . .', *E! True Hollywood Stories*, E! TV, 10 August, 1987.
'I'm not surprised . . .', *National Enquirer*, 6 May, 1992.

CHAPTER NINETEEN – PRINCE CHARMING

Prince Albert's Monaco . . .', *Washington Post*, 1 December, 1993.
'To come to me is not enough . . .', *Sports Illustrated*, 21 February, 1997.
Background on establishing tax free status in Monaco, ibid.
'It does look kind of funny', ibid.
Background on Prince Albert's competing in the 1992 Albertsville Winter Olympics, *Wall Street Journal*, 11 February, 1992.
'If I don't do well . . .', ibid.
All background on Prince Albert's affair with Stevie Parker, interview with Stevie Parker, 15 May, 1997, and 11 July, 1997.
Background on Albert's affair with Tamara Rotolo, interview with Bruce McCormack, 12 November, 1997.
Details on Rotolo suing for child support, *Today*, 17 December, 1992.
'He spent his whole time trying . . .', interview with Stevie Parker, 15 May, 1997.
'. . . punched out by a jealous husband', *Daily News*, 12 November, 1992.
Background on Daniel Ducruet, *Style & Travel*, 7 April, 1993.
'That woman stole my baby's father . . .', ibid.
'My mother came from Catholic Irish . . .', *Hello*, 6 June, 1992.
'My life has been one enormous doubt . . .', *Daily Express*, 2 June, 1992.
Prince Rainier's reaction to Stephanie's pregnancy, *People*, 15 June, 1992.
'She was willing to support him . . .', *The Grimaldi Dynasty: Life with Grace*, Meridian TV.
'My sister would have been very upset . . .', interview with Lizanne Kelly LeVine, 10 June, 1997.
Background on Caroline's annulment, *Grace*, by Robert Lacey, p 380.

CHAPTER TWENTY – FRACTURED FAIRYTALE

Background on National Day, *Washington Post*, 26 November, 1992.
Details of Larbi Daghmane's confession, *New York Post*, 12 November, 1992.
Daniel Ducruet's arrest and sentence, *Washington Post*, 26 November, 1992; and 13 December, 1992.
'It's been a drama . . .', interview with Lionel Noghes, 22 May, 1997.
Grimaldis snub Stephanie in hospital, *Hello*, 3 February, 1993.
Ducruet's deal with *Hello*, *Daily Express*, 6 February, 1993.
'our love is deeper now . . .', *Hello*, 5 December, 1992.
Rainier's heart attack scare, *National Enquirer*, 19 January, 1993.
'I live in Monte Carlo . . .', *USA-Today*, 16 September, 1992.
Theory that Rainier and Karl Lagerfeld had encouraged Claudia Schiffer's relationship with Albert, *Washington Post*, 1 December, 1993.
'I was never romantically involved . . .', ibid.
Report that Albert had accepted responsibility for Jazmin Grace, *Washington Post*, 19 January, 1994; and *New York Post*, 3 February, 1993.
Details on Pope John Paul II legitimizing Caroline's children, *New York Times*, 6 April, 1993.
Rainier's 70th birthday interview, *European*, 20 May to 23 May, 1993.
'He said that Albert must get married . . .', *The Grimaldi Dynasty: Life with Grace*, Meridian TV.
'Michael has a lot of respect . . .', *Star*, 25 May, 1993.
Caroline posing with Andrea and Charlotte, *Hello*, 12 June, 1993.
Background on Ducruet's hobbies, *New idea*, 24 April, 1993.
'And as Uncle Rainier . . .', *The Grimaldi Dynasty: Life with Grace*, Meridian TV.
'I really have to give Rainier . . .', interview with Judy Balaban Quine, 29 July, 1997.

CHAPTER TWENTY-ONE – COWBOYS AND INDIANS

Monaco's acceptance into the United Nations, *Woman's Wear Daily*, 16 July, 1993, and 10 October, 1993.
Background on Stevie Parker's trips to Monaco and Texas, interview with Stevie Parker, 15 May, 1997; and 11 July, 1997.
'We've made it a tradition . . .', interview with Michael Powers, 2 July, 1997.
'Well mother was hardly noticed . . .', *Today Show*, NBC, 3 August, 1966.
'When I was very young . . .', *20/20*, ABC, 1985.
'I just love the whole atmosphere . . .', interview with Prince Albert, 19 June, 1997.
'I slept by the pool . . .', interview with Stevie Parker, 11 July, 1997.
'He loves doing these fun . . .', interview with Michael Powers, 2 July, 1997.
Background on Prince Albert I's meeting with Buffalo Bill, interview with Prince Albert, 19 June, 1997; and Michael Powers, 2 July, 1997.
Background on Tamara Rotolo's visit to Cody, interview with Bruce McCormack, 12 November, 1997.
Description of Prince Albert's visit, *Powell Tribune*, 26 August, 1993.
'This is not about money,' *Cody Enterprise*, September, 1993.
'She's his own flesh and blood . . .', interview with Tamara Rotolo, 2 December, 1997.
'Jazmin's fully aware . . .', interview with Tamara Rotolo, 2 December, 1997.
'Albert kept flirting with me . . .', interview with Stevie Parker, 11 July, 1997.
'They were like little kids . . .', interview with Stevie Parker, 11 July, 1997.
'The real girlfriends . . .', *Tatler*, January, 1995.
'Princess Caroline's children . . .', interview with Kate Powers, 16 May, 1997.
'Grace would have loved to have seen . . .', interview with Lizanne Kelly LeVine, 10 June, 1997.
Stephanie's decision to donate her neck brace to charity, *New York Post*, 3 March, 1994.
'We have a small country . . .', *New York Times*, 20 February, 1994.
'I want to thank Prince Albert . . .', *Daily Mirror*, 4 May, 1994.
Background on Ducruet's pre-nuptial agreement, *Daily News*, 5 May, 1994.
Prince Albert's declaration, *Daily Mail*, 13 August, 1994.
'With the antics . . .', *W*, September, 1994.
'This book severely violates . . .', *New York Post*, 4 November, 1994.
Background on Prince Rainier's heart by-pass operation, *Hello*, 18 December, 1994.
Rumours of Rainier abdication, *New York Times*, 23 December, 1994.

CHAPTER TWENTY-TWO – SEND IN THE CLOWNS

Background on the Monte-Carlo International Circus Festival, *Hello*, 1 February, 1995.
Background on Prince Rainier's camper-bus, *Grace*, Robert Lacey, p 386.
'That servant . . .', *Sunday Express*, 13 October, 1996.
Princess Stephanie declines family invitations, *People*, 17 July, 1995.
Background on Stephanie's domestic life in Monaco, *Daily Express*, 1 February, 1996.
Stephanie favoured a big wedding, *Woman's Wear Daily*, 10 March, 1995.
'That's really the time . . .', *Prime Time Live*, ABC, 3 September, 1997.
On the occasion of their marriage . . .', *Daily Telegraph*, 28 June, 1995.
Background on Stephanie's wedding, *Independent*, 30 June, 1995.
Wedding gift list, *Evening Standard*, 13 June, 1995.
'The princess was effusive . . .', *People*, 17 July, 1995.
'I don't see her as often . . .', *Prime Time Live*, ABC, 8 January, 1997.
'She has found her own equilibrium . . .', *W*, September, 1994.

'At one point . . .', interview with Stevie Parker, 15 May, 1997.
'I wish he had said something . . .', interview with Stevie Parker, 11 July, 1997.
Background on incident at Pomp and Circumstance, *People*, 13 November, 1995; and *Daily News*, 31 October, 1995.
Prince Albert shaving his head, *Daily Express*, 8 December, 1995.
'I've juggled my schedule . . .', interview with Prince Albert, 19 June, 1997.
'Maybe I should communicate . . .', interview with Prince Albert, 19 June, 1997.

CHAPTER TWENTY-THREE – APOCALYPSE MONACO

Background on Salic Law, *Tatler*, December, 1996.
Biographical details on Prince Ernst of Hanover, *Tatler*, December, 1996.
Background on Caroline's break-up with Vincent Lindon, *Hello*, 13 January, 1996.
'Ernst was saying . . .', *The Grimaldi Dynasty: Life with Grace*, Meridian TV.
'They move in the same kind . . .', *People*, 30 September, 1996.
Caroline and Ernst's trip to Thailand, *Philadelphia Inquirer*, 21 February, 1996.
Caroline's 'cultural' statement, *Woman's Wear Daily*, 3 May, 1996.
Background on Caroline preparing to auction Princess Grace's belongings, interview with Janice Gregory, 15
    September, 1997.
'In conversation the Prince is there . . .', *Prime Time Live*, ABC, 8 January, 1997.
Details on Prince Rainier falling asleep in public, *Daily News*, 24 January, 1997.
Background on Monaco's 'slum' Zoo, *Sunday Times*, 5 May, 1996; and *The Planet on Sunday*, 16 June, 1996.
'I hope we can persuade . . .', *Sunday Times*, 5 May, 1996.
'What's stupid is that . . .', interview with Patrick Middleton, 21 May, 1997.
'I know Prince Rainier . . .', *The Planet on Sunday*, 16 June, 1996.
'To have found true love . . .', *TV Guide*, 4 May, 1996.
'We were born in two different . . .', *TV Guide*, 4 May, 1996.
Ducruet's first meeting with Fili Houteman, *Daily Express*, 28 August, 1997.
Background on Ducruet's afternoon with Houteman, *The Grimaldi Dynasty: Life with Grace*, Meridian TV.
'The trap was set . . .', ibid.
Details of the 1996 Red Cross Ball, *New York Post*, 12 August, 1996.
'I think the children should know . . .', *Prime Time Live*, ABC, 8 January, 1997.
'Lizzie my hair . . .', *E! True Hollywood Stories*, E! TV, 10 August, 1987.
Background on the escalation of Caroline's relationship with Prince Ernst, *People*, 30 September, 1996.
'It's a skin problem . . .', *People*, 30 August, 1996.
'Rainier was very relieved . . .', interview with Lizanne Kelly LeVine, 15 July, 1997.
'My mistake has destroyed me . . .', *Evening Standard*, 24 September, 1996.
Background on Princess Caroline in New York, *People*, 21 October, 1996.
'Looking terrific in a turban . . .', *Woman's Wear Daily*, 8 October, 1996.

EPILOGUE

'I think over the last few years . . .', *Prime Time Live*, ABC, 8 January, 1997.
Background on Monaco's budget deficit, *Time*, 20 January, 1997.
'Rainier was speaking . . .', interview with Judy Balaban Quine, 29 July, 1997.
'Sharpen his skills . . .', *Daily Telegraph*, 9 January, 1997.
'Monaco's fortune is based . . .', *Guardian*, 5 July, 1997.
'Dirtie Bertie . . .', *W*, November, 1997.
'Rainier says he's a little reluctant . . .', interview with Lizanne Kelly LeVine, 19 June, 1997.
'Well I thought about this . . .', interview with Prince Albert, 19 June, 1997.
Details on the 1997 SBM scandal, *New York Times*, 14 March, 1997.
Allegations of Princess Grace's involvement with the Order of the Solar Temple, *Secret Lives*, Channel 4, 29 December,
    1997.
'In certain newspapers . . .', *Daily Telegraph*, 19 December, 1996.
Background on Chantal Hochuli's split from Ernst, *Hello*, 12 March, 1997.
Prince Ernst and Caroline photographed aboard Pacha, *Hello*, 21 June, 1997.
Speculation that Caroline and Ernst would marry, *Hello*, 1 November, 1997.
'I don't know how long . . .', *Prime Time Live*, ABC, 8 January, 1997.
Stephanie's relationship with Claudio Buziol, *New York Post*, 14 September, 1997.
'She's doing very well . . .', interview with Lizanne Kelly LeVine, 10 June, 1997.
Background on Stephanie's relationship with Jean Raymond, *People*, 3 November, 1997.
'I think Grace and Rainier . . .', interview with Gwen Robyns, 21 August, 1997.

BIBLIOGRAPHY

Bradford, Sarah. *Princess Grace*. Stein and Day, USA. 1984.

De Massy, Baron Christian and Higham, Charles. *Palace: My Life in the Royal Family of Monaco*. Atheneum, USA. 1986.

Edwards, Anne. *The Grimaldis of Monaco: The Centuries of Scandal, The Years of Grace*. Ulverscroft, London. 1994.

Englund, Steven. *Grace of Monaco: An Interpretative Biography*. Sphere Books, New York. 1985.

Lacey, Robert. *Grace*. Pan Books, London. 1995.

Quine, Judith Balaban. *Grace Kelly and Six Intimate Friends: The Bridesmaids*. Pocket Books, New York. 1991.

Robinson, Jeffrey. *Rainier and Grace*. Pocket Books, London. 1997.

Robyns, Gwen. *Princess Grace: A Biography*. David McKay Company Inc, London. 1976.

Spada, James. *Grace: The Secret Lives of a Princess*. Doubleday Dell, New York. 1987.

Wayne, Jane Ellen. *Grace Kelly's Men*. St Martin's Press, New York. 1991.

INDEX